The Neo-pagans

The Neo-pagans

*Friendship and Love
in the
Rupert Brooke Circle*

Paul Delany

Macmillan London

For Elspeth

First published 1987 by
MACMILLAN LONDON LIMITED
4 Little Essex Street London WC2R 3LF
and Basingstoke

Associated companies in Auckland, Delhi, Dublin,
Gaborone, Hamburg, Harare, Hong Kong,
Johannesburg, Kuala Lumpur, Lagos, Manzini,
Melbourne, Mexico City, Nairobi, New York,
Singapore and Tokyo

British Library Cataloguing in Publication Data
Delany, Paul
The neo-pagans: friendship and love in the
Rupert Brooke circle.
1. Brooke, Rupert —— Friends and
associates   2. Poets, English —— 20th
century —— Biography
I. Title
821′.912   PR6003.R4Z/

ISBN 0–333–44572–4

Phototypeset in Linotron Sabon by Wyvern Typesetting, Bristol
Printed in Britain by Anchor Brendon, Tiptree, Essex

Each of either reaped and sown:
Rosiest rosy wanes to crone. . . .
Look with spirit past the sense,
Spirit shines in permanence.

George Meredith, *The Woods of Westermain*

Now, God be thanked Who has matched us with His
    hour,
  And caught our youth, and wakened us from
    sleeping,
With hand made sure, clear eye, and sharpened power,
  To turn, as swimmers into cleanness leaping. . . .

Rupert Brooke, *1914*

Never such innocence,
Never before or since . . .
Never such innocence again.

Philip Larkin, *MCMXIV*

Contents

Preface

It was Rupert Brooke's true fate to die young; posterity added a false one, that he died innocent. Though he left no children to guard his posthumous respectability, others appointed themselves to guard it anyway, and continued to do so even after the death of his mother in 1930 made their vigilance obsolete. Sir Edward Marsh at first, and Sir Geoffrey Keynes later, were the leading protectors of Brooke's reputation. If one asks what they really wanted to protect, the final answer has to be *themselves*: their own investment in Brooke of so much faith and love, their own share in the reflected glory of a national hero – the 'young Apollo, golden-haired.' Yet their claims on him were in fact weak; for Brooke never cared deeply about Marsh or Keynes, nor did they play any major role in his emotional history. When his memory was expropriated to promote an overblown myth of poetry and youth, his close friends and lovers preferred to keep silent about the actual – and far more substantial – young man they had known. By setting Brooke in the context of 'Neo-paganism', I have tried to restore him to the true company he kept, and in which he can best be judged.

The biographer, unlike other kinds of writer, soon discovers that there are people who don't want him to do what he has chosen to do – and are also in a position to hinder his doing it. This can still be the case when, as with this book, the people he writes about are all dead. There can be good reasons for opposing a biography: that family secrets would disrupt the lives of the next generation; or simply that the presumptive biographer might not do his job well. But many other objections arise for the biographer to contend with; signs of these struggles can be seen in the prefaces to biographies, often covered over by prose of an obsequiousness scarcely seen since the Grub Street dedications of the eighteenth century. Biographers must, it would seem, apologise for what they do. They are mistrusted for considering other people's affairs too curiously, for indulging a voyeurism that has only a feeble claim to being respectable. To find out secrets is indeed a pleasure; nevertheless, a secret is what best explains the façades that are built up to conceal it. There is more to biography, of course, than exposing secrets. Every life is built on a delicate and shifting balance between public and private experience. And only through respect for both the public and private self can biography find its true justification: to give its readers an expanded sense of possibility in the lives they are still engaged in living.

My first debt, therefore, is to those who expanded the possibilities of my own work, whether by advice, by an active pursuit of the evidence I needed, or simply by encouraging me to feel that the work was worth doing: Quentin Bell, Michael Hastings, Elizabeth Hollingsworth, Lucilla Shand and Michael Holroyd. Then I thank those who provided precious new material, either personal reminiscences or private documents that revealed the complex web of relations between the Neo-pagans. First among these must come Val Arnold-Forster, who answered a biographer's prayer by pulling out an old suitcase full of letters to her mother-in-law, Ka Cox, and asking me if I'd like to take it home for the weekend. My other helpers were Ann Olivier Bell, Bob Best, Christopher Cornford, Sylvia Curtis, Richard Garnett, Catherine Gide, Sophie Gurney, the late Angela Harris, Sir Geoffrey Keynes, Howard Moseley, the late Cathleen Nesbitt, H. A. Popham, Sophia Popham, Julia Rendall, Dr Benedict Richards, Jacqueline Rouah and Mary Newbery Sturrock.

Stephane Roumilhac provided a memorable lunch and tour of the Château de Prunoy, Yonne; Mr and Mrs J. Finlinson showed me their home, formerly The Champions, at Limpsfield; the librarians of Rugby and Bedales, and the housemaster of School Field, Rugby, were my guides to the two places where Neo-paganism had its roots.

Many others have added pieces to the story, whether in letters or conversation: Anna Anrep, Nicholas Barker, Alan Bell, Justin Brooke, Keith Clements, Jenny Dereham, Helen Duffy, Richard Garnett, Chloe Green, Tamsin Harris, Dr Tony Harris, Paul Levy, Ann Radford MacEwan, Patrick McVeigh, Perry Meisel, Lois Olivier, Peggy Packwood, Tristram Popham, David Pye, Mark Ramage, S. P. Rosenbaum, the Laird of Rothiemurchus, John Schroder, Robert Skidelsky and David Steel.

For archival sources I am specially indebted to Michael Halls, Modern Archivist at King's College, Cambridge, and to the late Peter Croft; to Peter Gautry of the Cambridge University Library; and to Lola Szladits of the Berg Collection, New York Public Library.

This book could not have its present form without the co-operation of the Trustees of the Rupert Brooke Estate, the late Sir Geoffrey Keynes, Jon Stallworthy and Andrew Motion; and the sympathetic concern of Tony Pocock and Frank Pike at Faber & Faber. At a difficult point in the book's progress I was encouraged by expert advice from Peter Ackroyd and Carol Blake.

I am indebted to Faber & Faber Limited for permission to quote from *The Letters of Rupert Brooke*, edited by Sir Geoffrey Keynes, and from Christopher Hassall's *Rupert Brooke*; and to the Hogarth Press and Harcourt Brace Jovanovitch for excerpts from the *Letters* and *Diary* of Virginia Woolf.

A Leave Fellowship from the Social Sciences and Humanities Research Council of Canada helped me to complete a first draft. Simon Fraser University supplied many kinds of help, including two President's Research Grants; and I owe individual thanks to Bob Brown, Dean of Arts, to Jerald Zaslove for arranging a crucial period of leave, and to Margaret Sharon of Computing Services. My research assistants, Jeff Berg and Jon Paul Henry, helped me to start the book, and to finish it. At the University of Waterloo, Gordon Slethaug smoothed the way for a visitor to his department.

I am fortunate to have an editor, Erwin Glikes of The Free Press, who has given me over the years such precious encouragement, friendship and intellectual challenge. My agents, Georges Borchardt and Richard Scott Simon, kept the book on course with their confidence and sound advice. At Macmillan, Philippa

Harrison and Adam Sisman have been editors such as every writer hopes for, but rarely gets.

David and Anne Murray, Bill and Benita Parry, and Marcia Marriott helped me to feel that Britain was still my second home. In Vancouver, Roger and Barbara Seamon have been a sympathetic audience for thoughts not yet articulated on the page. My wife, Elspeth McVeigh, has shared with me all the trials – and some of the pleasures – that a book brings; and the others too.

Paul Delany
Vancouver, 1987

Introduction

When Rupert Brooke was eighteen, James Strachey asked him if he approved of war. 'Certainly,' he replied. 'It kills off the unnecessary.' In 1915, it killed *him*. Did Rupert, in that school-boy joke, write his own best epitaph? To answer the question, we must look at the ten years in between. His emotional life in that period centred on a group of friends that gathered around him at Cambridge in 1908. Later Virginia Woolf gave them, half mockingly, a nickname: the 'Neo-pagans'. The core of the group was Rupert, Justin Brooke (no relation), Jacques and Gwen Raverat, Frances Cornford, Katharine ('Ka') Cox and the four Olivier sisters – Margery, Brynhild, Daphne, Noel. Together they were going to sweep aside the cobwebs of Victorianism, enjoy both friendship and love at the highest pitch, and prolong their youth into an indefinitely glorious future. 'We are living in the greatest time there has been, ever,' said Jacques Raverat in 1911, 'and yet, only preparing for still greater things to come – tomorrow, at dawn.'

We know only too well, now, that the great thing to come was the First World War: the Edwardian optimism blown to bits in the trenches, the hostilities that didn't really end in 1918 but have been going on ever since. But why had the Neo-pagans lost *their* optimism already, their friendships abandoned or fragmented only four years after they had come together? Why did Rupert Brooke march off to war, not just without regret, but actually with a sense of relief? And why did the image of Rupert among his Neo-pagan friends become a national ideal, even though their party had not been spoiled by the war, but by their own internal conflicts?

Neo-paganism was an appealing new version of the ubiquitous 'rural myth', that specially British form of escape from modernity. But myth has a double sense: was Neo-paganism just another fatuous lie about the Condition of Britain, or was it the kind of noble lie that allows people to love their country, to feel loyalty and nostalgia for a historic way of life? There is something in Rupert Brooke and Neo-paganism that still has power to charm, resist it or debunk it as we may. At the centre of that charm, I feel, is that this was a group of talented and attractive young people who were possessed by *hope*. It is an emotion that, in any collective form, seems almost extinct today – deposed by its bastard child, ambition.

The first duty of this book is to the truth about this ghostly company, who made a religion of youth and now are all dead. Truth has been hard to come by, ever since Dean Inge quoted Brooke's 'The Soldier' in his sermon at St Paul's on 5 April 1915, three weeks before the poet's poetic death in the Aegean. The congregation was made up of the widows, parents and orphans of those who had already fallen. Before Inge could speak, a man jumped up to make a passionate denunciation of the war, and had to be dragged away. Since that day, Brooke's reputation has gone through the whole cycle from adulation to contemptuous dismissal without any trustworthy account of the kind of person he really was.

When I began work on this book I went to see Brooke's senior Literary Trustee, Sir Geoffrey Keynes, who had known Brooke since prep school. He had gathered a mass of documentation on Brooke (now preserved in the Brooke Archive at King's College, Cambridge); he controlled it, and he was temperamentally unable, over the years, to allow unhindered use of materials he considered sensitive. 'Rupert was by far the most wonderful person I have ever known,' he told me, and that was how the world must know him too. Christopher Hassall's 1964 biography tells Rupert's story fluently and sympathetically, despite some major gaps. Rupert's letters to Brynhild Olivier and Elisabeth van Rysselberghe were not available to Hassall, and the correspondence between Rupert and Noel Olivier is still inaccessible. But the essential flaw of Hassall's work was that it had to please Sir Geoffrey, which meant that it gave a fundamentally distorted and incomplete view of Rupert.

The tensions underneath the carefree mask of Neo-paganism need to be revealed; but it should be acknowledged that many of their troubles came from expecting so much out of life. If their Bloomsbury friends were fundamentally ironic and classical, the Neo-pagans were euphoric and romantic. At Lulworth in 1910, Rupert and his friends read *Prometheus Unbound* aloud in the evenings; with Maynard Keynes's party at Everleigh in 1912, it was Jane Austen's *Emma*. The utopian socialism of the Neo-pagans was derided by the predominantly Liberal Cambridge 'Apostles'. Their 'womanising' was for Keynes and the Stracheys something that also deserved a snigger of contempt, for the Neo-pagans were a society in which someone of the opposite sex could be either a comrade or the object of idealistic love. Much of Bloomsbury's charm comes from its devotion to the eighteenth century (as an antidote to the oppressive Victorianism on which they had grown up); but that same devotion produced much of what is limiting about Bloomsbury, turning it inward towards privatism and petty sociability. The Neo-pagans had a wider horizon, stretching to the 'Great Dawn' of Rupert's revolutionary poem. Caught up in the Edwardian optimism about social change, they were the party of youth, who saw the future as theirs to inherit and enjoy.

The defeats and conflicts of the Neo-pagans came directly from their hopes, since before bitterness there must be enthusiasm. First of all they believed in themselves: 'We are earth's best,' say the lovers in one of Rupert's poems. They were not an elite of power, for their sense of superiority did not include a claim to rule others. Instead they were Children of the Sun, exempt from care and responsibility alike. No one is really exempt, of course, and they found this out by their mid-twenties. Beauty and breezy confidence are wasting assets; they may turn into burdens when too much is made of them for too long. Few of the Neo-pagans took much thought for the morrow. Rupert and Justin Brooke, Brynhild and Noel Olivier all shied away from marriage because it would mark so clearly the end of their carefree youth.

The highest form of personal hope is romantic love. For the Neo-pagans, being in love was more important than making love. They played a part in the beginnings of sexual permissiveness, but anything like the gleeful lecherousness of H. G. Wells they instinctively shunned. Today, somewhere near the end of that movement, the romantic chastity of the Neo-pagans looks much more sympathetic than it would have a decade or two ago. When they finally embarked on sexual life, they may indeed have bungled it; Rupert certainly did. But should the failure be blamed on the eight or ten years of celibacy that preceded it? This moratorium was an emotional apprenticeship, a time when friendship gained what sexual love renounced. In any era, the sexual problem is far more than the search for a suitable 'outlet', as Kinsey naively assumed. Neo-pagan sexuality reflected the possibilities of its time: the Victorianism still lingering in the responses of young men and women alike; the tentative emancipation, distinct from the feminism of the suffragettes; the cross-currents from the homosexual world of public school and Apostolic sex; the muddles over contraception and marriage. Having still enough muddles of our own, we may appreciate the sexual hopes of the past, and even find some current use in them.

Then there was the dream of social transformation, another way of fleeing the humdrum necessities of jobs and incomes. They lived in a sunny niche of the old order, while believing that the future was going to redeem their extravagant hopes. Between these extremes there was a loss of seriousness and continuity. When the war came, it seemed easier for Rupert to sacrifice all of life than to live on into maturity, which had for so long appeared neither desirable nor even substantial.

How, then, did Rupert become a national hero and Neo-paganism, as embodied in him, such a powerful image of the good life? If the favourites of the gods died young, it followed that the life of youth was best and most enviable. 'I first heard of him', said D. H. Lawrence in his famous eulogy, 'as a Greek God under a Japanese Sunshade, reading poetry in his pyjamas, at Grantchester, at Grantchester, upon the lawns where the river goes.' In fact, Rupert worked hard enough as scholar, poet and journalist; but in the myth he was the wildflower of English culture — supremely yet gloriously useless.

So many cherished British myths came together in those images popularised by Eddie Marsh and Henry James: 'Dining-Room Tea', punting on the Backs at Cambridge, breakfasting under the apple blossom at the Orchard, Grantchester, all the camping and bathing and 'so many parties'. The style was itself the message: that living in the country, in endlessly sociable youthful leisure was not just enviable (which, indeed, it was), but was what really mattered, what most deserved a tear when they started lobbing trench mortars into the picnic in 1914. The Fabian socialism was acknowledged in passing, without being allowed to tarnish the 'general sunniness' that Lawrence spoke of; while the Rupert who said 'I HATE the upper classes' during the December 1910 election disappeared completely from view.

The privileged life enjoyed by the Neo-pagans was pastoral and therefore 'innocent'. When you were 'living in a tent or a river', wearing few clothes and doing no harm, who could resent you? The Brian Howard kind of roguish *Sonnenkind*, hot in pursuit of champagne and mischief, was far from the Neo-pagan spirit; still less could it fit in with the renegade Apostles of the thirties, the generation of Anthony Blunt and Guy Burgess. But the pastoral escapism of Neo-paganism made it all the more centrally British. Rupert once observed flippantly that Noel Olivier had a chance of 'turning out less pointless than the rest' of her sisters. Noel's active professional life as a paediatrician may have proved Rupert right. Yet so long as there was still honey for tea, being pointless was exactly the glory to be aimed at. Not a fatuous glory, to be sure, but a life lived lightly — and given up lightly too, in Flanders or Gallipoli.

One returns to the hope that came so easily to them all, and that makes them so appealing. Yet the great lie of the Rupert Brooke myth was that the vernal optimism of 1909 was still untarnished in 1914, when it was brutally crushed by the war. In fact the hopes of 1909 had been slain, by their own contradictions, long before. The war was going to be a solution to their troubles, Rupert told Noel in October 1914 — not the end of their hopes, but a chance to renew them.

Was it wrong, though, to have such hopes and pleasures at the start: their political utopias, their plays and camps caught in the amber of the Edwardian summer? This is dangerous ground, when nostalgia and costume dramas seem to be the only growth industries that Britain has left. Why should people have cared so much for these dew-dabblers then; why, even more, should we care for them now? I have tried to show enough of the darker side of Neo-paganism to avoid the rose-tinted nostalgia of which we have had too much already. It should be obvious, also, that all those Neo-pagan festivities were enjoyed at someone else's expense: those who cooked and washed, and those whose labour created the massive surplus that financed the great Edwardian garden party.

When all that is said, there is still the question – of which Rupert Brooke was especially aware – of what *is*, after all, truly of value. The Neo-pagans, like Lawrence, knew that to work is not, finally, to live. They did not want merely to get rich and spend, like the plutocracy; or to be merely sociable and meditative, like the Apostles; or to build the 'crystal palace' of a rational bureaucratic state, like the Webbs. With all their delinquencies the Neo-pagans had a better agenda, for themselves and their country, than most of the groups around them. If they failed to carry it out – and one must concede that they did fail – it is still worth looking at how far they got, and at the flaws that undermined, even before August 1914, all those generous and extravagant hopes with which they began.

Part One

Assembling

I

Rugby, Bedales and Cambridge

The Old School Reformed: Rugby

'Where did you go to school?' is notoriously the most strategic question that one Englishman can ask of another. The man who, more than any other, made it strategic was Thomas Arnold, headmaster of Rugby School from 1828 to his death in 1842. When he came to Rugby it was not the most aristocratic or ancient or intellectually distinguished of the great public schools; but Arnold turned it into by far the most ideological one.[1] Largely because of Arnold, secondary schooling is a more important and divisive social issue in Britain than in any other country. Thanks to him, too, Cyril Connolly could become famous for his 'Theory of Perpetual Adolescence': that for many middle-class Englishmen school was such an intense experience that everything that happened afterwards was an anticlimax.[2]

Rupert Brooke was born at Rugby, where his father was a master. In due course he went up to the school, and even taught there briefly after his father's death. When he himself died on the way to Gallipoli in 1915, he was glorified as the supreme kind of national hero of the Great War: the public schoolboy who went unhesitatingly from playing cricket for the school to leading a platoon of infantry in the trenches. What could not be said at the time was that the 'young Apollo' of the cricket field and the King's Parade at Cambridge had the vices, as well as the virtues, of his kind. Nor was it understood that Brooke's ideals had been more radical and generous than his public image allowed; that there was more to him than ingenuousness, a talent for sub-Keatsian verse, and a classic profile.

The real Rupert behind the mask was best known to his intimate friends of 1908 to 1912, the 'Neo-pagans'; but in 1915 they were keeping quiet about what they knew. None of them had gone to Rugby, but several had gone to Bedales, a school fundamentally opposed to Rugby values. Yet it had grown out of Rugby, if only by reaction; and Rupert's attraction to the Bedales spirit revealed his own dissatisfaction with the narrow world in which he had grown up. Together, the two schools epitomise the struggle between emancipation and orthodoxy that was played out in Edwardian Britain, especially in the generation of youth for whom Brooke became such a great and sacrificial symbol.

Like the rest of Lytton Strachey's 'Eminent Victorians', Thomas Arnold was a visionary, a gifted organiser and a bit of a crank. As a young man he looked on his country and saw 'a mass of evil a thousand times worse than all the idolatry of India'.[3] The remedy for this terrible state was, to him, obvious. The Church of England must become a truly national institution, and Anglicanism must be the living religion of the whole people. This was no small task, of course; but in accepting the headmastership of Rugby Arnold felt that he was tackling a manageable piece of it. A genuinely Christian school could be the model for a future Christian state, and the nursery for those who could build it.

His first step was to clear the ground. The morals of Rugby were those of the country squires who sent their sons there; as Arnold saw it, no morals at all, mere paganism and disorder. 'Evil being unavoidable,' he proclaimed, 'we are not a jail to keep it in, but a place of education where we must cast it out to prevent the taint from spreading.'[4] A storm of floggings and expulsions soon put Evil to flight. Now Arnold could set up his own ideals: 'first religious and moral principle; secondly gentlemanly conduct; and thirdly intellectual ability'.[5] To show the unity of these aims, Arnold broke with public school tradition by making himself the school chaplain. Rugby would now be governed by a single, awesome head: King, Prime Minister and Archbishop of Canterbury rolled into one.

In 1835 Arnold's future biographer, A. P. Stanley, wrote an

article for the *Rugby Magazine* called 'School a Little World'. A public school was 'not only a place where boys are receiving knowledge from masters', he argued, 'but a place also where they form a complete society among themselves – a society in its essential points similar, and therefore preparatory, to the society of men'. But what kind of society? In fact, an ideal rather than a real one. 'The schoolhouse, the chapel, and the playground,' Stanley continued, 'forming as they do one united group, become a tangible focus, in which the whole of our school existence is, as it were, symbolically consecrated.'[6] School life would become a sacred drama, in which the boys' life became one anxious struggle after another: to pass the exam, to resist evil, to win the game.

Arnold deliberately narrowed the range of age and class in the school. Though ancient statutes required Rugby to educate a certain number of boys from the town, he found ways to keep the sons of tradesmen and farmers out. But he also discouraged the aristocracy from sending their sons, fearing that these boys would be too arrogant and dissipated to bend to his yoke. *His* students would be drilled like Plato's guardians, to become the future governors and thinkers of Britain. Girls, of course, would continue to be excluded, as they were from all the other Victorian public schools. In the old days, however, schoolboys could roam freely in the town, and some even kept whores. The reformed schools, following Arnold's example, cut off their students from almost all feminine influence. At home there were mothers, sisters and domestic servants (who might be seduced by their young masters). At school, only the housemaster's wife would give the boys any female affection or homely comfort.

Arnold's 'little world' was actually far more single-minded, ideological and ascetic than the world outside its gates. The main entrance to Rugby School – a little doorway set into a gate at the top of the town's bustling High Street – recalls the scriptural eye of the needle. After one passes through the School House quadrangle, the perspective opens out on 'The Close', with its great sweep of rugby pitches. On these 'fields of the Lord', the ritual contests of public school life are still re-enacted in games of rugby and cricket. School sports in the Victorian era became even more codified and symbolic than the pursuits from which they derived: hunting and warfare. When history called, the step from playing fields to Flanders fields appeared sweet and fitting, for it had been taken so often already in imagination.

If he had been no more than a beady-eyed autocrat, Arnold would never have had so wide an influence. But his nature also had its gentler side, when he turned to his pupils a face of warmth, understanding and Christian love. A true Victorian, he was deeply self-divided, and two different paths led from his work. One was the path of unthinking submission to the nation's cause; it inspired the 'Service Classes' that ran the British Empire and it culminated in the mass sacrifice of the infantry subalterns of the Great War. The other way pushed the Victorian ethic of improvement to its utopian limit; it led to sexual reform, Fabian socialism, the 'simple life', and other attempts to build the New Jerusalem in Britain. The straight road to Waterloo and the crooked road to Wigan Pier began, after all, from the same place – the playing fields of Eton.

Rupert Brooke began on the straight road, then in his Neo-pagan phase took up the banner of reform. But he found the tensions of an emancipated life too much to bear. He reverted to his first beliefs and found – even welcomed – an early death in embracing them. Whether he was indeed a national hero, or whether he epitomised a national failure of nerve and imagination, is one of the questions posed by this book.

His father, William Parker Brooke, came to Rugby in 1880 to teach classics. The son of a parson, he had taken a First at King's College, Cambridge, then spent six years teaching at Fettes, near Edinburgh. In 1879 Brooke married Ruth Cotterill, the sister of one of his colleagues at Fettes. She was young and pretty, and promised to ease the social duties that her shy, scholarly husband found hard to manage. But she was also domineering and fiercely moralistic, as one might expect of a daughter of the manse and a niece of the Bishop of Edinburgh. Parker Brooke, who was only five foot three, soon acquired a look of hiding behind his moustache; nor was it hard to see from whom he was hiding.

Fettes was a recently founded offshoot of Rugby, so it was a step up the ladder for Brooke to move to the 'home' school. Once established there, he never looked to any wider horizon. He taught at Rugby for thirty years, gaining fame for such exploits as giving marks from zero downwards, or bringing his dog to class and making it sit in the wastepaper basket. After eleven years he was made housemaster of the house called School Field. This was a crucial promotion for a public school master, since he could pad out his salary with a handsome profit on the food and accommodation supplied to the boys in his house. Mrs Brooke now became a combination of matron, lodging-house keeper and substitute mother to fifty boys. She kept one sharp eye on their morals and the other, equally sharp, on the cost of their food. Over the years, her husband had developed an unfortunate habit of nervously fiddling with keys in his trouser pocket while teaching. His pupils unkindly suspected him of fiddling with something else; they gave him the name of 'Tooler', and 'Ma Tooler' to his wife.

Rupert Brooke was born on 3 August 1887, the second of his parents' three sons, and named after the Cavalier general Prince Rupert, whom his father admired. His middle name, Chawner, came from one of his mother's ancestors who had been a fanatical Roundhead. The combination proved to be a good index of his divided soul. Mrs Brooke was disappointed that he was not a girl, for she had lost a baby daughter after her first son was born. As Rupert grew up, she was frightened by his delicate health. She was reluctant to let him get too far out of sight and sent him to a prep school, Hillbrow, that was only a hundred yards down the road. There he became friends with James Strachey, who was in his form, and met a Scottish boy two years older, Duncan Grant.

When Rupert entered Rugby School, at the age of fourteen, he went on living in his father's house. One could say that he now went to school by staying at home, a peculiar and anxious situation. He was one of the boys, and one of the family; he had to conceal from his friends how he felt about his parents, and conceal from his parents what his friends felt about them. Leading two lives under the same roof, his personality developed along two separate lines. One Rupert was a British stereotype: a model student who excelled at rugby and cricket, diligently studied the classics and kept up a façade of purity for his puritan mother. The other Rupert belonged to the upstairs dormitory, a

world that seethed with contempt for his parents, and also with
erotic intrigue.

In March 1912, while he was staying with his mother, Rupert
casually mentioned Ka Cox – who two weeks earlier had become
his mistress:

> 'Katharine Cox seems', she almost beamed 'to go
> *everywhere.*' 'Oh, yes,' I agreed: and then we were fairly
> launched on you. I felt the red creep slowly up – Damn! It's
> just as it always was; even from the time when the holiday
> mention, at lunch, of the boy of the moment, in the House
> (with apologies, dear!) left me the level red of this blotting-
> paper, and crying with silent wrath.[7]

In his schooldays and his first year at Cambridge, Rupert might
be called homosexual; but if he was, it was more by chance than
by choice. John Lehmann has argued that repressed homosexuality was at the root of Rupert's later emotional problems.[8] In
fact, his case was more complex than that.

Rupert's attraction to other boys was a mixture of fantasy and
the simple fact of living in an all-male society. Until he was
twenty, his cousin Erica Cotterill was the only eligible girl he had
known intimately. At Rugby he had been taken up by a local
author, St John Lucas, a homosexual aesthete who was nine
years older than Rupert. The relation seems to have been harmless enough. It was a gesture of revolt against public school
philistinism, and it gave the sixteen-year-old Rupert affection
and approval that were not supplied by his parents. Under
Lucas's guidance he read Wilde, Dowson and Baudelaire; he
wrote poems with titles like 'Lost Lilies' and an abortive novel
whose hero, Chrysophase Tiberius Amaranth, sat in a 'small pale
green room' smoking opium-flavoured cigarettes. During his last
months at Rugby he duly fell in love with Charles Lascelles, a boy
two years younger than himself. They were two of the prettiest
boys in the school, and first signalled their interest in each other
by exchanging photographs.[9] Rupert gave Lascelles the name of
'Antinous', after the Emperor Hadrian's minion, but almost
certainly the affair did not go beyond a few kisses and a great deal
of purple rhetoric. The love poems inspired by Lascelles are
decorously homoerotic ('My only god' . . . 'dreams of men and
men's desire'), seasoned with portentous hints of outlaw status

('I dared the old abysmal curse').[10] If Rupert was in love, he was also well aware of what being in love required of him:

> You wonder how much of my affaire is true. So do I. (So, no doubt, does he!) It does not do to inquire too closely. It is now very pleasant. Some day perhaps we shall grow old and 'wise', and forget. But now we are young, and he is very beautiful. And it is spring. Even if it were only a romantic comedy, a fiction, who cares? Youth is stranger than fiction.[11]

In a Victorian album, Rupert's mother had written that her favourite quality in a man was 'Earnestness of purpose'; but by the time he left Rugby for Cambridge, her son was already a jester and poseur – one who took with him, for all occasions, an invisible audience.

The New School: Abbotsholme and Bedales

The Victorian public schools and universities were total institutions. They would not have liked to admit it, but they still had much in common with the monasteries from which they had sprung. Total institutions have a way of begetting their own most ferocious adversaries: Luther the spoiled monk, Stalin the spoiled seminarian. One such adversary, though a much gentler one, was Edward Carpenter. In 1880, the year that Parker Brooke joined the staff at Rugby, Carpenter decided to turn his back on the educational system that had formed him. He had become a clerical fellow of Trinity Hall, Cambridge, in 1867, when he was twenty-three. The vacancy arose through the resignation of Leslie Stephen, who was suffering from grievous doubts about Christianity, and also wanted to marry. After six years of teaching Carpenter found himself becoming disillusioned in turn, though more with the academic than with the spiritual world:

> I had come to feel that the so-called intellectual life of the University was . . . a fraud and a weariness. These everlasting discussions of theories which never came anywhere near actual life, this cheap philosophizing and ornamental cleverness, this endless book-learning, and the queer cynicism and

boredom underlying – all impressed me with a sense of utter
emptiness. The prospect of spending the rest of my life in
that atmosphere terrified me.[12]

Carpenter decided to renounce both his fellowship and Holy
Orders. Soon, he had a vision of what he should do instead: 'it
suddenly flashed upon me, with a vibration through my whole
body, that I would and must somehow go and make my life with
the mass of the people and the manual workers.'[13]

For the next seven years Carpenter travelled the Midlands as a
University Extension lecturer, but by the end of this period he
was close to a nervous breakdown, tormented by unfulfilled
homosexual desires. He began to experiment with vegetarianism
and spells of manual labour. Finally he took Whitman's advice:
'The great thing for one to do when he is used up, is to go out to
nature – throw yourself in her arms – submit to her destinies.'[14]
In the summer of 1880 he moved from Sheffield to the hamlet of
Totley, where he lived with a scythe-maker named Albert Fearne-
hough. His companion had a wife and two children, but he seems
to have satisfied Carpenter's sexual needs as well. 'My ideal of
love', Carpenter wrote, 'is a powerful, strongly built man, of my
own age or rather younger – preferably of the working class.
Though having solid sense and character, he need not be specially
intellectual.'[15]

In 1883 Carpenter published his first major book, *Towards
Democracy*, and set up a utopian community at Millthorpe, on
the edge of the Derbyshire moors. Attracting a stream of disciples
and curious visitors, Carpenter made his home into a potent
centre of propaganda. Like Arnold's Rugby, Millthorpe achieved
an integrated way of life, designed by a dominant, single-minded,
magnetic personality. Its ideal was summed up in the phrase the
'Simple Life'.[16] Carpenter supported himself by growing veg-
etables and by writing; he proclaimed his comradeship with
manual workers; he dressed in tweeds and home-made sandals
(he called shoes 'leather coffins'); he sunbathed, swam nude in
the river at the end of his garden, and denounced the evils of the
town and the factory. His remedy for Britain's ills was socialism,
rural self-sufficiency and sexual reform.

The Millthorpe colony fascinated middle-class young men

who suffered from the classic late-Victorian anxieties: worries over sexual identity, dissatisfaction with politics, or simple 'neurasthenia'. That Carpenter had found the courage to leave Cambridge made him an oracle for those who remained there, and for the many other intellectuals who were fretted by industrialism and city life. Having consulted the oracle, people like Goldsworthy Lowes Dickinson or E. M. Forster returned to their conventional surroundings, but with a changed outlook. Millthorpe inspired its visitors to go out and build anew, to bring to the everyday world Carpenter's vision of a return to the essentials of life.

Carpenter had left the educational system in disgust; Cecil Reddie did so too, but then went back to try and renew it. Reddie came from the Anglo-Scottish middle class and went to school at Fettes, where Parker Brooke would have been one of his teachers. He took a science degree at Edinburgh, and a PhD in chemistry from Göttingen. In 1885 he returned to Fettes to teach, and soon became a thorn in the side of his headmaster. Reddie was an eager socialist and member of the Fellowship of the New Life, the utopian society from which the Fabian Society was born. Even more disturbing was the secret society he founded, 'The Gild of the Laurel', which had the curious ambition of preserving the sexual purity of his favourite students.

  After only two years at Fettes, Reddie was moved on to Clifton College, another satellite of Rugby. Here, he lasted only a year. He could not take orders from a superior and he loudly disagreed with every existing plan of education, especially in the public schools:

> Listen to the four maxims of a great English school perpetually dinned into the boy's ears. Be industrious; that is, try and get above your comrades. Be self-restrained; cork up your feelings and be cold, formal, and 'moral'. Be modest; that is, be prudish and affected, be 'gentlemanly' instead of natural and healthy. Be pure; that is, conquer and kill one lust ... but never a word against lust of money, lust of power, lust of comfort. ...
>   These are the 'moral' maxims of an immense school; but, as one boy, starved on these husks, said: 'But, oh, sir, affection is foreign to the whole spirit of this place.'[17]

Close to a breakdown, Reddie fled to Carpenter's Millthorpe to take stock of his life:

> In that quiet valley there was a wonderful peace. Our meals
> were simple, but marvellously satisfying. . . . We would go
> to the little brook at the bottom of his garden for a bathe;
> but we stripped rather for the sun and airbath. . . . [Carpen-
> ter] believed that mere nudity in sun and air and water was a
> blessed physician for body, soul, and spirit. He was opposed
> to excessive intellectuality.[18]

As he recovered, Reddie decided that he should go out and found a school of his own. Carpenter's father had died a few years before, leaving him £6000; he contributed funds, and Reddie started Abbotsholme School in 1889. Abbotsholme was a realisation of the *Manifesto for a New School*, issued by the Fellowship of the New Life in 1886. Its ideal was 'the nurturing and disciplining of the young child so that it might come to live the life of true freedom; to be a law unto itself, and a beneficent power in the world'.[19] Unfortunately, Reddie was an autocrat and a crank as well as an idealist, and he kept Abbotsholme in a perpetual uproar.

The aims of the school were sensible enough: co-operation rather than competition, the use of German pedagogical tech-niques, and training in practical country pursuits. But Reddie's personal style was completely at odds with his principles. He took it for granted that he should have absolute rule, not just over the boys, but over the staff too. Abbotsholme, he said, was like a battleship, and he was the captain on the bridge. Everyone in the school had to wear a 'Simple Life' uniform of his own design: a 'Norfolk suit' of grey tweed with big pockets and knee breeches, complete with thick woollen stockings and stout boots. The school became a revolving door for idealistic young teachers who could not stomach Reddie's overbearing style.

Racked by desertions and mutinies, the 'battleship' could not steer a straight course and Reddie suffered a series of nervous breakdowns. He could not recognise his own lust for power, nor his pederastic instincts. Between the ages of eleven and eighteen, he believed, schoolboys should go to a single-sex school, with only bachelor masters. 'Worship of the male type', he wrote, 'is the natural hero-worship of adolescence; and comradeship is the natural outlet for the affections among normal boys during this period.'[20] The school hymn, adapted from Whitman, was 'The Love of Comrades'; the chapel and grounds were adorned with statues of joyous, naked boys. In summer, there was compulsory nude bathing in the river.

Reddie was deeply fascinated by male adolescent sexuality – and deeply fearful of it. He decided that all the boys would be given 'scientific instruction' on sex, but also that he would 'organise silently and secretly a body of selected natures to undertake the helping of the sick, and the watching over the weak'. Probably Reddie was celibate; he lived alone, and if he was actively homosexual he would hardly have had such blatant tastes in statuary. 'The greatest crime against youth is the crime of accelerating puberty,' he observed. Like many talented men of his period, he never really developed beyond puberty himself. Of course Abbotsholme was plagued by scandalous rumours, and parents kept withdrawing boys.[21] When Reddie was at last forced to retire, in the 1920s, there were only three boys left in the school. He withdrew to Welwyn Garden City (another offshoot of the Fellowship of the New Life), where he campaigned for music to be written vertically and for the abolition of capital letters. The torch of reform had long passed into less colourful hands.

J. H. Badley made progressive education work. The son of a country doctor, he did not go to school at all until he was thirteen. His parents gave him lessons on everything from painting to anatomy, and he read widely in their library. After two miserable years at prep school he went on to Rugby, arriving at the same time as a new master: Parker Brooke. Superficially, Badley seemed to bend to the public school yoke. He became both the top pupil in classics and a member of the First XV at rugby. His ambition was to return to Rugby as a master. But at Trinity College, Cambridge, he joined the progressive cause, influenced by such friends as Roger Fry, Goldsworthy Lowes Dickinson and Carpenter himself. After Cambridge Badley made the standard pilgrimage to Germany. When Reddie founded Abbotsholme, Badley signed on as one of the first teachers. After three years, however, he broke with Reddie. He wanted two

things that were anathema to his headmaster: to make Abbotsholme co-educational, and to marry. 'My greatest friend at
Cambridge', he recalled, 'came of a rather well-known feminist
family – Garrett Anderson – and he converted me to co-educa-
tion as being the right thing to be done. Eventually I married his
sister, who was of course still more keen, and who insisted if we
had a school it must have boys and girls together.'[22]

Like almost everybody in this book, Badley had 'a bit of
capital' to back up his ideals. He found a country house called
Bedales near Haywards Heath, Sussex, at a safe distance from
Reddie, and opened his school in 1893. For the first five years it
was a school for boys only, since Badley had his hands full
without the added stigma of sexual mixing. At this time there
were very few co-educational boarding schools in Britain, mainly
Quaker and with little prestige or influence. 'Old Bedales', as it
came to be called, held faithfully to Carpenter's ideal of the
Simple Life. Here is what impressed one ten-year-old boy on his
first day there:

> Mr. Powell, the second master . . . wore clothes unlike other
> men's, a pale blue tweed suit with leather at the cuffs, grey
> stockings and a red tie, and on his feet were very large home-
> made leather sandals. Everything in his house was very
> clean; the walls were whitewashed with few pictures; there
> was plain oak furniture and bare boards. After the evening
> meal, Mr. Powell went into the kitchen to help his wife wash
> up.[23]

The atmosphere of the school was spartan. The boys (and later
the girls) had a large tub under their beds; they began the day by
filling it with cold water and jumping in.[24] They were driven on
long cross country runs; they froze in winter and were hungry
year round; they bullied each other and were beaten – though not
so regularly or savagely as at more conventional schools. The
local people were suspicious of Bedales – how could they not
have been? – but it found its clientele among the bohemian fringe
of the upper-middle class and grew steadily. In 1900 it moved
from Sussex to newly built quarters on a farm near Petersfield,
Hampshire, where it remains and flourishes.

Like many things at Bedales, the students' work on the land
combined idealism and practicality. When George Bernard Shaw

and his allies split off from the Fellowship of the New Life to found the Fabian Society in 1885, he said that they were leaving to organise the docks, rather than 'sitting among the dandelions'.[25] Badley certainly believed that nature was the best of teachers, but he also thought that there was more to be done than sit around in it. At harvest time, Bedalians put in a full day in the fields. The rest of the year they studied in the morning, and worked with their hands in the afternoon. Badley thought that this was a better way to build character than through the master-and-servant rituals of older schools. But he was also continuing the Abbotsholme tradition of preparing students for life in the colonies. The public schoolboy might go abroad as a policeman (like George Orwell) or administrator; the Bedalian would go as a producer. This was the theory, anyway, though Badley's pupils were more likely to till the land in Suffolk than in Saskatchewan.

The emphasis on country pursuits gave Bedales some reputation among the Continental landed aristocracy, such as the Békássys of Hungary. It also impressed Edmond Demolins, who sent his own son there and published in France two books that extolled the English educational ideal of character-building.[26] Monsieur Georges Raverat read them, and decided to send his son Jacques to Bedales too. Georges was making his pile as head of the Le Havre docks; but he was also an intellectual, a nature-lover and a vegetarian who ate for breakfast an exotic new dish called yoghurt. Nearly a fifth of the early Bedalians were foreigners, recruited by Badley to avoid the imperialist chauvinism of the established public schools.

Backed up by his wife, Badley took on the other kind of chauvinism in 1898, when four girls entered the school. 'We dubbed [them] "beastly shes",' recalled Peter Grant Watson, 'and set about to make their lives as intolerable as possible.' It was a typical Bedales paradox, however, that when Watson fell in love with one of the girls it was now his own life that was made intolerable, with one of the younger masters leading the hue and cry.[27] Girls were not to be baited for their sex, certainly, but neither were they to be put on a pedestal. When he was fifteen, Jacques Raverat was taken aside for a lecture by the captain of the school. 'The Chief (as Badley was called) doesn't like stupid and obscene jokes about women,' he was told. 'It's something much too serious to joke about – and also there's nothing funny about something perfectly natural. . . . Sooner or later you're bound to know what women are like. I myself have bathed with naked girls.'[28]

Seen through French eyes, Badley's ideas on sex were at once touching and absurd; and so were the female teachers that he dutifully hired:

> The mistresses were almost always advanced women, feminists, socialists, Tolstoyans, etc. They dressed according to their theories: sandals, hygienic jaeger fabrics, dresses without waists or shape called Gibbahs ... usually in a deliquescent green, thought to be artistic; no corsets, naturally – not hygienic – the hair drawn into flat *bandeaux*; in a word, everything needed to make women as unattractive as possible.[29]

Carrying all this ideological baggage, how did Badley succeed as well as he did? Unlike Reddie, he was no raving crank, and he was a highly gifted and devoted teacher. Because his capital was limited, he had to keep up the appearance of a reputable, fee-paying school for the middle class. There would be self-expression without anarchy, nudity without fornication. Badley's vaguely leftist ideals owed more to William Morris than to Marx. He wanted his pupils to appreciate arts and crafts, physical labour and country life. Industry and Empire, the great political issues of the day, were not pressing concerns for the rural, homespun-clad Bedalians. In the early years, little was done to prepare them for competitive examinations. Badley's religion was a cult of Jesus the man, rather than muscular Christianity. Instead of stringing his students up for the battle of life, he cultivated in them the arts of peace, leisure, domesticity.

At Bedales, the symbolic space of the public school was turned inside out. The buildings had no mock fortifications, nor did they enclose their playing fields. Instead they opened on the woods and meadows where the students would learn to cultivate the land, but could also roam at will. Badley's personality dominated his school as much as Arnold's had dominated Rugby; but one cannot imagine Arnold shovelling out the school's earth-closets for a waiting line of boys with wheelbarrows. There were cooking and sewing classes at Bedales – but only for boys, since

Badley thought that they were the ones who needed lessons. For the patriarchal mystique of Rugby, Bedales substituted an ideal of rational comradeship between the sexes.

Badley retired in 1935, though he went on living at the school; he died in 1967, at the age of 101. His successor was a Rugby science master, F. A. Meier, who had no previous ties to the progressive movement. Bedales did not repudiate its origins, but it has moved steadily towards the educational centre. Its time of glory ran from 1898, when it became co-educational, to the outbreak of the Great War.

Going to Cambridge

Rupert Brooke went up to King's College to read classics because his father had done the same, because his uncle Alan Brooke was dean of the college, and because he had won a scholarship. Until a few years before King's had been a college exclusively for Etonians and it still kept an atmosphere of aristocratic leisure. A standard career might be to go to King's from Eton, become a fellow of the college, then return to Eton as a master. One famous local character, the snobbish aesthete Oscar Browning, had reversed this course: dismissed from Eton on suspicion of moral turpitude, he had returned to be a fellow of King's. His rooms were across the hall from Rupert, but his *fin de siècle* affectations were too much for even Rupert to take.

Instead, Rupert found a replacement for St John Lucas in Charles Sayle, who worked at the university library. Sayle also had gone to Rugby, where he had had a sentimental friendship with J. H. Badley. Small, fussy and spinsterish, his nickname was 'Aunt Snayle'. Bertrand Russell called him 'a well known ass'.[30] Now forty-two, he had a little house at 8 Trumpington Street where he entertained a stream of students and fell tremulously in love with the prettiest ones. 'I do not know if these undergraduates love me,' he wrote in his diary, 'but I know that they love me to love them!'[31] He was also a paedophile – probably quite innocently – swooning over working-class boys, whom he called 'Angels of Earth'.

During his first two years at Cambridge Rupert was a constant visitor to Sayle's house. Geoffrey Keynes (a contemporary from Rugby) and the climber George Mallory were often there with him. Their intimacy was of a kind that has long vanished, and today it appears both touching and preposterous. As with St John Lucas, Rupert was drawn to an older man who could give him domestic tenderness and sympathy. He must have known that Sayle was infatuated with him, but almost certainly there was no sexual contact between them. In later years Rupert kept quiet about the friendship with Sayle, realising how pathetic his way of life might appear to an outsider. Sayle had no such second thoughts. 'I do not know in what language to moderate my appreciation of this great man,' he wrote in his diary, 'great in his ideals, great in his imagination, great in his charm. The world will learn to know him later on. It has been mine to know him now.'[32] Before dismissing this as mere gush, we should remember that it was exactly how most of Britain would judge Rupert in his posthumous heyday.

Justin Brooke (who was not related to Rupert) had come to Cambridge by a very different path. His father was a small grocer in Manchester who single-handedly built up his shop into one of the largest tea merchants in Britain: Brooke Bond.[33] Arthur Brooke could well afford to send his four sons to public school, but, like many progressive Northern businessmen, he mistrusted the education provided for the sons of the gentry. He wanted his children to keep their feet on the ground and their eyes on a future with the family firm. However, he was also open-minded enough to send three of his four boys to Mr Badley's new school in Sussex. Justin Brooke arrived at Bedales in 1896, when he was eleven years old. After two years his father transferred him to Abbotsholme. Three years after that, one of Reddie's regular scandals erupted and Justin was returned to Bedales, where he became head boy in his last year.

Justin's life and character fell under the long shadow of his father. Arthur Brooke had the characteristic powerful will and emotional incompetence of the Victorian self-made man. He forced Justin to give up his natural left-handedness when he was small. When Justin decided that he wanted to become a schoolteacher, like Badley, his father scotched that ambition too.

Justin's two older brothers had gone directly from school into the family firm; Justin, his father decided, could best serve the enterprise by qualifying as a lawyer. He duly went to Emmanuel College, Cambridge, in 1904, but took a backhanded revenge on his father by devoting most of his time and energy to the theatre.

Justin had been taught by Badley that the spoken word had more life in it than the written one. The high point of the school year at Bedales was a Christmas production of Shakespeare, directed by Badley and open to the local community. At Bedales Justin was a star actor, and he soon became a mainstay of the Cambridge Amateur Dramatic Club – specialising in leading ladies, since female students were forbidden to act alongside men. His neat, birdlike features and twenty-two-inch waist made him a natural *ingénue*. Not surprisingly, his looks appealed strongly to his own sex, though he chose not to return the interest. So far as Jacques Raverat was concerned, Justin did not return anyone's interest. Justin once admitted that he didn't understand what friendship was, and had never been sorry to say goodbye to anyone. His nature was an entirely superficial one, Jacques felt – 'incapable of passion, or even of deep affection. Nonetheless, we were very good friends on these terms and even, strangely enough, quite intimate.'[34] When Jacques was at Bedales, Justin had mostly been away at Abbotsholme, but they met again at Emmanuel in the autumn of 1906 and agreed to share lodgings. Jacques had gone to the Sorbonne for a degree in mathematics after leaving Bedales, and was now continuing his studies (somewhat lackadaisically) at Cambridge.

Justin could hardly miss a new arrival at King's who was already making a splash with his looks and neo-decadent style, and who had the same name as his elder brother. Obviously this Rupert Brooke and Jacques should meet, since they were both poets (though Jacques destroyed his verses without letting anybody see them). Jacques' first impression was not favourable. Rupert struck him as an affected schoolboy aesthete. After a while, he realised that this was how Rupert coped with so much pressing, open-mouthed admiration of his startling good looks:

> a childish beauty, undefined and fluid, as if his mother's milk were still in his cheeks. . . . The forehead was very high and very pure, the chin and lips admirably moulded; the eyes

were small, grey-blue and already veiled, mysterious and
secret. His hair was too long, the colour of tarnished gold,
and parted in the middle; it kept falling in his face and he
threw it back with a movement of his head.[35]

Soon Rupert and Jacques were talking from breakfast to midnight of poetry, art, sex, suicide; laughing at 'the ridiculous
superstitions about God and Religion; the absurd prejudices of
patriotism and decency; the grotesque encumbrances called
parents'.[36] Rugby and Bedales had found common ground, and,
since Justin and Jacques were two years older than Rupert, it
was the Bedales spirit that tended to prevail. In those lazy undergraduate days, with three young men who dreamed of entering
adulthood with a clean slate, Neo-paganism had its beginning.

Justin's main project that term was a production of Aeschylus'
Eumenides. Rupert had the right kind of glamour but
unfortunately suffered from stage-fright, so Justin cast him as the
Herald. All he had to do was stand downstage in a short skirt,
look interesting and say nothing. Eddie Marsh, Private Secretary
to the young Cabinet Minister Winston Churchill, experienced
the *coup de foudre* at his first sight of Rupert's 'radiant, youthful
figure'. James Strachey, now at Trinity and able to renew his
acquaintance with Rupert, left a note after the performance
telling him how beautiful he looked.[37] In a single evening, Rupert
had become Cambridge's pin-up of the year, and he threw
himself full tilt into the role of the gay and handsome *ingénue*.
Even the eminent Newnham classicist Jane Harrison was drawn
into the game, with a wry reference in a lecture to Rupert's *bon
mot* that 'Nobody over thirty is worth talking to.' So easily
infatuating others, Rupert was in danger of becoming fatuous
himself. Fortunately, he was able to take much of this adulation
as funny rather than threatening. His sense of humour was
fanciful, part of his gift for posing and dramatising, and when he
chose he could be the most amusing of companions. Because
beauty and humour seem rarely to go together, they are doubly
irresistible when they do.

However, Rupert was all too serious when he confided to
Geoffrey Keynes his plans for making a splash in Cambridge
society:

I shall be rather witty and rather clever and I shall spend my time pretending to admire what I think it humorous or impressive in me to admire. Even more than yourself I attempt to be 'all things to all men'; rather 'cultured' among the cultured, faintly athletic among athletes, a little blasphemous among blasphemers, slightly insincere to myself. . . .

However, there are advantages in being a hypocrite, aren't there?[38]

Today, the word for a character like Rupert's is 'inauthentic'. His playacting came from the strange circumstances under which he had grown up, and from his awareness that other people had become abnormally conscious of him. His schoolboy good looks 'feminised' his personal development and relationships. Suddenly he was flattered, sought out by both sexes, constantly noticed. Beauty meant being at other people's disposal, reflecting back to them whatever they wanted to see in him. He was forced into being secretive, even sly, because he was always juggling claims that had to be kept separate. He ended up living 'many subterranean lives', and taking a positive pleasure in being at the centre of a web of deceit.[39]

Beauty also threatened Rupert's sexual identity: because his looks appealed equally to both sexes, he was left feeling confused and angry about a sexuality that was imposed on him from without. Rupert's puritanical mother had deeply inhibited his sexual responses. By and large, he was not flirtatious. He held conventional ideas about sexual etiquette and would lash out against those whom he felt were pursuing him – especially if they were women, who seemed to him to be betraying their honour by taking the sexual initiative.

For Christmas 1906 Rupert went home to Rugby for a month. While he was there his brother Dick died of pneumonia, after only a week's illness. He was six years older than Rupert, and the two were not especially close. Dick was not as strong as Rupert, emotionally or physically, nor as brilliant – he had started a business career in London instead of going to university. But Parker Brooke took the death hard, and lost whatever authority he had kept within the family. Rupert now became both Mrs

Brooke's favourite son and the 'man of the family', the single focus of her ambition and her powerful will.[40]

A second blow followed on his brother's death. Rupert had been looking forward to seeing some of his younger Rugby friends when they returned for the new term, but instead he suddenly slipped off to Cambridge before they arrived. Most likely he had received a letter ending their relationship from Charles Lascelles, since he virtually disappears from Rupert's life after this point.[41] When he spoke later of the 'enormous period of youthful Tragedy with which [he] started at Cambridge', he meant both the loss of his schoolboy love for Charles Lascelles and the struggle to make a place for himself at King's after his 'effortless superiority' at Rugby.[42]

In April Rupert went to Florence with his brother Alfred, who was now a pupil at Rugby and living in their father's house. At their *pension* in Florence a fellow guest asked Rupert if he came from a public school, and after a minute's contemplation pronounced: 'Rugby!'[43] Nothing abashed, Rupert went off to place flowers on the graves of W. S. Landor and A. H. Clough: both poets who had died at Florence, and both old boys of – yes, Rugby. 'I have been happier at Rugby than I can find words to say,' he would write later to Frances Darwin.

> As I look back at five years there, I seem to see almost every hour golden and radiant, and always increasing in beauty as I grew more conscious: and I could not, and cannot, hope for or even imagine such happiness elsewhere. And then I found the last days of all this slipping by me, and with them the faces and places and life I loved, and I without power to stay them. I became for the first time conscious of transience, and parting, and a great many other things.[44]

There is no reason to doubt that this schoolboy happiness was indeed more real than almost all the emotions that Rupert experienced afterwards; more real because it was part of a more enclosed and less ambiguous world than anything he would know in later years.

II

Young Samurai

The Cambridge Fabians and H. G. Wells

Rupert Brooke arrived at Cambridge posing as a world-weary aesthete. Public school had not fostered much concern for the outside world; Rupert's early politics were staunchly Liberal, like his father and mother. Cambridge gave him wider and more radical prospects. With a kindred spirit at King's, Hugh Dalton, Rupert started a reading-club called 'The Carbonari', inspired by the secret society of Italian revolutionaries.[1] Jacques Raverat made him a follower of Hilaire Belloc, the strenuously Anglophile Frenchman who had become a British subject in 1902 and had been elected to Parliament in 1906 as a Radical Liberal. In June of 1907 Belloc came to speak at Cambridge. His habit was to keep a large hunk of cheese in his pocket, from which he could cut slices as needed, and wash them down with large draughts of beer. By the end of his speech he was incapable of going home unaided, and Rupert volunteered to shepherd him to his bed.

Belloc sided with the working class and the Irish, but was too eccentric and egotistical to march in step with the rising socialist tendency. In alliance with G. K. Chesterton he broke away from the Fabian socialists to promote 'Distributism', a neo-medieval alternative to modern capitalism. His ideal, as Rupert saw it, was to go back to the merry days before the Reformation when every Englishman had a cottage, a field and all the beer he could drink.[2]

Belloc's heartiness and love of the English countryside contributed one strain to the Neo-pagan sensibility. But there was also a bullying and suspicious side to his nature, including a rabid streak of anti-semitism. Jacques embraced this prejudice, and passed it on to Rupert. From now on, anti-semitic slurs were freely sprinkled in Rupert's letters, usually harping on the Jews as rootless, intellectually destructive outsiders. He and Jacques imagined that the traditional English way of life, based on the field and the village, was threatened by urban plutocrats of mongrel origin. Belloc himself went much further, wanting actually to revive the Middle Ages and restore the supremacy of Rome. He was a belligerently orthodox Catholic, an anti-Dreyfusard and an enemy of female suffrage (lecturing to an Extension class, he pointed to his women students and said 'These are not the kind of women we want to make our wives').[3] The Catholicism was too much for Rupert to swallow, but the anti-semitism and anti-feminism he adopted as incongruous elements in his socialistic beliefs. At this stage, these dislikes were perhaps only two of many other affectations. After his nervous breakdown in 1912, however, they took on a more obsessive and sinister tone as cornerstones for the aggressive philistinism of his last phase.

Belloc's campaign for 'Distributism' was really a one-man band, which meant that by late 1907 a leftist student at Cambridge was almost bound to gravitate to the 'scientific' socialism of the Fabian Society. George Bernard Shaw, H. G. Wells and Beatrice and Sidney Webb had been putting up an intellectual firework display that more than doubled the size of the Society, though it still had only about two thousand members.[4] Ben Keeling, a Trinity undergraduate and fiery revolutionary, set up a branch of the Young Fabians at Cambridge. He promoted a speech by the militant trade unionist Keir Hardie. When a mob of rugger-playing hearties vowed to prevent it, Keeling foiled them by deploying two counterfeit Hardies, rigged out with beards and red ties. In his room he had a large poster of the workers of the world striding ahead with clenched fists, over the slogan 'Forward the Day is Breaking'.[5] The only actual workers that the undergraduate socialists knew were their bed-makers, who would give them advance warning of raids by the hearties. Nonetheless, revolution was in the air and the Cambridge students were eagerly debating how it would come and what part they would play in it.

At first Rupert would put only one foot into their camp, signing on as an associate rather than a full member. His uncle Clement Cotterill, a disciple of William Morris, had just published a pamphlet whose title put Fabianism in a nutshell: *Human Justice for Those at the Bottom from Those at the Top*. Rupert told Cotterill that he hoped to convert the Cambridge Fabians to 'a more human view of things. . . . Of course they're really sincere, energetic, useful people, and they do a lot of good work. But, as I've said, they seem rather hard. . . . They sometimes seem to take it for granted that all rich men, and all Conservatives (and most ordinary Liberals) are heartless villains.'[6] To go even as far as this set Rupert on a different course from his two closest friends, Jacques Raverat and Justin Brooke. Both were the sons of rich men and expected to inherit a comfortable patrimony. Their fathers were liberal enough to send them to Bedales, but Badley's creed was the Simple Life rather than the expropriation of private property. Jacques remained a folk-revolutionary of the Belloc type, while Justin's passion was the theatre, not politics.

A crucial difference between the Fabians and Belloc lay in their attitude to the crusade for women's suffrage. Belloc was a patriarchal chauvinist, whereas the Fabians were coming round to equal rights for women (even if some of the male members found this hard to swallow). The Fabian Society became the first place at Cambridge where male undergraduates and the women of Newnham College could meet on equal terms. When Rupert joined and got on to the steering committee, a Newnhamite called Ka Cox had just become treasurer.

Ka was the daughter of Henry Fisher Cox, a Fabian who also had enough business sense to become a prosperous stockbroker. His first wife died young, leaving three daughters: Hester, Katharine and Margaret. Henry then remarried and had two more daughters before dying suddenly in 1905, when Ka was eighteen. Ka and her two grown-up sisters were left financially independent. She had a cottage near her father's old estate in Woking, and shared her sister Hester's flat in Westminster when she was in London. She was in the unusual position, for a young woman of her class, of being relatively free to live and travel – and even to love – as she pleased. Ka was not conventionally pretty, but she had a sweet nature and a fresh, clear-skinned look that appealed to many of her fellow students. They felt that she would accept and nurture them, soothing the trials of their young manhood. Rupert once called her 'a Cushion, or a floor'.[7] Her troubles would begin when she discovered needs and initiatives of her own.

When Rupert began working closely with Ka in the Young Fabians, he already knew her as a friend of Jacques and Justin. She had walked up the north coast of Cornwall in August 1907 with them and her sister Margaret, adopting the Bedales custom of going off for fifty-mile walks several times a year. Jacques had fallen mysteriously ill at Easter and had been obliged to abandon his studies; he had recovered enough to go on the Cornish tour, then collapsed again. He would feel deathly ill for no good reason, then suddenly feel better. The doctors could not even decide whether it was his body or his mind that was sick. He had always been prickly and temperamental – a 'Volatile Frog', Virginia Woolf would call him – but now his moods were more extreme and he often found it a strain to be in company. No one at all realised that he was already in the grip of a progressive and incurable disease.

Jacques' father took him back to France to recuperate, and by December he seemed well enough to join Rupert and his younger brother Alfred for a winter sports holiday at Andermatt in the Bernese Oberland. But he suffered a 'maniacal episode' on the train to Andermatt, and soon had to be removed from the hotel to a nearby sanatorium.[8] It is now recognised that acute hysteria in someone of Jacques' age, and with no history of mental illness, may signal the onset of multiple sclerosis. This was indeed his unhappy fate. But the disease was not diagnosed for another seven years, and in the meantime he was treated as if he had simply had a nervous breakdown. Everyone sensed that he was ill; no one, least of all Jacques himself, could do much to help it.

It was the latest craze for undergraduates to spend Christmas skiing and tobogganing in the Alps, where you could enjoy a fortnight's holiday – including train, hotel and enormous meals – for about a pound a day.[9] Moreover, about half the party were girls, many of them from the cloistered precincts of Newnham. They were strictly chaperoned, of course, by a friend of Rupert's mother called Mrs Leon, but at Cambridge it was forbidden for a male undergraduate even to go for a walk with a Newnham girl.[10] For Rupert, Andermatt was a crucial step out of the predominantly male world he had grown up in. Before going, he told his cousin Erica that the group would be 'Mostly young, heady, strange, Females. I am terrified.' When he got there he reported that they were not so terrible as he had feared – 'Several are no duller to talk to than males.'[11] Behind the facetiousness lay a real discovery: of the appeal of mixed company, and of one girl in particular, Brynhild Olivier.

. Bryn, as she was commonly called, was not a Cambridge student. She was brought by her older sister Margery, a leader of the Cambridge Fabians. Margery had been put in charge of her three younger sisters (the other two were Daphne and Noel) when their father, Sir Sydney Olivier, left England to become Governor-General of Jamaica in April 1907 and took Lady Olivier with him. Bryn, born in 1887, had been named after the wise queen in William Morris's *Sigurd the Volsung*. Her parents had many ties with the Morris and Edward Carpenter circles, and Sir Sydney had been one of the first Fabians (he and his friend Sidney Webb signed up in 1885).

The Oliviers were founding members of the 'aristocracy of the left' that had developed around the Fabian Society. The Webbs and the Shaws were childless, but families like the Oliviers, the Blands, the Peases and the Reeves had produced a clutch of progressively raised children who had grown up with the Society and were now young adults. The four Olivier sisters were all handsome and made an overwhelming impression when seen arriving as a party, even more when accompanied by their equally striking parents. Their cousin Laurence would become the most handsome and eminent of them all, though in 1907 he had only just been born.[12] But, of the sisters, Bryn stood out as the true beauty, with her father's riveting good looks. 'Most fetching,' was one contemporary's verdict, 'sweet, charming, gay. Very pale amber eyes.'[13] Rupert had met someone who could 'snap up every glance in the room' as effortlessly as himself.

The natural thing to do in the evenings, in those days, was to put on a play – and what could be better than *The Importance of Being Earnest*? As the obvious belles of the company, Rupert would be Algernon and Bryn, Cecily. To play the lover both in jest and in earnest was enough to sweep Rupert off his feet. 'There is One! . . . oh there is One,' he told his cousin Erica, 'aged twenty, *very* beautiful & nice & everything. . . . My pen is dragging at its bit to run away with me about her. I adore her, for a week.'[14] It was characteristic of Rupert to wonder whether he was experiencing his first love for a woman, or just playing the part expected of him in a holiday romance. What kept the affair within bounds was Bryn's ability to play the game without any risk of losing her head. She already had enough admirers to know how to take their measure; also, she was shortly to go back to Jamaica with her parents. Even if Bryn had been more pliant, a real love affair was not thinkable at Andermatt. The young ladies were closely chaperoned by the Leons and other respectable older couples. They still wore long skirts to go skiing. They were not expected, nor did they expect themselves, to go to bed with anyone before marriage. If they should break this rule, the current state of contraception put them desperately at risk of scandal.

Groups like the skiers at Andermatt had scarcely existed before the Edwardian years. In Victorian times propriety, and lack of an independent income, made it almost impossible for such mixed groups of middle-class youths to go on extended outings together. When they first appeared, around the turn of the century, their members still believed that the period between adolescence and marriage should be a sexual moratorium. Their erotic yearnings were not confined to a single beloved, but were shared out among all. Love could easily be felt for a whole cluster of friends, instead of being saved for the narrower pleasures of the couple. The wheel of sexual choice had begun to spin, but all had agreed to wait a few years before cashing in their stake. Too much sexual commitment could be the enemy of friendship. Prolonged courtship created the group, and the end of courtship would eventually destroy it.

When he arrived at Andermatt, Rupert had been much impressed that his party were 'nearly all Socialists, and . . . all great personal friends of H. G. Wells'.[15] For two years now, Wells had been trying to take over the Fabian Society and make it the instrument for a root-and-branch transformation of British life. He had been successfully boxed in by the Old Guard on the Fabian executive: the Webbs, Bernard Shaw, Hubert Bland and Edward Pease. But Wells had made more headway with several of the Old Guard's wives and children, who were attracted by his feminism, his eagerness to transform private as well as public life, and his sheer bounciness. He was the roguish uncle, always ready for a spree. As the children of his Fabian friends went to university Wells tried to recruit them, and at the same time to savour the undergraduate pleasures that had been denied him in his own hard-pressed student days at the Normal School of Science in South Kensington.

In February 1908 Wells gave a lecture to the Cambridge Young Fabians. Afterwards, he agreed to discuss 'the family' – which meant his new and dangerous ideas on sex – with a group of students and dons in Rupert's rooms at King's.[16] Rupert was by now a firm Wellsian, and he soon moved to become a full member of the Fabians by assenting to 'The Basis'. This called for the abolition of private property, rent and interest, and for the equal citizenship of men and women.

Wells had given Rupert two incentives to take the plunge and become a full-blooded socialist. There was, first, the wonderful painlessness of being a Wellsian revolutionary. 'Socialism may arrive after all,' Wells suggested, 'not by a social convulsion, but by . . . a revolution as orderly and quiet as the procession of the equinoxes.' The leader of this stately march would be the 'Constructive Socialist', who undertakes 'whatever lies in his power towards *the enrichment of the Socialist idea*. He has to give whatever gifts he has as artist, as writer, as maker of any sort to increasing and refining the conception of civilized life.'[17] The cynic might observe that this would allow Rupert to go on doing what he was doing already, but with a good social conscience. Ingenuous as always, Wells had just informed the *Labour Leader* that he didn't want people to live in slums on a pound a week, so why should he live that way himself? 'I am ready to go on working for [socialism],' he concluded, 'having just as good a time and just as many pleasant things as I can.'[18]

An opposite sort of appeal lay in the disciplined half of Wells's split personality. In *A Modern Utopia*, published three years earlier, he had imagined a new kind of ruling class, the high-minded and ascetic 'Samurai'. Unlike the existing British aristocracy, the Samurai would be an intellectual elite, living modestly and abstaining from alcohol or tobacco. However, their training would include a period of sexual experimentation – which pointed to the 'hidden agenda' that Wells was trying to insinuate into Old-Guard Fabianism:

> The majority of those who become *samurai* do so between twenty-seven and thirty-five. And, between seventeen and thirty, the Utopians have their dealings with love, and the play and excitement of love is a chief interest in life. Much freedom of act is allowed them so that their wills may grow freely. For the most part they end mated, and love gives place to some special and more enduring interest, though, indeed, there is love between older men and fresh girls, and between youths and maturer women.

Once a year the Samurai were required to spend a week alone in the wilderness, in order 'to secure a certain stoutness of heart and body in the members of the order, which otherwise might have lain open to too many timorous, merely abstemious, men and women'.[19]

This enticing curriculum was a reversal of Wells's own experience: he had practised self-denial in his youth, by hard necessity, and was now revelling in a promiscuous middle age. His Samurai rulers would work intensely and keep the lower orders under strict scientific control, but in their private lives they would be moral adventurers and a law unto themselves. Wells himself did not aspire to be a muscular Samurai mountaineer. His need for adventure was centred on the pursuit of 'fresh girls', as he ambiguously called them. It was splendid that his friend Sydney Olivier should become a Samurai Governor of Jamaica, improving the lot of the 'subject races' (as they were then called). But Wells needed something closer to centre stage. He liked invitations from the society hostess Lady Desborough, or making thousands of pounds on his popular novels, or chasing the daughters of his Fabian colleagues. He was so made, furthermore, that part of the enjoyment of these actions was to ensure that everyone could see what he was up to. His recklessness ensured that he would before long be in hot water, both with the outraged right and the puritanical left.

'Yours Fraternally'

While Rupert was deepening his commitment to Fabianism he also found himself, almost accidentally, joining a different kind of self-appointed elite. When James Strachey made him a declaration of love after the performance of the *Eumenides* in November 1906, Rupert made it clear that he wanted nothing more than friendship – and probably not even that unless James could control his infatuation. But James went on pursuing him, getting as close as he dared and then retreating when Rupert turned skittish. He followed Rupert into the Fabians, abandoning his former conservatism without a pang. But in the company of political enthusiasts like Ben Keeling, or of emancipated 'new women' like Ka Cox or Margery Olivier, James was bound to look pallid and peripheral. He was finicky, hypochondriac and graceless. What use was it to be loyal and intelligent when you had the personality and status of a schoolboy swot? If he wanted to shine in Rupert's eyes, he would have to get him on to his own ground and in a more intimate setting. The ideal way – the only way – to do this was to promote Rupert's election to the Apostles, of whom James had been a member since February of 1906.

By now the Apostles or 'The Society' must be the world's least secret secret society.[20] Until the turn of the century (it was founded in 1820) it had been an exclusive and idealistic circle of male friends. They referred to each other as 'brothers', and signed their letters 'Yours fraternally'. Several Apostles of the 1880s and 1890s, such as Eddie Marsh, G. L. Dickinson, J. McT. E. McTaggart and G. E. Moore, were romantically drawn to their own sex, but they were shy of giving their feelings a physical expression, and might even have denied that they had such feelings at all. From 1901 to the beginning of the war, however, a majority of those elected were actively homosexual, and among these Lytton Strachey and John Maynard Keynes were most influential in setting the Society's tone. Under their regime, talk about philosophy and the good life was combined with compulsive flirtation.

Gradually, the 'brothers' divided into two distinct types. Some – Lytton and James Strachey, Keynes, J. T. Sheppard – were intellectually and sexually on the prowl, often as a way of making up for feelings of physical inferiority. To be both clever and ugly was their uneasy fate. Then there were those whose ticket of entry was their boyish good looks and the passion they had inspired in someone from the first group: people like Arthur Hobhouse, Cecil Taylor and Brooke himself. Whatever intellectual gifts they had, these were not the main reason they had been elected. Within a few years, the Society had been reorganised around the sexual couple.

For years before his election, Rupert had been a closely watched candidate, or 'embryo' in the Society's jargon. 'I wasn't particularly impressed,' Lytton reported to Keynes in September 1905 (when Rupert was starting his last year at Rugby). 'His appearance is pleasant – mainly, I think, owing to youth. . . . He's damned literary, rather too serious and conscientious, and devoid of finesse.'[21] Nonetheless, Rupert became an Apostle on 25 January 1908, shortly after his return from Andermatt. He owed his election mainly to James Strachey, who had to overcome heavy opposition from unnamed quarters.[22] Three years earlier, Lytton Strachey and Keynes had pushed through the election of another yellow-haired public school hero, Arthur Hobhouse. He had turned out to be a grave disappointment, both sexually and intellectually. His sponsors probably feared that Rupert would be a pea from the same pod, but finally gave in to James's pleadings.

Rupert held his own as an Apostle, however. For the Easter vacation of 1908 he was asked to join G. E. Moore's reading party at Market Lavington, on the edge of Salisbury Plain. Since he scarcely knew Moore, this was a notable endorsement from the man whose *Principia Ethica* (1903) had made him the unchallenged intellectual leader of the Society. Being invited to one of Moore's reading parties was the entry into an inner circle that included most of the Apostles who became members of 'Bloomsbury'.[23] Reading parties were an old Oxbridge tradition, and Rupert had already been on a few with his schoolfriends. But the gathering at Market Lavington was in a different league altogether. Besides Moore there were Keynes, the poet Bob Trevelyan, the barrister C. P. Sanger, the economist Ralph Hawtrey, the critic Desmond MacCarthy, and Lytton and James Strachey. For someone who had scraped through his preliminary classics exams with a shaky second the previous May, Rupert might seem to be in over his head. But his looks, good humour and native wit pulled him through. 'Rupert Brooke – isn't it a romantic name?' Lytton told Virginia Woolf, '– with pink cheeks and bright yellow hair – it sounds horrible, but it wasn't. . . . I laughed enormously, and whenever I began to feel dull I could look at the yellow hair and pink cheeks of Rupert.'[24]

In fact, Rupert's animal spirits were badly needed by the group at the Green Dragon Inn. Moore's philosophy fitted in cosily with the aesthetic interests of a few congenial souls, but it counted for very little in the world beyond Trinity and King's. Many of the Apostles gathered at Market Lavington had been struggling with arrested development, spinsterism, hypochondria and inanition. In the egregious Saxon Sydney-Turner these traits had been raised to the level of a vocation, and James Strachey was an equally sad case. He was 'a creature, not a man', in Gwen Raverat's eyes, 'and pitiable for all his brains. He would sit curled up on the sofa looking like a cat that is afraid of wetting its feet.'[25] 'Excessive paleness is what I think worries me most,' Lytton had once confided to Leonard Woolf. 'The Taupe [E. M. Forster] . . . saw this about me, and feeling that he himself verged upon the washed-out, shuddered.'[26] One measure of the 'paleness' of the 1908 reading party was that everyone there, except MacCarthy, either married late or not at all.

In becoming an Apostle, Brooke was committing himself to having two separate sets of friends at Cambridge. One set would follow the Bedalian style of country living, theatricals and an easy mingling of men and women. The other was exclusively male and devoted to philosophical speculation; it was also clandestine, which made it hard for Rupert's other friends to understand why he spent so much time with people they mistrusted – and why he disappeared every Saturday night during term. He had to divide his loyalties, and cunningly keep one life separate from the other. Though he became a loyal 'brother', he would never give himself wholeheartedly to the Society. He had played the game of schoolboy homosexuality, and he didn't mind catering to the Society's obsessive interest in the subject of 'copulation' (as they called it). But Rupert flatly refused to become the lover of James, or of any other 'brother'.[27] Though his *coup de foudre* with Brynhild Olivier had not led to a real love affair, it showed the way that he was inclined to go.

James Strachey, meanwhile, was so doggedly devoted to Rupert that he tried to move the Society into his beloved's orbit. The result was a brief and uneasy alliance between the Society and the Cambridge Fabians. The previous generation of Apostles were virtually all lukewarm Liberals; they tended to look down their nose at politics and to mock Rupert's passion for social improvement. But James danced to Rupert's political tune and managed to get another Fabian – Gerald Shove – into the Apostles, at the beginning of 1909. One consequence of James's manoeuvrings was that the Fabian Society at Cambridge became less of a meeting-ground for male and female undergraduates, and more of a young men's social club with a distinctly homo-sexual tinge. This step backwards was reinforced, paradoxically, by the heterosexual indiscretions of H. G. Wells.

Fabian Daughters: Making Love, Falling in Love

On 10 May 1908 the Cambridge Fabians gave a dinner in honour of Sir Sydney Olivier, who was on a brief visit home from Jamaica. It was a 'socialist meal' of one course followed by fruit, served to twenty-five people in Ben Keeling's rooms. Two guests came in late, and had to sit on a window sill: Olivier's old friend H. G. Wells, and a bright-eyed Newnham student called Amber Reeves. Amber was the daughter of a leading Fabian couple, Maud and William Pember Reeves; her father was soon to be appointed director of the Webbs' new foundation, the London School of Economics, and Amber herself had served as treasurer of the Cambridge Young Fabians.

Wells was in hot water at the time with the Fabian executive.

He had written a letter supporting the Liberal candidate, Winston Churchill, in a Manchester by-election, even though there was also a socialist in the running.[28] At the Fabian annual meeting on 22 April he had tried to defend his letter, then walked off the platform in a huff. The row over the Churchill letter was only the visible tip of a bitter quarrel between Wells and the Fabian Old Guard that had been seething for three years. Publicly, Wells had annoyed them by pressing the Society to support children's allowances, as a means of undermining the 'masculine proprietorship' of women. Privately, he enraged them by drawing their wives towards feminist ideas, and their daughters towards sexual emancipation – in the form of going to bed with *him*. In 1905 he had a brief affair with Rosamund Bland, the nineteen-year-old daughter of Hubert Bland. Wells claimed that he was not especially attracted by Rosamund's plump and brown-eyed charms, but wanted to save her from her father's incestuous advances. Nonetheless, he and Rosamund planned to run off together, but the affair was nipped in the bud when Wells made the mistake of telling too many people what he planned to do before he had actually done it.[29]

In the spring of 1908 Wells was involved, more deeply this time, with Amber. She was the same age as Rupert Brooke, not quite so good-looking but just as much of an eye-catcher. Beatrice Webb was one who gave Amber a long look, and did not much like what she saw: 'an amazingly vital person and I suppose very clever, but a terrible little pagan – vain, egotistical, and careless of other people's happiness. This may be a phase, for she is a mere precocious child, but the phase is unpleasant and not promising for really sound work. . . . if Amber were my child I should be anxious.'[30]

Amber was precocious sexually, as well as intellectually. After some months of friendship with Wells, she took advantage of his visit to Cambridge for the Olivier dinner to tell him that she was in love. When he asked her 'with whom?', she threw herself into his arms. Wells was not one to miss an opportunity, and they went to bed without more ado. What gave this passionate encounter an extra spice was that it took place in Amber's room at Newnham, to which Wells had been admitted on the claim that he was an old friend of the family![31] Both of them were

exactly the sort of people who would enjoy being, in all likeli-
hood, the first couple to use a Newnham room for such a
purpose. However, their embrace had to be incomplete because
H.G. had failed to stop at a chemist first. Having agreed to meet
again soon in Soho, for a more leisurely encounter, they made it
to Trinity in time for dinner. It would be interesting to know
what excuse they gave for being late.

Amber told her parents that she needed to go away on a
reading party to prepare for her finals; in fact she went to
lodgings in Southend with H.G. Returning to Cambridge in high
spirits, and armed with useful tips from her mentor, she took a
First in Part II of the moral science tripos. Wells's formal
resignation from the Fabian Society, six months later, was made
inevitable when news of his affair with Amber started to leak out.

Rupert's infatuation with Brynhild Olivier had no such swift
consummation. Two months after the Christmas party at
Andermatt Bryn went to Jamaica, and stayed there for most of
1908. However, her three other sisters were in Cambridge for the
dinner in their father's honour. It was Rupert's first meeting with
Daphne and Noel, who had come back to England with their
parents after several months in Jamaica. Rupert found himself
opposite Noel at dinner. Just enrolled at Bedales, she liked to
wear the school uniform of blouse and embroidered tunic
wherever she went. She was barely fifteen, and her contribution
to the dinner party was to look shy and break a coffee cup. One
would expect Amber Reeves to put her completely in the shade,
but despite Noel's awkwardness – perhaps because of it – Rupert
was immediately stricken. For Bryn he had felt infatuation; for
her younger sister, he developed a more serious and sustained
passion.

Noel was a lover of the forest, and her father may have chosen
Bedales for her because of this. She would roam the woods with
David ('Bunny') Garnett, looking for dead animals to dissect. In
time this led her to a career in medicine, but as a childish pursuit it
points to a core of coldness and firmness in her character. When
Rupert met her she was still very much the schoolgirl: pure, self-
contained and keen on games. In looks she was her father's child,
with chiselled features and long dark hair. The family used to

tease her by calling her 'the plain child', but when she grew up only Bryn outshone her, and of all the four girls she was most able to inspire romantic devotion in her admirers. 'Noel talked much less than her sisters,' observed Garnett, 'and listened and thought more. She was their superior in intelligence and her superiority became more noticeable with the years.'[32]

Why should Rupert fix his attention on a girl so young, quiet and unformed, instead of on someone more in his own set? Noel was not much interested in politics, nor was she a flamboyant heart-breaker like her older sister Bryn. Fabian daughters like Rosamund Bland or Amber Reeves were avidly grasping the freedoms summed up in the figure of the 'New Woman' – the type propagandised by H. G. Wells. But Rupert, in his deeper self, held to the firmly conventional ideas about young women that had been drilled into him by his mother. A remembered snippet of conversation catches his style:

> *Rupert:* When I marry I shall settle absolutely everything in my own house. My wife must completely obey me.
> *Justin* [Brooke]: (*taking him seriously*) Oh Rupert, I should hate that! I *do* want a wife who can stand up to me.
> *Rupert:* No. I shall settle *everything*.
> [Frances] *Darwin:* But may she never have her own way even about the children?
> *Rupert:* I suppose she may just settle little things about them when they are quite small. That's all.[33]

Behind the joking there was sympathy for his hen-pecked father, but also something more. In Rupert's progressive beliefs, there was a complete gap when it came to feminism, whether of the militant suffragette or milder Fabian slant. He never liked women to take the initiative, and when they wooed him sexually he could not bear it. A sonnet inspired by Noel, 'Success', lays bare his conflict:

I think if you had loved me when I wanted;
If I'd looked up one day, and seen your eyes,
And found my wild sick blasphemous prayer granted,
And your brown face, that's full of pity and wise,
Flushed suddenly; the white godhead in new fear
Intolerably so struggling, and so shamed;

Most holy and far, if you'd come all too near,
If earth had seen Earth's lordliest wild limbs tamed,
Shaken, and trapped, and shivering, for *my* touch –
Myself should I have slain? or that foul you?

Though he was five years older than Noel, in his poems to her
Rupert makes himself young and wayward, while his beloved is
'full of pity and wise'. She is loved as a dryad, a chaste and elusive
creature of the woods; and if *she* were to fall prey to lust for a
man – 'shaken, and trapped, and shivering' – the poet would feel
horror and disgust. Noel's hold on Rupert, then, lay precisely in
his knowing how impervious she was to his charm. An easy or
natural maturing of their affection was hardly to be expected;
nor, deep down, did Rupert want it to mature. Any woman he
loved was expected to be, like his mother, the keeper of his
conscience and censor of his desire.

III

Neo-pagans

Neo-paganism

What was Neo-paganism, and where did it come from? As Rupert moved into his Neo-pagan phase, in the summer of 1908, he announced that he was 'becoming a wild rough elementalist. Walt Whitman is nothing to me.'[1] If Whitman was Neo-paganism's spiritual grandfather, its godfather was Edward Carpenter, with his gospel of nudity, sunbathing and sandals. In 'Civilisation: Its Cause and Cure', Carpenter had predicted the coming of a new and glorious post-Christian man:

> The meaning of the old religions will come back to him. On the high tops once more gathering he will celebrate with naked dances the glory of the human form and the great processions of the stars, or greet the bright horn of the young moon which now after a hundred centuries comes back laden with such wondrous associations – all the yearnings and the dreams and the wonderment of the generations of mankind – the worship of Astarte and of Diana, of Isis or the Virgin Mary; once more in sacred groves will he reunite the passion and the delight of human love with his deepest feelings of the sanctity and beauty of Nature; or in the open, standing uncovered to the Sun, will adore the emblem of the everlasting splendour which shines within.[2]

By living closely with nature, one could learn her secrets and become one of her favourite children. The same message could be found in George Meredith, who was eighty years old in 1908.

Revered as the sage of Box Hill, where he lived in seclusion, he was a powerful influence on Rupert's poetry. The flavour he gave to Neo-paganism can be found in poems like 'Earth's Preference' (for the young over the old), 'Daphne' or 'The Woods of Westermain'. Both Carpenter and Meredith venerated female chastity, unlike the more full-blooded paganism of D. H. Lawrence, or the libertinism of H. G. Wells. Meredith's woods are full of dryads, mystic and sensuous girls who always outrun the young men who seek them out.

The spirit of Meredith was brought down to earth in the new forest suburb of Limpsfield Chart, a few miles east of Box Hill along the Surrey downs. In 1895 Sydney and Margaret Olivier moved there with their daughters, into a converted double cottage called the Champions. Sir Sydney (as he became in 1907) was a man of commanding presence – handsome, athletic and formidably intelligent. He had decided that the best way to put his Fabian principles into practice was to work within the Colonial Office for a more humane administration of the British Empire. His only weak point, perhaps, was his inability to put himself in the place of his less gifted fellows. 'He was a law unto himself,' Bernard Shaw observed, 'and never dreamed of considering other people's feelings, nor could conceive their sensitiveness on points that were to him trivial.'[3]

With no brothers to restrain them, the Olivier girls took their cue from their father's Olympian manner. 'They were all aristocratic creatures,' David Garnett wrote of them, 'pride was the moving force of their lives; they felt contempt easily; pity did not come naturally, except for animals.'[4] Their self-containment was reinforced by their parents' disdain for conventional schooling. The three older girls did not go to school at all, but were intermittently tutored at home. All of them spent much of their childhood roaming the woods for miles around; they were fearless tree-climbers and could outrun most men across country. The family style, Bunny Garnett recalled, was an indescribable 'combination of Meredith and ancient Sparta'.[5]

Soon after the Oliviers moved to Limpsfield, Edward and Constance Garnett followed, to build a house at The Cearne. Their only child, Bunny, would have a playmate his own age, the three-year-old Noel, and Constance could translate her Russian novels in the peace of the country. Others were drawn to this nucleus of the Oliviers and Garnetts: political exiles from Russia like the Kropotkins and Stepniaks; Fabians like the Peases and Hobsons; literary visitors like Conrad or Ford Madox Ford. Limpsfield was different from both the planned utopian community of Welwyn Garden City and the 'beer and cricket' flavour of villages then being colonised by middle-class intellectuals. 'There was no church within two miles,' recalled Bunny Garnett, 'no rookery, no immemorial elms, no ancient red brick or mellowed ashlar walls, no water, no fertile soil. Instead there was a great horizon, solitude, and the encompassing forest.'[6] Leading such unbounded lives, the children there grew up contemptuous of established society. Rupert admired this freedom of spirit in the Olivier sisters, especially Noel, and tried to emulate it. But his own upbringing and temperament were far more constricted. In Neo-paganism there would always be an uneasy coexistence between the pastoral anarchy of Limpsfield and the pastoral reaction of Belloc; and between the new Bedales and the old Rugby.

When the Neo-pagans came together at Cambridge in 1908, many ways for the new generation to escape from Victorianism were in the air, but they had no thought of any formal manifesto to found their group. They were friends of Rupert, and friends of each other, who had a common style of youthful unconventionality, and overlapping links to Bedales, Fabianism, Cambridge and the Simple Life. The central group was Rupert, Justin Brooke, Jacques Raverat, Gwen and Frances Darwin, Ka Cox and the Olivier sisters. Fringe members included Bunny Garnett, Geoffrey Keynes, Ethel and Sybil Pye, Dudley Ward, Godwin Baynes, and Ferenc Békássy. But they were not even called 'Neo-pagans' until three years later – and then by outsiders, and half in derision.

Apart from liking each other, they had various dislikes in common. They agreed that the social conventions of the previous century needed to be consciously trampled on. For some members of the group – Rupert in particular – this meant judiciously snubbing their parents. There were other negative definitions. Being Neo-pagan was something that Young Fabians did when they were not being Fabians, or that the children of Fabians did as a way of not following in their parents' footsteps. They were keeping alive the ideals of Wells's *A Modern Utopia*, after the purging of its author and his ideas from the Fabian Society. They were the friends to whom Rupert turned when he wanted to keep James Strachey and the other Apostles at a distance, and in whom Justin Brooke found refuge from his father and Brooke Bond tea. Neo-paganism was, finally, the antidote to the creed of 'John Rump', a retired public school housemaster who was the butt of one of Rupert's satirical poems. Rump ascends to heaven, with top hat and umbrella, and tells God that what *he* believes in is:

Safety, regulations, paving-stones,
Street-lamps, police, and bijou-residences
Semi-detached. I stand for Sanity,
Comfort, Content, Prosperity, top-hats,
Alcohol, collars, meat.[7]

When Beatrice Webb called Amber Reeves 'a dreadful little pagan', she was invoking the paganism of Aphrodite and the new feminism of cigarette-smoking and careers, free thought and free love. Neo-paganism was not nearly so radical or aggressive. It was, rather, the paganism of Diana and Juno: of free-thinking but chaste young women, who would live as comrades with both sexes, before entering a devoted and domestic marriage. They thought of themselves as an emancipated new generation, and flouted convention by consorting with young men unchaperoned. But they drew a sharp line at sexual freedom; there, they were as much the 'gatekeepers' as their mothers before them. Paradoxically, it was this restraint that allowed the Neo-pagans to continue as a stable group of friends for several years. Rosamund Bland and Amber Reeves, the ripe and un-inhibited Fabian daughters, both found themselves married in 1909. Given the current state of contraception, and of middle-class morality, any sexually active young woman became a loose cannon that had to be quickly tied down. For women, the cycle from licence to confinement was bound to be short. But Amber and H.G. were not thinking this out when they gleefully took their pleasure within the cloisters of Newnham.

Nonetheless, the Neo-pagan ideal of comradeship was bound

to clash with the realities of sexual desire and possessiveness in young men and women alike. Even in the purely male comradeship of the Apostles there was a similar conflict between the 'Higher Sodomy' (idealistic) and the 'Lower' (sensual or lowerclass). Was a young man to be looked on as a soul-mate or a bedmate? Was a girl to be an untouched nymph, a concubine or a wife? The Victorians had firm answers to these questions, but the more thoughtful young Edwardians would not accept them. They were determined to make new rules, out of their own imagination and experience. If Neo-paganism was a false start at coping with the modern world – as perhaps it was – should the blame be laid on youth, or on the old world that hemmed them in so closely when they tried to make all things new?

Comus

It seems right that Rupert and Noel's first shared activity, and the project that made the Neo-pagans into a group, with Rupert as its leader, should be a production of Milton's *Comus*. Here was a masque about a young virgin who loses herself in a forest, is accosted by a silver-tongued seducer, but is saved through the intervention of an Attendant Spirit – played by Rupert. The production was sponsored by Christ's College to celebrate the tercentenary of the birth of its former student and Cambridge's greatest poet.[8] Justin and Rupert were enlisted as directors, but Justin also had finals to think about, so Rupert found himself both stage manager and playing the longest part.

Justin had already begun a revival of the Elizabethan drama at Cambridge. In the autumn of 1907 he decided to produce Marlowe's *Doctor Faustus*. He first tried to persuade the Amateur Dramatic Club to put it on, instead of their usual Victorian farces; when they refused, he set up what became the Marlowe Dramatic Society. Justin wanted to do at Cambridge what Badley had already done at Bedales: to present Elizabethan verse as living, rhythmic speech (instead of stilted recitation), and to cast women in the female roles. Unfortunately, the authorities of Newnham were not yet willing to let their young ladies take part in such a dubious venture. Nonetheless, *Faustus* was performed on 11 and 12 November 1907. The general verdict was that it was odd but effective, despite having no music, scenery or footlights. Rupert played one of the leads, Mephistophilis, though he made no great impression. In everyday life he was theatrical to a fault and could read poetry brilliantly to his friends, but on stage he tended to 'choke'.

Because *Comus* was a masque rather than a play, and was being produced out of term, Justin and Rupert could cast their net much more widely than previous student directors and even have women in the female roles. Francis Cornford, a young classics don from Trinity, would play the seducer Comus; Jane Harrison recruited young ladies from Newnham (including Dorothy Lamb as Sabrina); Albert Rothenstein came from London to paint the scenery. Two cousins, Frances and Gwen Darwin, were given the job of designing the costumes. Neither of them was at Newnham, but as granddaughters of Charles Darwin they could claim deep roots in the Cambridge intellectual aristocracy. Frances's father, Francis, was an eminent botanist and a fellow of Christ's. She had inherited from her grandfather the prognathous jaw and vaguely simian features that inspired the famous Victorian cartoon of the man blending into the ape. Her looks were comely enough, though more striking than winsome. She was already sensitive, artistic and a poet when Rupert met her, and her photographs suggest that she liked striking a pose almost as much as he did.

Frances was a year older than Rupert, but when the production of *Comus* began she had just returned to Cambridge after four years in limbo. Her mother's death, when Frances was seventeen, had caused a series of nervous breakdowns; she had been shuttled from one cure to another in Cannes, Switzerland and England. In later life she would again suffer from bouts of depression, yet she had a base of stable common sense that her friends would often rely on in troubles that lay ahead.

Gwen Darwin's father, George, was another leading scientist, a professor of astronomy and a fellow of Trinity. Like Frances, Gwen belonged to the first generation of academic children that appeared when dons were permitted to marry from 1878 on. Her girlhood, in the tight-knit and high-minded society of Victorian Cambridge, had not been easy; she was 'fat and clumsy and plain' – and shy and bespectacled for good measure. But these awkward years had developed her gifts of sense and observation. In the year of *Comus* she was twenty-three – a year older than Frances – but only just emerging from her powerful family. She had wanted to be a painter since she was thirteen. Her parents had finally acknowledged that her talent for drawing was more than just a childish knack, and had agreed that she could go to London and enroll at the Slade. It was the start of her career as a minor but exemplary British artist.

Frances and Gwen drew in other young women: to help with the costumes, like Ka Cox and Sybil and Ethel Pye (neighbours of the Oliviers at Limpsfield), or just to clean brushes, like Noel. But most of the power gravitated to Rupert, who became effectively the producer, director and star. As head of his house at Rugby he had learned how to direct others, and his talent for organisation had a lot to do with his becoming the central figure of the Neo-pagans. Any social event is, after all, a kind of dramatic performance. Someone must decide a time and place for the action, arrange transportation and props, give the participants some hint of the roles they are to play. From Justin, Rupert had learned the actor's knack of making himself a centre of attention. His friends became his daily audience – an insidious bond, perhaps, but one that gave intensity to casual gatherings, and raised them into occasions that lingered in memory.

The pleasures of the group required also that each should care more for the ensemble than for any favourite partner. So Rupert was not entirely facetious in asking his collaborators on *Comus* to swear that none of them would get engaged to be married within six months of the masque's performance.[9] Having assembled a group of friends of which he was the unchallenged leader (unlike his subordinate role in the Apostles or the Fabians), Rupert wanted to steer them into the future with closed ranks.

Frances Darwin saw how Rupert's beauty and charm made him into a symbol for his admirers. Noticing once that his blond locks were highlighted by the sun from a window above the stage, she sketched a little poem on her vision:

A young Apollo, goldenhaired
Stands dreaming on the verge of strife

Magnificently unprepared
For the long littleness of life.

After Rupert's death, the poem became merely sentimental – a
cultural cliché of the Great War. But Frances had grasped the
contradiction in Rupert's position: the golden boy of his tribe
who could not live up to his pedestal, fatally undermined by his
own weakness and by the adulation he provoked. His long hair,
casual dress and schoolboy-hero manner were the target for
every kind of gush and sentimentality. More than could be true of
any beautiful young woman at that time, Cambridge made
Rupert into a *mystified* sexual object. But it could not have done
so if he had not accepted the role. Frances describes how the girls
taught him to hang his head upside down and shake out his hair;
afterwards he could be seen 'rumpling his fingers through the
front and gazing in the glass with melancholy flower-like eyes. "I
can't get it right. Is it right now? Will my hair do now?"'[10]
    For all Rupert's care, the actual performances of *Comus*, at the
New Theatre on 10 and 11 July, fell short of a triumph. The
literary world outside Cambridge was well represented. Thomas
Hardy came up from Dorset, and Rupert was invited to breakfast with him. He summed him up memorably as 'incredibly
shrivelled and ordinary, and said faintly pessimistic things in a
flat voice about the toast'.[11] Also present on the first night were
Alfred Austin, the Poet Laureate; Robert Bridges, who left early;
and Edmund Gosse – who when someone congratulated him on
having heard *Comus* replied, 'I have overheard it.'[12] Lytton
Strachey's review in the *Spectator* gave the fairest summing-up of
what the production had achieved:

> How infinitely rarely does one hear, in any theatre, the
> beauty that is blank verse! From this point of view, the
> performance at Cambridge was indeed memorable. . . . The
> existence of such a body of able and enthusiastic lovers of
> poetry and drama must be welcomed as at least an augury of
> a better state of things.[13]

    The weakness of the Marlowe Society was that their produc-
tions had more poetry than drama. Rupert loved gorgeous
language, but he had little sense of creating a character or

working in an ensemble. There was still a gulf between the universities and the London stage: few of the Marlovians became professional actors, and they were complete novices at present-ing a natural interplay between men and women. The whole production was a kind of glorified charade, like the set-pieces of so many Edwardian parties. After the final performance, a cast party followed at Newnham Grange – Gwen Darwin's home on the river – where the actors remained in costume to mingle with their guests. Rupert's tunic was so short and tight he couldn't sit down; he could have danced, along with the rest, except that dancing was something he could never bring himself to do.

When the party ended, Mrs Brooke carried off her son for three months in Rugby (including a subdued twenty-first birth-day, on 3 August). She was disturbed by his seeming to be over-tired and over-excited; by his cloudy academic prospects, since he had let his studies slip; and by the company he kept. The girls, especially, seemed ominously 'fast'. She could see the impact of Rupert's looks on his peers, and intended to keep him under her eye – not to say under her thumb – as much as she could.

Summer with Beatrice

The only real break in Rupert's tedious summer at home with his parents was a week at the Fabian Summer School at Llanbedr, near Harlech. The first one had been organised the year before by Bernard and Charlotte Shaw. For thirty-five shillings a week Fabians were offered board, lodging, outings, and lectures on marriage or socialism by G.B.S.:

> some hundred members of both sexes and all ages living in 3 Houses and camping out roundabout there, listening to lectures in the morning, and bathing and rock-climbing in the afternoon, discussing in the evening – food almost vegetarian and clothes of the most unconventional – ladies in 'Gyms' and men in any description of flannels. . . . Mixed up with these university men and girls, were some score of elementary teachers and minor civil servants – some of the new pension officers – the whole making a most varied little world, living in intimate companionship one with the other.[14]

It is easy to laugh at the vegetarian food, the Swedish drill in the morning, and the dress code: tunics for the ladies, knee-breeches for the men, sensible shoes for both. But the crankishness was incidental to the desire for a classless community of plain living and hard thinking. The Fabian Summer School's values owed a good deal to Carpenter's Millthorpe. Unlike Millthorpe, however, it had no erotic agenda and no connection with the long rhythms of country life. It was a temporary encampment, designed to energise its participants and then send them back to the front lines of social reform in the cities.

The first session went so well that Beatrice and Sidney Webb decided to attend in person for four days in 1908. Beatrice, who was staying at Leominster before going to the Summer School, issued a blanket invitation to any Fabians heading for Llanbedr to stay the night. Rupert and James Strachey duly turned up, accompanied by Ben Keeling, Dudley Ward, Hugh Dalton, Arthur Waley and Gerald Shove.[15] Ward, a new friend of Rupert's, was reading economics at St John's. His manner was shy, bumbling but likeable, his appearance humdrum, his politics vigorously Fabian. Although Rupert became very fond of him, Ward never quite stood out; he was always 'dear old Dudley', making himself useful somewhere in the background. Beatrice, however, was favourably impressed by him, and still more by Dalton: 'one of the most astute and thoughtful of our younger members – by nature an ecclesiastic – a sort of lay Jesuit – preparing for political life'.[16]

The Webbs were at this time much concerned with eugenics and the virtues of the 'highly regulated races' who had sex well under control, like the Japanese and Germans.[17] They hoped that the Young Fabians could be made into a kind of socialist Jesuit order, with Beatrice and Sidney standing in the place of the Pope. 'There are some', Beatrice had noted in her diary, 'who wish to reach a socialist state by the assertion of economic equality – they desire to force the property-owners to yield to the non-property-owners. I prefer to have the forward movement based on the obligation of each individual to serve the state, in return getting maintenance.'[18] What this really meant was that a disciplined, self-denying elite of civil servants would regulate the lives of everyone else. The Webbs found an impressive precedent for this in the Salvation Army, who were setting up rural colonies for the destitute:

> They represent in part a true 'Samurai' class. . . . If the State undertakes the drainage system the Salvationists are quite the best agency to deal wisely with some of the products of this drainage system. . . . Their spirit of persistent work, their extraordinary vitality – even their curious combination of revivalist religion, with the technique of a very superior and reformed 'Variety Artist' exactly suits the helpless, hopeless, will-less man, a prey to sexual impulses, to recover his virility and faculty for regular life and regular work.[19]

For the Webbs, the main purpose of the Summer School was to provide hard training for future political leaders; it was not to be a holiday camp or an experiment in living. Unfortunately for them, many of the students went there in search of novelty and, simply, a good time. The young university men and women took a malicious pleasure in shocking their straitlaced elders and flouting the rigid rules of chaperonage. By the fourth school, in 1910, Beatrice's dissatisfaction was focused on the Cambridge 'clique' of Brooke, Dalton, James Strachey, Clifford Allen and William Foss:

> They are inclined to go away rather more critical and supercilious than they came. . . . 'They won't come, unless they know who they are going to meet,' sums up Rupert Brooke. . . . They don't want to learn, they don't think they have anything to learn. . . . The egotism of the young university man is colossal.[20]

It was quite true that they skipped lectures and generally ignored the school rules. But James's main reason for going was the hope of getting his mattress next to Rupert's, in the stable where the young men slept. Rupert provided Lytton Strachey with titillating reports of fun and games after lights-out:

> Daddy [Dalton] was a schoolboy in dormitory; and conceived a light lust for James – who, I thought, was quite dignified about it. He would start up suddenly behind him and tickle him gently under the armpits, making strange sibilant cluckings with his mouth meanwhile. And when

James was in bed Daddy stood over him, waving an *immense* steaming penis in his face and chuckling softly. Poor James was nearly sick.[21]

One suspects that such campy outbursts helped to keep the Newnhamites away from the Summer School. Ka Cox, for one, refused to go even when urged by Rupert; perhaps she did not care to compete for his attention when he was constantly shadowed by James. Beatrice Webb certainly sniffed out something rotten in the Cambridge Fabians and Apostles, though she was off the mark in blaming it for the break-up of Bertrand Russell's marriage in 1911:

> he is a bit of an 'A' – Artist, Anarchist and Aristocrat, and inspite of his acquired puritanism, is apt to be swept away by primitive instincts. . . . I am sorry now that Bertie went to Cambridge – there is a pernicious set presided over by Lowes Dickinson, which makes a sort of ideal of anarchic ways in sexual questions – we have, for a long time, been aware of its bad influence on our young Fabians. The intellectual star is the metaphysical George Moore with his *Principia Ethica* – a book they all talk of as 'The Truth'! I never can see anything in it, except a metaphysical justification for doing what you like and what other people disapprove of! So far as I can understand the philosophy it is a denial both of the scientific method and of religion – as a rule, that is the net result on the minds of young men – it seems to disintegrate their intellects and their characters.[22]

But there was more to Rupert's position, at least, than Apostolic metaphysics. He was not the kind of person to sit quietly while, for example, the actor–manager Harley Granville-Barker argued that under socialism 'all women will have dresses of the same material and wear them for the same length of time.'[23] Still inspired by the myth of the golden age, Rupert was a utopian and a humanist who shrank from the juiceless planned societies of Shaw and the Webbs. His only 'socialist' poem, 'Second Best', ended with a vision of post-revolutionary brotherhood, a joyous celebration by the Children of the Sun:

Yet, behind the night,
Waits for the great unborn, somewhere afar,
Some white tremendous daybreak. And the light,

Returning, shall give back the golden hours,
Ocean a windless level, Earth a lawn
Spacious and full of sunlit dancing-places,
And laughter, and music, and, among the flowers,
The gay child-hearts of men, and the child-faces,
O heart, in the great dawn!

For the Apostles, such a vision would be too vague and lush; the Webbs would have made the same criticism, if for different reasons. Rupert's brave new world was neither a coterie nor a technocracy, but a place where personal life was made radiant. It was inspired by William Morris, by Wells and by Campanella's vision of a 'City of the Sun'. It was not enough for Rupert to be just a Fabian (especially now that Wells was on his way out), or an Apostle, or even both in turn. He needed to cut himself a bigger slice of life, to have an integrated vision that would make the world a better place, and himself a more complete person. Neo-paganism was Fabian hope – without the asceticism of the Webbs – and Apostolic intimacy – without the claustrophobic intellectualism and hypochondria. For Rupert it was an essential escape route, a breaking out of stuffiness into the open air.

Couples: *the Near and the Far*

Neo-paganism might have an image of breezy freedom and friendship, but it needed to make a place for love as well – and there could be the rub. Less than three months after *Comus* the cast learned that Frances Darwin and Francis Cornford had broken their vow of loyalty to their friends and become engaged.[24] Their courtship had been carried on entirely by correspondence, while Frances was in Ireland with her father. The *éminence grise* of the whole affair had been Jane Harrison, a kind of honorary Neo-pagan who preached nude bathing and similar pastimes as tributes to the ancient Greeks. She had long been Francis Cornford's mentor, and recognised that his painful shyness might be thawed by the intense and emotionally vulnerable Frances. The match between Frances and Francis was of her making, and proved a credit to her insight.

The years when Frances might have been at university had been taken up with rest cures, or with home life under the watchful eye of her father. But she was content to be an academic wife and let others pursue more worldly ambitions. Her taste had always been for art and poetry, in any case, and marriage to Francis was no bar to becoming a poet. By marrying a well-established don who was twelve years older than herself, she would put herself on the fringe of the Neo-pagans even before they were well launched. Having the security of domestic life, she was often cast into a maternal role by her friends, and was made exempt from most of the 'soul-making' that lay ahead.

Jacques Raverat and Ka Cox also conducted a courtship by letter in 1908, though they spent most of the year without actually seeing each other. After Jacques had recovered from the acute phase of his breakdown, his father brought him from Switzerland to England in the hope of finding an effective treatment. When Rupert broke down four years later, he said that he and Jacques had gone mad for the same reason: the burden of too many years of sexual frustration.[25] If it is true, as doctors say, that nobody dies of pain, then perhaps nobody goes mad from chastity either. Nonetheless a remarkable number of the Neo-pagans, of both sexes, had nervous breakdowns in the years between puberty and marriage.[26]

Jacques' problem was organic, of course, but he still had to cope with the same problems as his friends, no matter how ill he felt. If lack of sexual companionship was a burden, it can hardly have helped that the accepted treatment for nervous collapse was to keep the sufferer almost completely removed from society. Jacques was not allowed to see anyone for months at a time, except for a few old and trusted friends such as Justin or Geoffrey Lupton, another old Bedalian. He stayed for some time at Froxfield Green, near the school, where Geoffrey plied his trade of making archaic furniture. Jacques wrote to Ka that he would like a similar future for himself:

> I cannot tell for certain whether I shall be up next term or whether I shall not finally throw to the winds all this folly and wisdom, the pomp of knowledge and the vanity (e'en)

of learning, and come and live up here: a clean life, and ply some trade (such as bookbinding or hand printing) for my living (?) and take plenty of holidays (for walking tours and a pilgrimage to Florence, etc.)[27]

Ka, meanwhile, was also to pursue the Simple Life in a cottage. Reading between the lines, it seems obvious that Jacques hoped to share it with her. If his letters to Ka often seem bombastic and grandiose, it may be partly due to the euphoria that is a common symptom in the early stages of MS. Often there are swings to the opposite pole, also, and when Jacques came up to Cambridge in May he was too weak and nervous to see either Ka or Rupert. After a week he collapsed again and was taken to Richmond by his father. From there he went up to London each day for treatment by Dr J. M. Bramwell, one of Britain's leading hypnotists:

> Dr Bramwell is to cure me in a fortnight, simply by sugges-
> tion, a delightful process: I simply sit and say Prospero's
> speeches to myself or bits out of Lear whilst he just 'speaks'
> to the subliminal self. You soon get into a state not vastly
> different, I imagine, from the Buddhist Nirvana and your
> heart and soul are soon filled with an ineffable peace and
> quiet and silence hardly broken by his whisper. And in three
> days he has made me better than I had been for months.[28]

After six weeks, Jacques and his father took Bramwell with them for a long holiday at Finistère in Brittany. Jacques lay nude in the sun, read Housman, Henley and Meredith, and let Bramwell operate on his subconscious. For all that, it was November before he could return to England, staying again with Geoffrey Lupton (who was now building a house for the writer Edward Thomas, using traditional methods of carpentry and plastering).[29] Jacques was still afraid to visit Cambridge, he told Ka, because it would be 'like a return from the land of the dead to the land of the living. . . . I should hardly know a soul and those I knew, they will have travelled so far from where we parted.'[30] In December he and Ka were finally reunited, after a year's separation. They went to the theatre and to the Old Bedalian dance, then Jacques had to return to the Continent before Christmas for more months of travel and convalescence. Although he had spent only about four of his twenty-three years in England, it was the place of freedom for him, of his deepest friendships and of a wished-for home. But after nearly two years of illness he still had no firm hope of even seeing Ka and his friends regularly, still less of settling down with any of them.

In his emotional life, Rupert found himself by the autumn of 1908 almost as nervous and frustrated as Jacques, though for different reasons. To fall in love with Noel on a couple of hours' acquaintance, in May, seemed easy and inevitable, but what sequel could there be? She was a fifteen-year-old schoolgirl, who answered Rupert's love letters, but would give him no more. The production of *Comus* cannot have allowed for more than a few snatched hours together, after which they did not see each other for months. Rupert spoke of himself as frantic, at the Fabian Summer School, with a 'purulent ulcer of *hysterica passio*' – of loving Noel with no prospect of expressing it freely.[31]

Because he could not openly woo Noel, Rupert hit on the subterfuge of cultivating an intimacy with Margery Olivier, using their joint work for the Fabians as a pretext. From time to time, he hoped, Margery would bring him into contact with Noel. The policy paid off in an invitation for Rupert to join Margery and Noel on another Christmas ski trip, to Klosters in Switzerland. The group of about thirty was, again, mostly from Cambridge. One of them, who became a new friend, was Godwin Baynes, a well-known Cambridge rowing blue who was now a medical student.

Rupert summed up the holiday as 'Switzerland fair (I morose) Noel Olivier superb.'[32] Noel celebrated her sixteenth birthday at Klosters, on Christmas day. The time Rupert was able to spend with her confirmed his love, but nothing was settled about what it could lead to. Noel was still firmly virginal and virtuous – like almost all girls of her age and class – with no intention of having a real affair with Rupert. But it was not just sexual caution that kept their relationship unripe. Three and a half years later Rupert told James Strachey, with real bitterness, that Noel seemed remarkable when one was in love with her, and was very kind, but didn't have any real emotions.[33] He had persuaded himself, by then, that the whole Olivier family were 'adamantine' –

people who didn't respond to others because they simply didn't understand what they were feeling.

Many of Noel's friends, and almost all her suitors, seemed to end up judging her in similar terms. Much of her seeming impassivity may have been because she was less self-confident than she looked. She had grown up in the shadow of three strong-minded elder sisters, and had convinced herself that her pretty face was offset by 'an ugly little body'.[34] Her skin broke out easily, and there was always the shadow of her overwhelmingly beautiful older sister Bryn. For whatever reason, she mistrusted passion, and never yielded to it until she was entering middle age.

Rupert's problem was rather different. He didn't keep passion at arm's length, but he tended to have several passions at once. They conflicted with each other, and left him confused about what was flood and what was froth. Like Noel, he was virginal and virtuous – but finding it more and more oppressive to be so. The side of him that believed in virtue was nourished by his ideal passion for Noel; the other side wanted sensual fulfilment, but devalued any woman who seemed ready to give it to him. The more lonely and dissatisfied he felt, the wider the split in his emotional make-up. And his mother was always there as the third point of any triangle he found himself in. He went directly to her from Klosters, playing the dutiful son, then quarrelled with her constantly as if to work off his resentment that it *was* a duty. He now commonly called her 'the Ranee', the wife of an oriental despot; though her husband's power in the home had dwindled away and the real despot was herself.[35]

Preparing for the end of his undergraduate days at King's, in the spring of 1909, Rupert felt squeezed between unfulfilled desire and unappealing duty. He decided to take his Easter break in 'the greenwood', as E. M. Forster would call it. The line of escape was to the south-west – the Neo-pagan 'Land of Heart's Desire'. Rupert's first three weeks were spent at Beckey Falls, near Manaton on Dartmoor, working on a new design for living:

> I am leading the healthy life. I rise early, twist myself about on a kind of pulley that is supposed to make my chest immense (but doesn't), eat no meat, wear very little, do not part my hair, take frequent cold baths, work ten hours a

day, and rush madly about the mountains in flannels and
rainstorms for hours. I am surprisingly cheerful about it – it
is all part of my scheme of returning to nature.[36]

Rupert was supposed to be working for his classics tripos, but
his actual reading was English poetry and Beatrice Webb's
Minority Report of the Poor Law Commission. From Beckey he
went on to the Lizard, in Cornwall, for Moore's Apostolic
reading party. It was freakishly warm, and Rupert spent the days
swimming in the surf and lying on the beach to dry. His new pose
of being a child of nature put James Strachey under a severe
strain. 'This afternoon,' he reported to Lytton, 'for the first time
in my life, I saw Rupert naked. Can't we imagine what *you*'ld say
on such an occasion? . . . But *I*'m simply inadequate, of course. So
I say nothing, except that I didn't have an erection – which was
. . . fortunate?, as I was naked too. I thought him – if you'ld like
to have a pendant – "absolutely beautiful".'[37] Once again, James
plucked up courage to invite Rupert to his bed (as he had done
intermittently since 1906), and once again he was bluntly
refused. Rupert preferred to spend his nights in trying to beat off
Moore's relentless attacks on Fabianism. Moore was notoriously
gifted and persistent at deflating other people's enthusiasms. He
did not deflate Rupert, but his ascendancy over the Apostles at
this time meant that Rupert would have to look elsewhere for
friends who would share his beliefs.

As he sparred with the Apostles, Rupert was laying an elabor-
ate plot to join a very different party. Having got word that
Margery and Noel Olivier were going to be in the New Forest, he
persuaded Dudley Ward to find out where they would be and
arrange to drop in on them 'accidentally'. The rendezvous was a
discovery of Ben Keeling's: the hamlet of Bank, no more than a
few houses set around a clearing deep in the forest. A superb cook
called Mrs Primmer let out rooms in her cottage, which became a
favourite with the Cambridge Fabians. Margery Olivier had
arranged a Newnhamite reading party there, with her friends
Evelyn Radford and Dorothy Osmaston. Noel would come
down from Bedales to be under her older sister's watchful eye.
For Rupert, the meeting with Noel was an enchantment, by
which he could slough off his old self and start afresh:

I was lost for four days – I went clean out of the knowledge of anyone in England but two or three – I turned, and turned, and covered my trail; and for three–four days, I was, for the first time in my life, a free man, and my own master! Oh! the joy of it! Only three know, but you shall. . . . For I went dancing and leaping through the New Forest, with £3 and a satchel full of books, talking to everyone I met, mocking and laughing at them, sleeping and eating anywhere, singing to the birds, tumbling about in the flowers, bathing in the rivers, and, in general, behaving naturally. And all in England, at Eastertide! And so I walked and laughed and met a many people and made a thousand songs – all very good – and, in the end of the days, came to a Woman who was more glorious than the Sun and stronger than the sea, and kinder than the earth, who is a flower made out of fire, a star that laughs all day, whose brain is clean and clear like a man's and her heart is full of courage and kindness; and whom I love.[38]

This is about as far as one can get from the languid aesthete of three years before, but Rupert's new attitude was no less suspect. Suspect even to himself, since he went on to assure his correspondent that he was 'not unlike the R.B. you used to find, as you say, learning Ernest Dowson by heart'.[39] What is he up to this time, one wonders: learning by heart to be a Child of Nature? Rupert in the role of Pan is not altogether convincing, especially when he prances in constant fear of the Ranee, who waits for him suspiciously in her boarding-house at Sidmouth – and expects him to arrive from the west rather than from the east, requiring more subterfuge on Rupert's part.

What were the real emotions of those four days at Bank? Pictures show us Rupert in boots and Norfolk jacket (made popular by G.B.S.), looking more hearty and less conscious of the camera than usual. His hair is shorter, too – perhaps because he expects to confront the Ranee before long. Noel, in her Bedales tunic, looks down with a shy smile; she is at the opposite end of the group from Rupert, with Margery planted warily in the middle. In fact, things were not so quiet as they look in the picture. The trouble, which would fester for years, was that Rupert had succeeded too well in pretending an interest in Margery. She had fallen in love with him, and Noel's presence must have seemed an irritation and a stumbling-block.

Meanwhile, Noel was slipping away for soulful meetings with Rupert among the great trees that surrounded their cottage.

On Rupert's side, there are two revealing poems inspired by the days at Bank. One is really his first breakthrough into serious and mature poetry: 'Oh! Death will find me, long before I tire / Of watching you.' The speaker, who has died before his beloved, finally sees her arrive in the underworld:

Pass, light as ever, through the lightless host,
Quietly ponder, start, and sway, and gleam –
Most individual and bewildering ghost! –
And turn, and toss your brown delightful head
Amusedly, among the ancient Dead.

The beloved, whom he has never possessed in life, acknowledges his gaze, but does not respond to it. Her aloofness, we suspect, is just what makes her lovable. 'The Voice' gives their relation a darker outcome. It begins at twilight, with the poet brooding on his love:

Safe in the magic of my woods
    I lay, and watched the dying light. . . .
And there I waited breathlessly,
Alone; and slowly the holy three,
The three that I loved, together grew
One, in the hour of knowing,
Night, and the woods, and you –

But when the girl comes through the woods to join him, her 'flat clear voice' breaks the spell:

You came and quacked beside me in the wood.
You said, 'The view from here is very good!'
You said, 'It's nice to be alone a bit!'
'How the days are drawing out!' you said.
You said, 'The sunset's pretty, isn't it?'

*   *   *

By God! I wish – I wish that you were dead!

After lavishing sentiment on his absent beloved, the poet turns hysterical when the real person appears and fails to sense his mood. However euphoric Brooke may have been at Bank, his happiness seems to have rested on the *lack* of any real dialogue between himself and his love.

When the days of academic reckoning came in May Rupert had not worked steadily at Greek or Latin for many months, and he cared more for picnics or sleeping out on the Backs than for examinations. Conceivably he was constructing another pose – the schoolboy who never swots but does brilliantly on the exam – and had worked secretly and hoped to do well. In any case, he only managed a Second. Frances Darwin (who was in the know) refrained from telling him that he almost got a Third.

Surely there was something deliberate in Rupert's neglect of the classics and his mediocre result. His father had won his First at King's, gained a fellowship there and taught classics for a living. Rupert had to succeed in his own way, avoiding a mere repetition of his father's early triumphs – which had led only to his present eclipse at School Field. If this entailed a conspicuous failure to live up to high expectations, then so be it. In any case, Rupert had his own hopes, which by now had crystallised into the belief that he could be one of the English poets. When Hugh Dalton had come to visit him at Rugby the previous October, Rupert showed him the memorial in the school chapel to Arthur Hugh Clough, who had composed 'Say not the struggle naught availeth' on his death-bed in Florence. Rupert pointed to the bare wall beside it and said: 'They are keeping that for *me*.'[40] Was it just a joke, or was he already weighing the odds? Clough had died at forty-two; Rupert would be up on the wall in less than ten years – a portrait medallion from one of Sherrill Schell's over-blown photographs. Can he have imagined, already, that it would take an even more romantic death to put him there?

Part Two

An English Heaven

IV

'At Grantchester, Where the River Goes'

Camping Out

When Rupert failed to carry off the laurel in his tripos, he had his
retreat already planned: a picturesque exile in Grantchester,
three miles upstream on the Cam. He claimed that he moved out
of King's, and out of Cambridge altogether, because he was
'passionately enamoured of solitude'.[1] But people who really
want to be hermits should not take lodgings in a charming spot
within an hour's stroll from scores of acquaintances. Before he
moved there in June 1909 Grantchester was already one of
Rupert's favourite places, for tea in the famous orchard or bathes
in Byron's Pool, a secluded stretch of the river a few hundred
yards from the village. When he took rooms in a cottage there, his
nominal exile made him even more of a Cambridge celebrity and
the village became the ideal backdrop for his performance as a
student Simple Lifer. The picture he painted for Erica Cotterill is
a study in planned spontaneity:

> I work at Shakespere [*sic*], read, write all day, & now &
> then wander in the woods or by the river. I bathe every
> morning & sometimes by moonlight, have all my meals
> (chiefly fruit) brought to me out of doors, & am as happy as
> the day's long. I am chiefly sorry for all you people in the
> world. Every now & then dull bald spectacled people from
> Cambridge come out & take tea here. I mock them & pour
> the cream down their necks or roll them in the rose-beds or
> push them in the river, & they hate me & go away.[2]

Later, when he had briefly dropped his mask, he would admit

to James Strachey that 'Solitude is my one unbearable fear.'[3] Like many magnetic personalities he was at his best with enough people to count as an audience, and became ill at ease as the number dwindled. His new image – the elfin vegetarian socialist, roaming barefoot through the meadows and leaping naked into the river – was a guaranteed star turn. His friends flocked to see and imitate it. With careless art, Rupert had created a new student style, which caused him and his followers to be nick-named 'the dew-dabblers'.

Rupert showed how it was done in two riverside picnics he organised at Overcote, outside Cambridge. The picnickers included Justin Brooke, who drove everyone in his new Opel car (the first intrusion of the motor age), Gwen and Margaret Darwin, Ka Cox, Dorothy Lamb, Geoffrey Keynes and Donald Robertson.[4] Activities included boating (in the newly popular Canadian canoes), wrestling, riding horses bareback, plaiting daisy-chains, swimming in the nude (men and women separately) and falling in the river. Rupert crowned the day by reading Herrick's great ode to the pleasures of May:

Come, let us go, while we are in our prime,
And take the harmless folly of the time!
We shall grow old apace, and die
Before we know our liberty.

When all goes right, such gatherings can be remembered as milestones in a life. It was in Rupert's gift, at his best, to create events that felt as concentrated and complete as a lyric.

If this seems too high a claim, consider that Rupert now submitted his talents to the most discerning of judges, and passed the test with acclaim. Henry James was invited by Geoffrey Keynes and Charles Sayle to sample a round of Cambridge pleasures, from breakfasting with Maynard Keynes to going down the river with Rupert. Standing on the punt in his white open-necked shirt and flannels, Rupert did what he called his 'fresh, boyish stunt' to killing effect. James was susceptible to pretty young men, even while keeping a nice sense of what prettiness was worth. 'He reappears to me,' James wrote in his later tribute, 'as with his felicities all most promptly divinable, in that splendid setting of the river at the "backs".[5] Does 'promptly' carry a hint that Rupert's felicities were too blatantly on the surface, too readily trotted out for a famous visitor? James was too downy a bird, surely, to swallow Rupert's myth whole. He even entertained the idea that Rupert was a 'spoiled child of history'. But, at the news of his death in the Aegean, he wept.

After James, John. The swarthy bohemian Augustus John turned up in July to pitch his camp at Grantchester. Thirty-one years old and already famous, John had been commissioned to paint a portrait of Jane Harrison at Newnham. If Rupert was flirting with the Simple Life, John had flung himself into it head over heels. Obsessed with the threatened extinction of the gypsy way of life, he decided to become a gypsy himself, leaving his Chelsea home to travel with an entourage of 'six horses, two vans, one cart, six children, Arthur [a groom], a stray boy "for washing up", a broken-down wagon, Dorelia [Dorothy McNeil] and her younger sister Edie'.[6] The children, all boys, were by his wife Ida and his mistress Dorelia. John had lived with the two women in a *ménage à trois* until Ida died in childbirth two years before.

Another of John's mistresses, Lady Ottoline Morrell, came to sample his gypsy-style lodgings, but retreated to her home in London after one night. Rupert was delighted to hang around John's encampment and romp with his pack of children (and also with the five-year-old Gregory Bateson, another resident of Grantchester). Nonetheless, he did not copy either John's riotous dress (gypsy hat and sandals) or riotous sex-life. Inspired by Whitman and Meredith, John posed as 'a robust pagan with a creed that personified Nature as a mother'.[7] Indeed, he got so deeply into his pose that it effectively ceased to be one, whereas Rupert's wildness and roughness were mostly on paper. He was never able to provide himself with one wife, let alone John's long train of wives and mistresses. Nor was he able to support himself on his own talent, as John already did. Though he affected to be free as a bird, Rupert at Grantchester was only pushing back a little the bounds of the academic life-style. He had neglected his classical studies in order to pursue the new and promising field of English literature; and his excuse for living at Grantchester was that it was an ideal place to write a thesis on the Elizabethan dramatist John Webster, and thereby win a fellowship at King's.

In July Rupert joined an outing more ambitious than a mere picnic, instigated by the young and enterprising Bunny Garnett. Bunny found an ideal spot to camp on the River Eden near Penshurst, a short ride from his country home at The Cearne and the Olivier house at Limpsfield. After a week he was joined there by Godwin Baynes, the herculean medical student who had been on the last Christmas excursion to Klosters. Godwin was 'open-hearted, warm, affectionate and generous', Garnett recalled. 'Having escaped from a strict nonconformist upbringing at home, with prayers muttered into the seats of chairs before breakfast, he had become an enthusiastic neo-pagan.'[8] Instead of hymns in the parlour, he now sang Wagner arias as he strode along the ridges of Snowdon. Bryn, Noel and Daphne Olivier arrived next, with Dorothy Osmaston; then Harold Hobson (an engineer friend of Bunny's) and Walter Layton – soon to be engaged to Dorothy.[9] Finally Rupert and Dudley Ward turned up – by the same 'coincidence' that had brought them to Bank at Easter. But this time Margery was not there to keep a jealous eye on his walks with Noel.

A story of Bunny's catches the true Olivier style – panache or blind arrogance, depending on one's prejudices:

> On Sunday morning the rustics of Penshurst came down and leant in a line upon the parapet of the bridge, staring into the pool in which we were to bathe.
> 'Come on,' said Daphne. 'They're not going to stop us.'
> Nor did they. We bathed, ignoring them, and Noel, not to be put off from her high dives, picked her way along the parapet between the rows of wrists and elbows, politely asked for standing-room in the middle, and made a perfect dive into the pool. With florid expressionless face, the nearest labourer shook his black Sunday coat-sleeve free of the drops which had fallen from her heel.[10]

Camping out was just coming into style. It was more adventurous than the traditional reading parties for undergraduates, and more likely to include women (often, it must be said, because they understood the mysteries of cooking and washing up). At Bedales camping was actually part of the curriculum and Old Bedalians were reunited at an annual camp, invariably attended by 'The Chief'. Badley returned to nature for *discipline*; his students would not become sensual Children of the Sun, but hardier citizens of the existing world. He welcomed the Boy Scout movement, founded by Baden-Powell in 1908 to prepare British youth for colonial life and, when necessary, for colonial warfare. Scouting, Badley argued:

> satisfies ... the universal craving for adventure and for open-air life which is particularly strong in the 'Red Indian' phase of growth; a phase through which children normally pass in their recapitulation of the social and economic development of mankind just as they have passed, before birth, through a recapitulation of organic evolution.[11]

Instead of a cadet corps with uniforms and drill, Bedales had a scout corps, whose training was modelled on the Boer commandos. The open field was more appealing than the parade-ground, but students did not go there just to dabble in the dew.[12] Like everything else at Bedales, camping had plenty of rules:

> The Camp is always pitched near a bathing-place, for Bedalians, like fish, cannot live long out of water. . . . The Camp itself consists of four tents – the cook tent, one sleeping tent for the girls, and two for the boys. Bedding of straw, bracken, or heather is provided, and each camper brings with him three blankets, one of which is sewn up into a sleeping-bag. Pillows most of us scorn; the most hardened do without, the others roll up their clothes, and thus make a good substitute. . . .
>
> Every other day, at least, is spent in a good tramp across the country – ten or fifteen miles at first to get into training, but this may be increased to twenty, or even twenty-five, later on. . . . We take sandwiches with us for lunch, thus avoiding an elaborate midday meal, and on the longer walks find tea on the way, arriving back at Camp in time for a bathe and supper. Then we adjourn to the neighbouring farmhouse (whence we get our bread, butter, eggs, and milk) and for the rest of the evening sit lazily, while the Chief and another take turn and turn about in reading aloud some novel.
>
> After a strenuous day of walk, a slack day in Camp usually follows, with plenty of bathing and perhaps a short walk in the afternoon to get up an appetite for supper. Too many slack days, however, should be discouraged, as they

mean extra work for the cook, and anyway we don't come
to Camp to slack.[13]

At Penshurst, Noel and Daphne Olivier showed their Bedalian
spirit by joining the men to bathe nude in the river – under cover
of darkness, but using a bicycle lamp to show them where to
dive.[14] 'There is much to be said', Badley proclaimed, 'for the
practice, where possible, of nudism as a means of mental as well
as of bodily health. . . . Under right conditions, amongst friends
and at camp for instance, it is perfectly possible and, I believe, all
to the good. But I have never wished to make it the rule for all, as
there are some whom it makes unwholesomely sex-conscious.'[15]
He settled on these rules: mixed nude bathing in the junior school
(to age twelve or thirteen); then boys separately in the nude, girls
with their choice of nudity or a costume; at mixed events all wore
costumes. At an Old Bedalian weekend, Noel Olivier once
scandalised Badley by diving nude off the high board in sight of
everyone. He insisted on bathing suits after that. Badley was
trying to carry water on both shoulders, even if the side of
restraint outweighed that of liberation. Neo-paganism had
similar contradictions. There was the cult of the body beautiful
and scorn for social conventions; but there was also a strict, self-
imposed chastity before marriage. It was an unstable mixture of
impulses, and for some an explosive one.

Bunny Garnett saw Rupert for the first time at the Penshurst
camp:

> His complexion, his skin, his eyes and hair were perfect. He
> was tall and well built, loosely put together, with a careless
> animal grace and a face made for smiling and teasing and
> sudden laughter. As he ate in the firelight I watched him, at
> once delighted by him and afraid that his friendliness might
> be a mask. What might not lie below it?[16]

Rupert's poem 'Jealousy' shows one emotion that lay below. A
girl whom the poet once admired for her coolness and wisdom
is now 'Gazing with silly sickness' on a fool, whose 'empty
grace . . . strong legs and arms . . . rosy face' suggest Godwin
Baynes. Godwin did propose to Bryn a couple of months after the
camp, and, if they are models for the two lovers, the poet cast a

sickly eye on their affection. He imagines them married: the husband's strength running to fat, their love sinking into habit, until the last act:

And you, that loved young life and clean, must tend
A foul sick fumbling dribbling body and old,
When his rare lips hang flabby and can't hold
Slobber, and you're enduring that worst thing,
Senility's queasy furtive love-making. . . .
That's how I'll see your man and you? –
                                        But you
– Oh, when *that* time comes, you'll be dirty too!

   Rupert started with a pastiche of seventeenth-century satire, but soon his own preoccupations took over. For him, 'dirtiness' is moral rather than physical, and is caused by sexual experience.[17] His Neo-paganism was a wilful, sometimes desperate attempt to escape from his engrained puritanism. The Olivier girls, raised by free-thinking parents, were more instinctually pagan than he could ever be. Bunny Garnett, whose parents were even more enlightened, was happily free of Rupert's sexual self-consciousness:

> to fall asleep within a yard or two of a lovely girl without a thought of trying to make love to her was natural to me at eighteen. It was simply part of the social climate in which I was brought up and had nothing to do with innocence or its reverse, not a matter of morality but of manners.[18]

Bunny did not start his epic amorous career until two years after the Penshurst camp, when he was initiated by a married woman just separated from her husband. He seemed able to practise chastity or lust with equal ease, but Rupert, unhappily for him, could never be comfortable with either.

Basel Station, May 1933

Going to Cambridge had not made Rupert free of his gloomy parental home. He was still regularly summoned back to Rugby for weeks of seclusion, while his mother anxiously watched him for signs of illness or strain. In the summer of 1909 he decided to break the tedium of family life by bringing his friends to his family. He persuaded his parents to rent a large Victorian vicarage at Clevedon, on the Severn estuary, and there they awaited the invasion. The Ranee, however, was already on her guard. At Rugby she had met a young lady who knew the Oliviers. '"My, yes!" the Person shrilled, "the Oliviers! they'd do *any*thing, those girls!"'[19] It was shocking enough that the Oliviers roamed around Britain unchaperoned, but what really frightened Mrs Brooke, we may guess, was the risk of an imprudent early marriage that could scotch the career of her favourite son.

For the first two weeks at Clevedon there were few visitors, and Rupert was ill. 'My only way of keeping in touch with "life"', he told Dudley Ward, 'is playing tennis barefoot. It's not so effective as living in a tent and a river with three Oliviers: but it annoys the family. ... The family atmosphere is too paralysing.'[20] Then the guests started to arrive in packs and the family – which meant the Ranee – was even more annoyed. Most irritating was Bryn, with her complete disregard of drawing-room convention. 'It's such a responsibility taking Bryn about,' Margery had written to Rupert. 'People always fall in love with her.'[21] Not the Ranee, however. 'I prefer Miss Cox,' she told Gwen Darwin, 'her wrists are very thick and I don't like the expression of her mouth, but she's a sensible girl. I can't understand what you all see in these Oliviers; they are pretty, I suppose, but not at all clever; they're shocking flirts and their manners are disgraceful.'[22]

The failure at Clevedon underlined the homelessness of the Neo-pagans. Ka's parents were dead, the Oliviers' mostly out of the country, Jacques' in France. There were advantages, however, to being orphans. In lodgings, still more in a tent or a river, they could live by their own rules. Gwen Darwin, whose parents were alive and highly respectable, was not allowed to go on these frolics unless she could convince them that a suitable chaperone would be there too. 'Sometimes I think that every one ought to be killed off at 40,' she had written to her cousin

Frances, 'when I see what a misery all parents are to their children.'[23]

Another solution to the problem of parents was to make sure that when one got older one would be nothing like them. Walking on the cliffs at Portishead, Rupert, Margery, Bryn, Dudley and Bill Hubback hit on a scheme to bring this about.[24] They were talking about the poet John Davidson, who had just drowned himself in Cornwall at the age of fifty-one. The year before, in *The Testament of John Davidson*, he had glorified the life of the road as the only antidote to age and death:

I felt the time had come to find a grave:
I knew it in my heart my days were done.
I took my staff in hand; I took the road,
And wandered out to seek my last abode.
Hearts of gold and hearts of lead
Sing it yet in sun and rain,
'Heel and toe from dawn to dusk,
'Round the world and home again.'

What if Davidson had only faked suicide? they fantasised. Perhaps he was now enjoying a secret life, after casting off all his responsibilities:

> The idea, the splendour of this escape back into youth, fascinated us. We imagined a number of young people, splendidly young together, vowing to *live* such an idea, parting to do their 'work in the world' for a time and then, twenty years later, meeting on some windy road, one prearranged spring morning, reborn to find and make a new world together, vanishing from the knowledge of men and things they knew before, resurgent in sun and rain —[25]

The walkers made a solemn pact to meet for breakfast at Basel station on 1 May 1933. Turning their backs on England, they would start a new life, 'fishing for tunnies off Sicily or exploring Constantinople or roaring with laughter in some Spanish inn'. Jacques was invited in November; Godwin Baynes, Ka and a few others would also get the call.[26]

'The great essential thing is the Organized Chance of Living

Again,' Rupert told Jacques, instead of becoming 'a greying literary hack, mumbling along in some London suburb. ... middle aged, tied with more and more ties, busier and busier, fussier and fussier ... the world will fade to us, fade, grow tasteless, habitual, dull'.[27] It is unclear why 1 May 1933 was the target date, except that by then they would all be twice their present age, and Mayday was a festival of springtime and youth. They could hardly have foreseen that by the appointed day Rupert and Jacques would be dead, Margery insane, the others carrying burdens that would make the gathering unthinkable. What really mattered, anyway, was the vision as it first came to them, for Rupert's long letter of invitation to Jacques is the closest thing we have to a 'Neo-pagan manifesto'.

Their great aim was to throw off the natural accumulations of age: houses, jobs, spouses, children. One was not made old just by living long, but by accepting a place in society without protest. To avoid being like your parents, you had only to get rid of what your parents had got. 'We'll be children seventy-years, instead of seven,' Rupert vowed in conclusion. 'We'll *live* Romance, not *talk* of it. We'll show the grey unbelieving age, we'll teach the whole damn World, that there's a better Heaven than the pale serene Anglican windless harmonium-buzzing Eternity of the Christians, a Heaven in Time, now and for ever, ending for each, staying for all, a Heaven of Laughter and Bodies and Flowers and Love and People and Sun and Wind, in the only place we know or care for, ON EARTH.'[28] It was a paradise that would turn the Christian one on its head; but what else would it do? The only concrete decision that emerged from Rupert's sense that everything needed to be changed was the vow that 'I am *not* going to be a resident fellow of Kings, nor a lecturer in Leeds, I am going to be a Bloody POET.'[29]

Going to Town

The Clevedon vision of escaping over the hills was a reaction to the awkward shift that the Neo-pagans now had to make, from student life to a serious vocation. Rupert could live the poetic life at Grantchester, but most of them would have to make their way in London, and their outings would now be holidays from the work that held them in the capital. From 1909 London began to replace Cambridge as a centre for their shared lives. Even Rupert needed a *pied-à-terre* there, so he joined the National Liberal Club. As clubs went, it was cheap and politically progressive. At one visit or another, Rupert must have bumped into a fellow contributor to the *Westminster Gazette* called Raymond Chandler, a year younger than himself. They both wanted to be poets, but Chandler soon gave it up; his success, unlike Rupert's, would be late, and achieved by cynicism rather than sentiment.

Justin Brooke and Gwen Darwin responded differently to the move away from Cambridge. For years Gwen had been chafing at home. She did not have enough to do, her health was uncertain, and she felt smothered by an extended family that was almost an institution in Cambridge. She wished she had been born a man, so that she could follow her interests without interference. In the autumn of 1908 her parents finally let her study art at the Slade School, in Chelsea. She would live with her uncle William, but to be an apprentice artist in the anonymity of London was to her a liberation and a joy.

Justin's fate was quite the reverse. He had moved to London at the same time as Gwen, and was now sinking into despondency. At Cambridge he had lived for the theatre. Now he was articled to solicitors in Chancery Lane, and his life was in pawn to his father's company, which he would join when he completed his training. When Jacques came to settle in London, he found that Justin was now much worse off than him. 'It is odd', he told Ka, 'how he and I have changed parts: that I now should be playing the comforter to that skylark.'[30]

In the course of 1909, Jacques had steadily got back on his feet. He visited Florence in March, and in discovering the Old Masters he also found a vocation for himself: to be no longer a mathematician, but an artist. By June he was back in England, fit enough to rejoin his old circle of friends. He met Rupert at Petersfield and Grantchester in June, the first time they had seen each other in a year and a half. Instead of the mannered decadence of Rupert's first year at Cambridge, Jacques now found him in the open air, with a young woman who had 'the startled beauty of a nymph taken by surprise'.[31] This was

Brynhild Olivier, and Rupert was eagerly discussing with her how to reform the Poor Laws. His personal style had been revised to match his politics:

> he had given up tobacco and any kind of alcohol, he lived on vegetables and fruits and dressed in a dishevelled style that showed off his beauty very effectively. He was well aware of it, and relished the romantic and Byronic impression given by his long hair and open-necked shirt.[32]

In the morning Jacques and Rupert bathed in Byron's Pool before setting off to London to see Shaw's banned play, *The Shewing-up of Blanco Posnet*. There Jacques met Margery and Daphne Olivier. He sensed that Rupert was in love with all the sisters at once, but most seriously with Noel.

After picking up the threads with Rupert and his new friends, Jacques went off walking in Wales with Ka, then to a production of Ibsen's *Love's Comedy* put on by a group of Old Bedalians at the country mansion of Justin's father. He returned to his regimen in France for three months afterwards. Justin, Ka and Geoffrey Keynes visited him at Prunoy in October. By November he was ready to live in London, renting rooms in Chelsea. He was taken on as an apprentice at the Ashendene Press, where his project was to typeset Blake's *Marriage of Heaven and Hell*. In the afternoons he studied drawing at the Central School of Art under Noel Rooke and Bernard Adeney. After Christmas he transferred to the Slade, which brought him into daily contact with Gwen.

Ka had decided to spend a fourth year at Newnham while she pondered the choice of a career. She wavered between trying to write and putting her socialism to the proof by, as Jacques put it, 'burying herself in the slums'.[33] Her social work projects often brought her to London, and the flat in Westminster that she shared with Hester became a centre for her Neo-pagan friends. Gwen Darwin, having escaped from her own dominating family, was especially charmed by Ka's way of life – a home without parents:

> Ka's flat was a pleasant place. It seemed to belong to her alone, for Hester was always out at some gaiety or other. There we lolled in chairs, and sat and lay on the floor, and

smoked and talked; talked easily, openly, intimately, while Ka treated us all like children, with indulgent affection.

There was always tea for us, or coffee in the evening, and we used to put the light out and sit with the fire light flickering on the walls and casting odd shadows on the ceiling. . . . I used to lie on the sofa, while Justin perched like a bird on the end; Ka sat with her white hands on her lap, and Gwen would be on the floor by the hearth, leaning her tired head against the chimney. And sometimes Brynhild would drift in like a gentle fragrance; or Noel with her bag of books, to tease Justin until they came to blows in childish horseplay. And Geoffrey would talk big and tell wild stories, to be laughed at after he had gone; and James would come in out of the rain like a distressed cat, to look at Rupert with adoring eyes. And then rather early, Gwen would say she must go or Aunt Emily would be frightened; and one by one we would drift off to affairs of our own, until only one or two of us were left alone with Ka, talking, talking till late at night. . . . Long silences would fall upon us when we sat together thus; often we all went off into dreams of our own and forgot to talk; and the fire jumped and flickered, and the cabs rumbled by outside.

And – I don't know what the others felt – but to my mind, always hidden among the shadows behind our backs, was Death – Death waiting to catch us who were so young and full of hope; Death, ready to snap us up before our work was done – Death, barely hidden, waiting to destroy all our youth and beauty and grace.[34]

The Knight's Move

After Clevedon, Mrs Brooke sequestered Rupert at Rugby for three weeks and subjected him to 'nightly anti-Olivier lectures' (which meant attacks on Bryn, whom the Ranee wrongly suspected of being Rupert's favourite Olivier).[35] Meanwhile Margery Olivier attacked him from the other side. Rupert had got Jacques to take him to Bedales in June, where Noel was surprised to look out of a window and see him below; and he had evaded Margery's vigilance by turning up unannounced for the Penshurst camp. But Margery made sure that Noel did not come to Clevedon, and made it clear to Rupert that his attentions to her were not welcome. When he went home to Rugby, Margery followed up with a long letter that kept him up all night with anxiety. Rupert would only do harm to himself and Noel, Margery argued, if he declared his love outright and tried to draw her sister into a premature commitment:

> Love, for a woman, she said, destroyed everything else. It filled her whole life, stopped her developing, absorbed her. 'You'll see what I mean if you look at women who married young,' she grimly adds. 'No woman should marry before 26 or 27' (why *then*? if it kills them). And later 'if you bring this great, terrible, all absorbing thing into Noel's life now ... it will stop her intellectual development', etc. It's a bloody thing, isn't it? The Logical outcome is that one must only marry the quite poor, unimportant, people, who don't matter being spoilt. The dream of any combined and increased splendour of the splendid you, or the splendid I, with the splendid X – that's gone. We can't marry X. At the best we can, if we try to marry X, marry her corpse.[36]

Despite Rupert's fulminations, he was probably being given good advice – even if it was tinged with Margery's self-interest. Of the four sisters she was the most committed to intellectual and political causes; she was also, it must be said, the one with the least beauty. She was trying to be a 'New Woman' and she wanted the same for Noel – a free space in which to work out her destiny. But it was naive to speak of Noel's or Bryn's destiny without accepting that their beauty was inevitably part of it. Nor did Margery admit how much she wanted to keep Rupert away from Noel in order to have more of him for herself.

In laying claim to Noel, Rupert also had his own inner divisions to contend with. One side of him longed for marriage, to move from fitful immaturity to love and sexual fulfilment. But the other side loved Noel precisely because he imagined her as a 'dryad', a nymph who would vanish into a thicket if pursued. This Rupert, in his poems, harped on the physical and mental unsavouriness of old age. 'Menelaus and Helen', for example, fills in what Homer left untold:

He does not tell you how white Helen bears
Child on legitimate child, becomes a scold,

Haggard with virtue. Menelaus bold
Waxed garrulous, and sacked a hundred Troys
'Twixt noon and supper. And her golden voice
Got shrill as he grew deafer. And both were old.
Often he wonders why on earth he went
Troyward, or why poor Paris ever came.
Oft she weeps, gummy-eyed and impotent;
Her dry shanks twitch at Paris' mumbled name.
So Menelaus nagged; and Helen cried;
And Paris slept on by Scamander side.

When he wrote the poem, Rupert was revealing his fear of actually sharing a life with any of the young women he loved. By the time he sailed to the modern wars of Troy at Gallipoli he was consciously acting the poem out: preferring a warrior's early death to the long anticlimax – as he feared it – of married life.

To back up her views, Margery simply left Noel immured at Bedales, refusing to bring her out for any occasion where she might meet Rupert. He was unable to see her at all for five months after Penshurst. As autumn closed in at Grantchester, he began to suffer from fits of loneliness and depression. He had barely scraped through his exams, he was cut off from the girl he loved, he had struck so many attitudes that he no longer knew who he really was, and he was mired in sexual frustration that seemed likely to drag on indefinitely.

It was in this mood that, sometime in October, Rupert decided to dispose of his irksome virginity. He could not go to Noel or any other young woman he knew, so he must achieve his end indirectly – 'the knight's move'. In July he had boasted to his cousin Erica that he knew all about 'people in love with people of the same sex as themselves'.[37] He may indeed have known, but he had not fully experienced. On the weekend of 29 October, he decided quite cold-bloodedly that it was time to move from idea to act, taking advantage of the visit of a friend his own age from Rugby: Denham Russell-Smith. Rupert had been closer friends with Denham's older brother Hugh, but evidently found Denham more physically appealing. During his nervous breakdown, three and a half years later, he told the story of that weekend to

James Strachey. It was probably the most revealing letter he ever wrote:

> How things shelve back! History takes you to January 1912 – Archaeology to the end of 1910 – Anthropology to, perhaps, the autumn of 1909. –
>
> The autumn of 1909! We had hugged & kissed & strained, Denham & I, on and off for years – ever since that quiet evening I rubbed him, in the dark, speechlessly, in the smaller of the two small dorms. An abortive affair, as I told you. But in the summer holidays of 1906 and 1907 he had often taken me out to the hammock, after dinner, to lie entwined there. – He had vaguely hoped, I fancy, – – – But I lay always thinking Charlie [Lascelles].
>
> Denham was though, to my taste, attractive. So honestly and friendlily lascivious. Charm, not beauty, was his *forte*. He was not unlike Ka, in the allurement of vitality and of physical magic. – oh, but Ka has beauty too. – He was lustful, immoral, affectionate, and delightful. As romance faded in me, I began, all unacknowledgedly, to cherish a hope – – – But I was never in the slightest degree in love with him.
>
> In the early autumn of 1909, then, I was glad to get him to come and stay with me, at the Orchard. I came back late that Saturday night. Nothing was formulated in my mind. I found him asleep in front of the fire, at 1.45. I took him up to his bed, – he was very like a child when he was sleepy – and lay down on it. We hugged, and my fingers wandered a little. His skin was always very smooth. I had, I remember, a vast erection. He dropped off to sleep in my arms. I stole away to my own room: and lay in bed thinking – my head full of tiredness and my mouth of the taste of tea and whales, as usual.[38] I decided, almost quite consciously, I *would* put the thing through next night. You see, I didn't at all know how he would take it. But I wanted to have some fun, and, still more, to see what it was *like*, and to do away with the shame (as I thought it was) of being a virgin. At length, I thought, I shall know something of all that James and Norton and Maynard and Lytton know and hold over me.
>
> of course, I *said* nothing.
>
> Next evening, we talked long in front of the sitting room fire. My head was on his knees, after a bit. We discussed sodomy. He said he, finally, thought it *was* wrong. . . . We got undressed there, as it was warm. Flesh is exciting, in firelight. You must remember that *openly* we were nothing to each other – less even than in 1906. About what one is

ry Brooke, a strong-willed puritan, dominated the males in her family. Her sons were
hard, Rupert (here aged eleven) and Alfred (here aged seven). The standing of her
band, Parker Brooke, can be measured by a story current at Rugby School – whether it
true hardly matters – that his wife sent him out at night to collect horse-droppings for
garden.

lone of Mary Brooke's sons reached thirty. Richard died of pneumonia at twenty-five;
ert of septicaemia at twenty-seven; Alfred was killed in France while serving with the
t Office Rifles, less than two months after Rupert's death.

The Olivier family was the reverse of the Brookes, with a dominant father and all daughters instead of all sons. Sir Sydney Olivier had a commanding intellectual and physical presence: 'a law unto himself', said his friend George Bernard Shaw, who 'never dreamed of considering other people's feelings.'

When this photograph of the Olivier sisters was taken at Limpsfield, Surrey, around 1900, none of the girls had gone to school (from left: Margery, Daphne, Brynhild, Noel). Much of the time they ran wild in the woods, building secret tree houses and calling themselves the 'Reivilo' tribe. David Garnett called the family style 'a mixture of Meredith and ancient Sparta'. One sees in them their father's 'look of proud command'; also, an isolation from the everyday world that could lead to disaster

Sydney Olivier was colonial secretary in Jamaica, 1900–4, and Governor-General from 07 to 1913. From left: Margery, Daphne, Brynhild, Noel, Sir Sydney, about 1903.
The Olivier sisters grew up in their own company, often with Margery nominally in charge ile their parents were in Jamaica. Rupert Brooke, meanwhile, led a curious double life: as oarder at Rugby, but in a house – School Field – headed by his parents. Here he sits second m right, in his First XI cap; his closest friend, Hugh Russell-Smith, stands at upper left.

David Garnett called the Olivier sisters 'aristocratic creatures ... who felt contempt easily.' Certainly their beauty was without seductiveness, or even much concern for the spell it cast on others. Here Brynhild (left) is in her late twenties, Margery (right) about twenty. By her mid-thirties, Margery was hopelessly insane.

Justin Brooke (not related to Rupert) was the son of a self-made northern businessman, founder of Brooke Bond tea. Before going up to Cambridge, Justin (left) went to two newly established progressive schools: Abbotsholme and Bedales. At Bedales he met Jacques Raverat (right), also from a wealthy but liberal family.

edales was based on Edward Carpenter's creed of 'the Simple Life'; its curriculum included o-education, fresh air, nude bathing, work on the land, and classes in cooking and sewing — r boys only.

Katharine ('Ka') Cox, the orphan daughter of a wealthy stockbroker, met Rupert Brooke at the Cambridge Young Fabian Society in 1907. It took her five years to fall in love with him. James Strachey, on the other hand, loved Rupert abjectly and unrequitedly from the time they met at Hillbrow prep school in Rugby.

James (left) *and Lytton Strachey, 1912.*

stin Brooke directed Aeschylus's
umenides *at Cambridge in 1906. Rupert*
'ayed the Herald (downstage, right), *a silent*
irt that made the most of his profile.

Justin was also a gifted actor, trained by the headmaster of Bedales, J.H. Badley. Female undergraduates were not allowed to act with men at Cambridge; here, Justin (left) shows o his twenty-two-inch waist as Miss Hardcastle in She Stoops to Conquer, *and Rupert (right) Stingo in the same production.*

In an out-of-term production of Marlowe's Doctor Faustus, *Brynhild Olivier (top) was allowed to play Helen of Troy. It was another silent part; all she had to do, Brynhild said, was practise walking like a lady.*

with Bunny (who so resembles Denham). Oh, quite distant!

Again we went up to his room. He got into bed. I sat on it and talked. Then I lay on it. Then we put the light out and talked in the dark. I complained of the cold: and so got under the eiderdown. My brain was, I remember, almost all through, absolutely calm and indifferent, observing progress, and mapping out the next step. Of course, I had planned the general scheme beforehand.

I was still cold. He wasn't. 'Of course not, you're in bed!' 'Well then, you get right in, too.' – I made him ask me – oh! without difficulty! I got right in. Our arms were round each other. 'An adventure!' I kept thinking: and was horribly detached.

We stirred and pressed. The tides seemed to wax. At the right moment I, as planned, said 'come into my room, it's better there. . . .' I suppose he knew what I meant. Anyhow he followed me. In that large bed it was cold; we clung together. Intentions became plain; but still nothing was said. I broke away a second, as the dance began, to slip my pyjamas. His was the woman's part throughout. I had to make him take his off – do it for him. Then it was purely body to body – my first, you know! I was still a little frightened of his, at any too sudden step, bolting; and he, I suppose, was shy. We kissed very little, as far as I can remember, face to face. And I only rarely handled his penis. Mine he touched once with his fingers; and that made me shiver so much that I think he was frightened. But with alternate stirrings, and still pressures, we mounted. My right hand got hold of the left half of his bottom, clutched it, and pressed his body into me. The smell of sweat began to be noticeable. At length we took to rolling to and fro over each other, in the excitement. Quite calm things, I remember, were passing through my brain 'The Elizabethan joke "The Dance of the Sheets" has, then, something in it.' 'I hope his erection is all right' – – – and so on. I thought of him entirely in the third person. At length the waves grew more terrific: my control of the situation was over; I treated him with the utmost violence, to which he more quietly, but incessantly, responded. Half under him and half over, I came off. I *think* he came off at the same time, but of that I have never been sure. A silent moment: and then he slipped away to his room, carrying his pyjamas. We wished each other 'Goodnight.' It was between 4 and 5 in the morning. I lit a candle after he had gone. There was a dreadful mess on the bed. I wiped it as clear as I could, and left the place exposed in the air, to dry. I sat on the lower part of the bed, a blanket round me, and stared at the wall, and thought. I thought of innumerable things, that this was all; that the boasted jump from virginity to Knowledge seemed a very tiny affair, after all; that I hoped Denham, for whom I felt great tenderness, was sleeping. My thoughts went backward and forward. I unexcitedly reviewed my whole life, and indeed the whole universe. I was tired, and rather pleased with myself, and a little bleak. About six it was grayly daylight; I blew the candle out and slept till 8. At 8 Denham had to bicycle in to breakfast with Mr Benians, before catching his train. I bicycled with him, and turned off at the corner of –, is it Grange Road? –. We said scarcely anything to each other. I felt sad at the thought he was perhaps hurt and angry, and wouldn't ever want to see me again. – He did, of course, and was exactly as ever. Only we never referred to it. But that night I looked with some awe at the room – fifty yards away to the West from the bed I'm writing in – in which I Began; in which I 'copulated with' Denham; and I felt a curious private tie with Denham himself. So you'll understand it was – not with a *shock*, for I'm far too dead for that, but with a sort of dreary wonder and dizzy discomfort – that I heard Mr Benians inform me, after we'd greeted, that Denham died at one o'clock on Wednesday morning, – just twenty four hours ago now.[39]

The impact of Russell-Smith's early death belongs to the story of 1912. In 1909 his role was to give Rupert an escape from his sexual impasse – and perhaps to confirm the saying that 'no man is a hypocrite in his pleasures'. What the episode does not show, however, is that Rupert was simply a 'repressed' homosexual. His case resembles that of D. H. Lawrence. Both were emotionally drawn to men, yet were restrained from a homosexual life by the censorship of their formidable puritan mothers. But both also had genuine heterosexual ideals, and genuine scepticism about homosexual society. In Rupert's case there was a jealous recognition that, for someone of his class, homosexuality opened a much easier and earlier path to sexual satisfaction. He may have felt 'great tenderness' for Denham, but his main object was clearly 'the boasted jump from virginity to Knowledge'. Having taken the jump, his interest in Denham soon dwindled. There is no suggestion that Rupert felt for his sexual partner anything like the deep passion that James Strachey had long cherished for *him*; nor did his one-night stand with Denham make any difference to his love for Noel or to his determination to marry her. Finally, this first experiment did not lead to further homosexual affairs.[40] Given the many attempts by men to seduce him, his experience of homosexuality seems, if anything, to have confirmed that his sexual tastes did *not* run in that quarter.

Rupert now knew about 'all that James and Norton and Maynard and Lytton know and hold over me'; but he made no move to join their circle as an initiate. It was part of Denham's attraction that he was unknown to Rupert's regular friends. The affair exacerbated his self-division, between the 'dirtiness' of copulation and the 'purity' of romantic love. 'I thought of him entirely in the third person' sums up the relation between Rupert and his lover. And his secretiveness was stronger than ever, since he could hardly have discussed his escapade with any of his still virginal woman friends – least of all Noel.

'The Charm' shows how Noel fed Rupert's imagination, but not his need for everyday love or companionship:

In darkness the loud sea makes moan;
And earth is shaken, and all evils creep
About her ways.
                         Oh now to know you sleep!
Out of the whirling blinding moil, alone,
Out of the slow grim fight,
One thought to wing – to you, asleep,
In some cool room that's open to the night,
Lying half-forward, breathing quietly,
One white hand on the white
Unrumpled sheet, and the ever-moving hair
Quiet and still at length! . . .

Rupert wrote this within a month of his erotic adventure with Russell-Smith – which should perhaps be included among the evils that creep around the world at night! Certainly the 'unrumpled sheet' on which the beloved lies contrasts with the 'dreadful mess' on the bed of lust. Rupert's sexual initiation, instead of giving him a more realistic vision of Noel, led him to make her even more of a wax figure, unconscious of desire.

After a frenetic social round in London – including an

appearance at the Slade Arts Ball in a recycled version of his *Comus* costume – Rupert left for his third Christmas in Switzerland, this time at Lenzerheide. Margery Olivier organised the party; she included Daphne but not Noel or Bryn. Ka and Justin begged off also, though Jacques came, to make up for his awkward exit at Andermatt. Rupert blamed Noel for failing to appear. He was in rather a surly mood for the holiday and, as it turned out, there would be no more Christmases in Switzerland for the Neo-pagans. Four months after the plan for their reunion at Basel, here they were in Switzerland and already far from unanimous in spirit or commitment. The forces that would eventually drive them apart were starting to work, for those who had eyes to see them.

V

Ten to Three

Father's Footsteps

Towards the end of 1909 Justin Brooke had been in articles in Chancery Lane for over a year, and had found it completely unbearable. He was, in fact, close to a nervous breakdown. By November he had convinced his father that he had to break free, at least for a while. He wanted to get as far away as possible: not just to North America, but to the far west of California and British Columbia. On 14 January 1910, he went off with Jacques' enthusiastic blessings:

> Last friday afternoon at five o'clock, I offered a sacrifice – spiritual – to the Gods of perpetual youth: And Justin bade farewell to this old and dark and dusty land, sailing toward the isles of sunset, the new Atlantis, America – and liberty; 'like Paracelsus, who went to find his soul'. And my heart was filled with joy. . . . Imagine the joy of broken fetters, of the escape from Chancery lane and all the petty quibbling of lawyers, and the joy of being alone – alone with his soul, after all these months and that loathsome promiscuity (pah!) – in a new country.[1]

Justin had six months of freedom and solitude before he went back into harness. As he left, Rupert also became free of *his* father, though not by any conscious act of rejection. Soon after he returned from Lenzerheide, his father's health began rapidly to break down. 'He has been unable to see more than men as trees walking . . .' Rupert told Dudley Ward. 'It has been bad to see him tottering about the House, or sitting thinking and brooding over the future for hour on hour, never speaking, and always in pain.'[2] Parker Brooke had been in decline since his son Richard's death three years before, but now he had suffered a stroke. Within two weeks he was dead, at fifty-nine. After his early brilliance at school and university he had slowly dwindled into hen-pecked mediocrity. His career must have helped create Rupert's almost pathological fear of age.

After the funeral, Rupert took stock of his family's fortune. Parker Brooke had built up, through savings and inheritance, a private income of £600 a year. The Ranee would give Rupert an allowance of £150 a year out of this. It was enough for him to live on until he went to war in 1914, with some modest further earnings from freelance writing and winning academic prizes. Rugby agreed that he should run School Field until April, taking leave from Cambridge. This continued his father's salary and gave his mother time to find a new home. The Fabian Society, of which Rupert was now president, was entrusted to Hugh Dalton and a rising young student politician, Clifford Allen.[3]

Rupert had fifty-three boys to look after (though not to teach) for two months. It was the only time in his life that he held down a regular job, apart from his seven months in the Navy at the end of his life. He rated himself 'an efficient schoolmaster, tired & high-voiced & snappish' – and not afraid of discipline. Giving a flogging was an 'extraordinary sensation', he told James Strachey. 'He had broken his furniture to small pieces with a coal-hammer. But I had no consciously sexual emotions.'[4]

Taking over his father's job closed the circle of Rupert's upbringing. He had been born in a house owned by Rugby School, and now he had become a master there. The worst thing about it, he found, was the company of the other masters. He wrote an exasperated poem to Dudley about his eagerness to escape, but one passage showed how much affection he still had for schooldays – or rather, for schoolboys:

They do not know the Light.
They stink. They are no good. And yet . . . in spite
Of the thousand devils that freeze their narrowing views
(Christ, and gentility, and self-abuse)
They are young, direct, and animal. In their eyes

Spite of the dirt, stodge, wrappings, flits and flies
A certain dim nobility. . . . So I love . . .

                              each line
Of the fine limbs and faces; love, in fine,
(O unisexualist!) with half a heart,
Some fifty boys, together, and apart,
Half-serious and half-sentimentally. . . .[5]

By unisexualist, Rupert meant someone who combined male and female qualities. The poem shows that his attraction to young males was inseparable from the world of public school, so redolent, for him, of past triumphs and youthful ardour. This was the sentimental side of his homoeroticism and it left, by his reckoning, a quarter of him that loved his own sex outright and a half that loved women. It seems a fair division of his sexual allegiances.

As he wound up his housemastering, Rupert also helped his mother to retire from School Field. With her modest income, she would retain more status in the neighbourhood of the school than anywhere else. She ended up a quarter of a mile away: in a large semi-detached house at 24 Bilton Road, separated from the traffic only by an exiguous front yard. 'It's the first time I have ever lived at a number,' Rupert reported. 'I've always been at a house with a name, before. The difference is extraordinary.'[6] The difference was that Mrs Brooke had slipped down a rank or two within the middle class, and the kind of hospitality she could offer Rupert's friends was correspondingly reduced. The contrast between his home and such places as the Oliviers' cottage in the woods at Limpsfield, still more the Raverat château at Prunoy, was now much wider. Rupert had become one of the least well-off in his circle of friends.

Lack of grandeur might have been made up by charm, but 24 Bilton Road had only pretentiousness and gloom. In a misguided attempt to create privacy, its architect had put the entrances of each semi-detached around the side, in a dark little porch with columns; the stuccoed façade had a sinister blankness, as if the inhabitants had been bricked up inside. Rupert's younger brother Alfred was now at Cambridge too, so Mrs Brooke would live mostly alone. When her sons visited, they would enter a sealed environment. Rarely, now, would disturbing young ladies or men from Cambridge, with their breezy manners and unsound beliefs, cross the threshold. The memories of schoolboy prowess that Rupert enjoyed when he visited School Field were gone. Bilton Road was a constant reminder that his family was in decline.

Parker Brooke's death consolidated the Ranee's emotional hold on Rupert. The death itself did not move him deeply, or not visibly so at least. It was part of the Neo-pagan creed to claim that they and their parents belonged to utterly different worlds. For Rupert, however, no real separation was possible. When he visited his mother, he slipped into his father's vacant role. He bowed to her moral authority, even as he chafed under the yoke and looked forward eagerly to the time of release. But always, before long, he would be drawn back. He could never make himself a permanent home anywhere else during the five years of life that remained – as if to do so would be disloyal to the woman who followed his affairs, with anxious love and reproof, from Bilton Road.

'And then you suddenly cried, and turned away'

From late 1909 onwards, Rupert wrote a series of poems complaining about Noel's failure to live up to their trysts earlier in the year, in the New Forest and at Penshurst. In 'The Hill', the most romantically appealing of these poems, the beloved turns away on a momentary impulse:

Breathless, we flung us on the windy hill,
Laughed in the sun, and kissed the lovely grass. . . .

'We are Earth's best, that learnt her lesson here.
Life is our cry. We have kept the faith!' we said;
'We shall go down with unreluctant tread
Rose-crowned into the darkness!' . . . Proud we were,
And laughed, that had such brave true things to say.
– And then you suddenly cried, and turned away.

'Desertion' says little more about her reason for slipping apart:

> Was it something heard,
> Or a sudden cry, that meekly and without a word
> You broke the faith, and strangely, weakly, slipped apart?
> You gave in – you, the proud of heart, unbowed of heart!
> Was this, friend, the end of all that we could do?

Rupert's long separation from Noel ended when he wangled an invitation to the annual Shakespeare play at Bedales. He went down on 18 December 1909 with Jacques and Geoffrey Lupton. We do not know what passed between Noel and Rupert, but he was bitterly disappointed by the meeting. Margery managed to keep Noel from joining Rupert at Lenzerheide after Christmas, and may not have been above trying to turn her against Rupert by passing on gossip about him. Perhaps Margery saw Rupert flirting with Bryn at the riotous Slade Arts Ball; perhaps Margery, there or in Switzerland, decided that Rupert was flirting with herself. Whatever the provocation, or the interference by Margery, Noel clearly decided around this time that Rupert was too ardent and needed to be cooled off.

Bunny Garnett had been infatuated with Noel since the age of about four, and regularly tried to breach her defences. In a letter of April 1910 she tried to explain her elusiveness. Bunny's father, meeting her on the train from London to Oxted, had told her that all the Oliviers were afraid of emotional commitment, of 'giving themselves away' to another person. That was not quite it, Noel said; in fact, she *had* fallen in love, and more than once (she surely had Rupert in mind in saying this). But for her, youth meant that one had such passions while knowing, at the same time, that they wouldn't last. Therefore, one wasn't touched to the quick or deeply threatened by them; and the whole charm of being young, for her, was precisely in recognising that one's feelings weren't permanent.[7]

It is not clear whether Noel offered this as an explanation or an excuse. She was secretive to a high degree – not from any fondness for intrigue, like Rupert, but because she was just 'close' by nature. Mary Newbery and Noel liked each other well enough when they were at Bedales to share a bath regularly, but Noel never said anything about her love affairs. Men who were attracted to Noel found her maddeningly impervious and invulnerable. They could scarcely appreciate how she was able to 'bracket off' her spontaneity in the interest of extending her youthful freedom. Indeed, Noel found that after years of holding back her emotions they did not appear on cue when she decided that she was ready to commit herself at last. She did not truly fall in love until she was nearly forty, and then she did so with all the risk and abjectness that she had so carefully steered away from in her teens.

During the winter of 1909–10 Rupert saw Noel only once, and he felt that she was deliberately hiding from him. Trapped in his schoolmastering at Rugby, he longed to see her as soon as he was released in April. What he got instead was an offhand note: 'you don't climb at Easter, so good-bye for some time.'[8] He tried to intercept her train at Birmingham when she passed through on her way to Wales, but missed her and was left standing like a fool on the platform. All he could do was fall back on the Society and go to Lulworth Cove for a week with James and Lytton Strachey. Lytton was nursing a frustrated desire for George Mallory, the most recent athletic beauty to catch his eye. With Rupert pining for Noel they got on better than before, and would remain good friends until the upheavals of 1912.

The Oliviers, and several other Neo-pagans, were keen Morris dancers and rock climbers. Although he had been capped for both rugby and cricket at school, Rupert would neither dance nor climb. He feared, one assumes, the different kinds of exposure that went with these pastimes. At Bethesda, near Snowdon, Noel joined Bryn, Jacques, Godwin Baynes, Rosalind Thornycroft, Bill Hubback, Eva Spielman, Mary Newbery and H. A. (Hugh) Popham – a Cambridge diving champion who struck Ka Cox as 'an odd silent lonely sort of party'.[9] It is not known what climbs they did, but one can be sure that Bryn and Noel had plenty of the calculated self-control that every rock climber needs. This was Jacques' first opportunity to get to know Noel, and his description of her suggests what Rupert was up against:

> She was fairly short, but very strong and well set on her feet.
> Much later a rejected lover could say that she looked just

like a chest of drawers and, to be malicious, the comparison had just enough truth in it to be funny. She had an admirable head, admirably set on her handsome round neck, brown hair, flat complexion, the face very regular and unexpressive, even a bit hard. But it was lit up as if by the beam of a lighthouse when she turned her large grey eyes to you. One could hardly bear their gaze without feeling a kind of instant dizziness, like an electric shock. They seemed full of all the innocence in the world, and of all the experience also; they seemed to promise infinite happiness and wonderful love for whoever could win her. . . . But one would be quite wrong. Like her sisters, she had been raised according to the most modern and advanced principles, in almost complete liberty. They had picked up a few practical ideas about life, and above all an emancipated and determined appearance. But their parents, overly intellectual, had not given them the breathable milieu that they needed in order to develop. One sensed that they all lacked something. . . . You didn't have to know Yseult [Noel] for very long to see that her great beauty, and her excessively perfect health, were matched by only a good average, practical intelligence, little sensitivity, no tenderness, no imagination.[10]

Edwardian Summer

That spring, Rupert tried hard to beat down his love for Noel, since she was so firmly and painfully resistant to his ardour. 'There's a stage where one believes she's a "great creative genius",' he told James Strachey two years later. 'It's rather a nice one. It lasted 22 months with me. Conversation with her breaks it down in the end –'.[11] Conversation, at least, was more possible once the summer got under way. In late January Margery and Daphne had gone to see their parents in Jamaica, not returning until early October. With only Bryn to watch over her, Noel became more accessible physically, if not emotionally. At the end of April Rupert went down to Limpsfield with Jacques for four days. They walked cross-country to Toy's Hill with Noel, Bryn and Ethel Pye, savouring the first bluebells in the spring woods and the smell of the wet earth. In the pub where they had tea there was a canary which, it was decided, looked exactly like Jacques.

Bryn came up to Cambridge soon after and the high summer of Neo-paganism came into full swing. This was the golden age of mass breakfasts under the apple-blossoms in the orchard at Grantchester: the women still primly attired in shirt-waist blouses and skirts, the men in ties – except for Rupert in his open-necked blue shirt (matching his eyes), orchestrating the day's amusements. A punt was moored at the foot of his garden, for long excursions up and down the river. Inviting Bunny to visit, Brooke promised him 'apple-blossom now, later . . . roses . . . bathing and all manner of rustic delight, cheeses, and fruit'.[12]

This friendly invitation had some guile mixed in. Bunny was nice enough, but he was barely out of school. His major attraction was knowing the Oliviers so well. Encouraged by Rupert, he set up a cruise on the Norfolk Broads for five days at the end of June. Their companions would be Godwin Baynes, now the Medical Officer of Health for Hampstead; Bryn and Noel; and an old family friend called Dr Rogers to serve as chaperone. Bunny shared a cabin on the wherry *Reindeer* with Rupert, and found him 'simple, sincere and intimate, with a certain lazy warmth'.[13] Rupert had plenty of warmth, to be sure, but not much simplicity. Bunny does not seem to have suspected that he was being cultivated by Rupert for the sake of Bryn and Noel, whom they could hear laughing in the next cabin at night.

In his dissatisfaction with Noel, Rupert was again finding Bryn very appealing. The long days on the water showed off her gaiety, and her supple figure, to advantage. One sister for lust and liking, one for love; he pondered this riddle as he sat on the deck writing a long essay for the Harness Prize (which he won) on the English puritans. Inspired by his Neo-pagan company, Rupert jeered merrily at the absurdities of the puritan mind. He had not yet realised how much puritanism there was in himself, and how violently it was due to erupt.

Three weeks later, after much scheming, Rupert managed to see Noel briefly at Bedales. He had made friends with the writer Edward Thomas, who lived in a cottage near Petersfield. Noel could come there to have tea with him, though she had to be accompanied by another girl and have a pass signed personally by The Chief.[14] A fortnight later they were together again at Bucklers Hard, on the Beaulieu River in Hampshire. Bryn and

Dudley Ward had scouted the place after the cruise on the Broads. They found hay fields, a splendid landing-stage from which you could dive, and two rows of old brick cottages with a grassy street between them. It was then a remote clearing surrounded by woods, far from the over-built mecca for trippers that it is today.

The Beaulieu camp was carefully organised in proper Bedalian style. There was a large cook-tent, borrowed from the school, and a small lugger rented for the two weeks they were there. Most of the days were spent either in or on the river. Rupert and Dudley came from a Fabian caravan tour to join Ka Cox, Godwin Baynes, Jacques, Noel and Bryn. An outer circle included Harold Hobson, Hugh Popham, Bill Hubback and Eva Spielman (now engaged to each other), Sybil and Ethel Pye, and their younger brother David.[15] One quiet evening – it may have been on his twenty-third birthday, 3 August – Brooke went aside with Noel to gather wood and asked her to marry him. They had known each other for over two years, but she was still only seventeen. Her response was a half measure: to accept Rupert's proposal, while not allowing him to tell anyone of her decision.[16] But it was obvious that something was up between them, and Jacques' vignette suggests how it may have appeared to the other campers:

> she accepted the homage of his devotion with a calm, indifferent, detached air, as if it were something quite natural. No doubt she was flattered by his attentions, for she cannot have failed to see something of [Rupert's] beauty and charm; also, she saw how he was sought out, admired, showered with adulation on every side. But he did not inspire respect in her; she found him too young, too chimerical, too absurd.[17]

An engagement that was kept secret, and set no date for the wedding, was hardly a real engagement at all. Neither Rupert nor Noel had a clear understanding of how far they were bound to each other. Nor were they any more free to spend time together. But they could at least be in touch for another fortnight, when they moved on from Beaulieu to work on an encore performance of Marlowe's *Faustus*. It was staged on 17 August, for a group of visiting German students. Women could join the cast this time,

because it was not an official university production. Justin
Brooke, who returned from tramping around California and
British Columbia at the beginning of July, was immediately
recruited to direct the play. He cast Francis Cornford as Faustus,
Jacques as Mephistophilis and Rupert as the Chorus. There were
appropriate supporting roles for various other Neo-pagans. Bryn
made a dazzling Helen, in a low-cut robe with powdered gold in
her hair. She didn't have to speak, just make the audience believe
in 'the face that launched a thousand ships'. The only thing she
had to rehearse, she joked, was how to walk like a lady. Ethel Pye
embodied the Deadly Sin of Lechery – perhaps her extreme
admiration for Rupert had been noticed? – and Ka was Gluttony.
Noel was a humble understudy to Envy.

Again, the play itself seemed secondary to the preparing and
celebrating of it. Bryn, Noel and the Pye sisters stayed at the Old
Vicarage, a stone's throw from Rupert's lodgings in Grantchester. Sometimes they came home from rehearsals by water,
Rupert skilfully guiding the canoe along the dark and winding
river. Their diversions, when they stayed home, were swimming
and reading aloud. Whatever Rupert's stiffness onstage, he was a
magnetic reader in company. He needed a sympathetic audience
to release his expressiveness, and he had a shrewd eye for setting,
like reading *Paradise Lost* high up in a chestnut tree with Noel
and Sybil. In the evenings it might be *Antony and Cleopatra* or
Meredith's *Modern Love*, over at the Old Vicarage:

> Our sitting room was small and low, with a lamp slung from
> the ceiling, and a narrow door opening straight onto the
> dark garden. On quiet nights, when watery sounds and
> scents drifted up from the river, this room half suggested the
> cabin of a ship. Rupert sat with his book at a table just below
> the lamp, the open door and dark sky behind him; and the
> lamplight falling so directly on his head would vividly mark
> the outline and proportions of forehead, cheek and chin; so
> that in trying afterwards to realize just what lent them, apart
> from all expression, so complete and unusual a dignity, and
> charm, I find it is to this moment my mind turns.[18]

Sybil was in love with Rupert, of course, and saw him through
hungry and uncritical eyes. Jacques' view of those days of
rehearsal was much less sentimental:

He read [Noel] his poems – poor Charles [Rupert] – and others too – Donne, Milton, Yeats, Swinburne – in his slow, slightly affected voice; she listened politely but a little bored and often, I think, completely mystified; she would have understood Chinese poems as easily. I still remember seeing Charles, when he was painting some piece of scenery, touch the tip of Yseult's nose caressingly with his brush, as she came over to watch; she seemed to find this joke much more to her taste than serious readings or conversations. It was, it must be said, more suited to her age. In all, she felt for him only a certain affection, tinged with a little disdain. But Charles did not take it too hard. He was completely given over to his adoration of her; bitterness – along with desire – had not yet entered into his heart.[19]

To break the tension there was always Byron's Pool, where, Rupert teasingly told Lytton, 'It wouldn't stiffen you even at all to hear of what it was the rosiest chatteringest delirium for me to do – bathing naked by moonlight with the ladies. For I, of course, am with Jane [Harrison] in these matters.'[20] Sybil Pye remembers him coming from the river and hanging upside down from a poplar tree to dry his long hair, a pose that reminded her of a Blake woodcut. Rupert was playing the game of 'to the pure all things are pure' with his entourage of four comely young women. They *were* pure, so far as we can tell; but Noel was naturally without shame, whereas Rupert was consciously trying to deny his puritan heritage. And at what point would the game become earnest, when they all had to make their sexual choices, and live with them? Gwen Darwin expressed the longing of many of them that their maturity should never arrive:

I wish one of us could write a 'Ballade des beaux jours a Grantchester'. I can't bear to think of all these young beautiful people getting old and tired and stiff in the joints. I don't believe there is anything compensating in age and experience – We are at our very best and most livingest now – from now on the edge will go off our longings and the fierceness off our feelings and we shall no more swim in the Cam – – and we shan't mind much. I am still drunk with the feeling of Thursday afternoon. Do you know how one suddenly stops and sees them all sitting round – Rupert and Geoffrey and Jacques and Bryn and Noel – all so young and strong and keen and full of thought and desire – and one

knows it will all be gone in 20 years and there will be
nothing left. They will all be old and tired and perhaps
resigned. . . .

    If one of those afternoons could be written down just as it
was exactly it would be a poem – But I suppose perhaps a
thoroughly *lived* poem can't be written – only a partially
lived one. O it is intolerable, this waste of beauty – its all
there and nobody sees it but us and we can't express it – We
are none of us great enough to express a thing so simple and
large as last Thursday afternoon. I don't believe in getting
old. I hate it, I hate it –[21]

Helping the Poor

While balancing all these friendships and loves, in the summer of
1910, Rupert was also keeping his political conscience alive. In
July, just before the Beaulieu River camp, he travelled through
Hampshire and Dorset with Dudley Ward, making speeches for
reform of the Poor Law. A Commission on the Poor Law had
reported in February 1909. Its majority had argued for piecemeal
reform, but Beatrice Webb had written a Minority Report saying
that the whole system needed to be overthrown. To fight for her
views in the political arena, she and Sidney Webb formed the
National Committee for the Prevention of Destitution. There
was a tinge of absurdity in Rupert and Dudley going from one
village green to another, haranguing the yokels, but they were
part of a well-organised campaign with thousands of supporters.
Nonetheless, the campaign failed, for reasons that struck at the
root of the Fabian idea.

    Since the time of Dickens, the Poor Law and its Boards of
Guardians had been a stink in the nostrils of enlightened opinion.
The ruling idea of the Poor Law was *deterrence*: the infirm, aged
or unemployed should be kept alive, but at a level well below that
of the poorest employed workers. The giving out of relief was a
typical British muddle, a haphazard combination of state and
private charity, of workhouse and 'outdoor' (i.e. home) relief.

    Sorting out ancient British muddles was meat and drink to the
Webbs. They wanted to replace the local Boards of Guardians

with a national system of boards to provide health care, pensions and relief. But the central issue was what to do with the able-bodied unemployed, and here the Webbs could not break with the principle of deterrence. They viewed poverty as a social disease that needed to be quarantined, then treated. Whether the poor wanted to be treated was irrelevant. The state should operate like the Salvation Army, indoctrinating the people it helped and dividing them into grades. 'It is essential', Sidney Webb wrote, 'that the [unemployed] should be always moving up *or* down, by promotion or degradation.'

Meanwhile the Liberal Chancellor of the Exchequer, Lloyd George, was incubating a comprehensive scheme of state unemployment insurance. For Beatrice, this had 'the fatal defect that the state got nothing for its money – that the persons felt they had a right to the allowance whatever their conduct. . . . That is, of course, under the present conditions of human will, sheer madness, whatever it may be in good times to come.'[22] Rupert signed up for the Webbs' campaign, but in fact his views on unemployment relief sounded more like Lloyd George:

> When we are in trouble or danger from other people, we throw ourselves on the State in the shape of the policeman or the law court. This 'loss of independence' does not weaken the character; it leaves men free to use their energies more profitably. For a working-man to spend his time in unaided, individual encounters with thieves, disease, and the devil of unemployment, certainly may (if he is always victorious) foster and widen his sense of personal responsibility and self-reliance, but it is still more certainly a *ridiculous and sentimental waste of time and trouble*. . . . It is not possible, as Society is organized, for every man to get work.[23]

Rupert's and Dudley's decision to tour the southern countryside, rather than the industrial North, showed their roots as Simple Lifers and devotees of Olde England. Their choice of a caravan followed the example of Augustus John rather than the Webbs, who insisted on bourgeois amenities and efficient working conditions. There was no reason, except nostalgia, to travel by horse-power instead of by train or bicycle. Starting near Winchester, Rupert and Dudley went south-west through the New Forest as far as Corfe and then came back, speaking on village greens and street corners as they went. At Wareham it came on to rain and their cat was run over by a car, so they retreated to a hotel for beds and a lobster tea. No doubt the rustics of Wessex were bemused to be told about poverty by two fresh-faced young men from Cambridge, but it took determination and moral courage to stick at it for twelve days, and few of Rupert's friends would have been able or willing to do as much in a good cause.

Jacques Raverat, for example, was taken along to a Fabian dinner by Dudley Ward and Margery Olivier and detested everything about it:

> What beasts! What swine they are! Long before midnight Keeling and [R.H.] Mottram and three or four others were as drunk as lords and much more loathsome. It would be difficult to imagine any sight more revolting, more pitiably mean, tawdry, contemptible and joyless. ... Dudley, Margery, Evelyn [Radford] and I drank, with empty glasses to 1933. Then I went home, treading on air, never before so conscious of the bestiality of men, and my immeasurable pride.

Nonetheless, Jacques spent a week canvassing in Walworth for the Liberal candidate in the General Election, and was surprised to find how well he could do it. 'The enthusiasm was quite spurious,' he told Ka Cox, 'and I'm afraid I haven't any political sense after all: I remain quite impartial and aloof, really, thinking how foolish all this turmoil and how vain, and how much misspent these energies. I think my democratic principles are purely intellectual; and my instincts ——— well, the less said about *them* the better.'[24] Jacques' instincts, and Justin's too, were shaped by having rich fathers. They wanted to claim their independence, but by way of bohemia rather than political activism. Frances Cornford and Gwen Raverat gave priority to their art. Ka spent much of her life on good causes, but in a more traditionally feminine style of nurture, nursing the sick or aiding refugees during the war. Of the Oliviers, only Margery showed much political sense. Having been brought up on Fabianism from the nursery, they looked elsewhere to find their adult identities.

It would be a mistake, then, to see the Neo-pagans as simply a younger generation of the Fabian movement. They were free to enjoy an aesthetic way of life, if they liked, with only slight connections to politics. Their radicalism leaned towards the quirkiness of those E. M. Forster characters whose private incomes give them the luxury of following their impulses. Their temperaments were nostalgic, anti-industrial, dedicated to leisure and personal freedom. Whether their breezy unconventionality should be admired, or derided as the self-indulgence of a privileged clique, is an open question.[25] But Rupert was the only one of them who tried conscientiously to make an equal commitment to public and private life.

Even so, he had little relish for the political process itself. Working in the second General Election of 1910, he complained about the conflict he felt in being both a Fabian and a disciple of G. E. Moore:

> It is not true that anger against injustice and wickedness and tyrannies is a good state of mind, 'noble'. Oh, perhaps it is with some, if they're fine. But I guess with most, as with me, it's a dirty mean choky emotion. I HATE the upper classes.[26]

When he wrote a personal credo to Ben Keeling, the Apostle clearly had the upper hand. Keeling had been made manager of one of the new Labour Exchanges, at Leeds; evidently he had found the workaday world a let-down after Cambridge, and Brooke had to lecture him on his 'pessimism':

> I suddenly feel the extraordinary value and importance of everybody I meet, and almost everything I see. . . . That is, when the mood is on me. I roam about places – yesterday I did it even in Birmingham! – and sit in trains and see the essential glory and beauty of all the people I meet. I can watch a dirty middle-aged tradesman in a railway-carriage for hours, and love every dirty greasy sulky wrinkle in his weak chin and every button on his spotted unclean waist-coat. I know their states of mind are bad. But I'm so much occupied with their being there at all, that I don't have time to think of that.[27]

These moments of euphoria would have been viewed with suspicion by the Apostles, who held that a good state of mind was less valuable when it was experienced by an inferior person. In

January 1909 the Fabian Gerald Shove joined the Society, but Rupert was still isolated. 'Sheppard delivered an indictment on poor Rupert', J. M. Keynes told Duncan Grant, 'for admiring Mr. Wells and thinking truth beauty, beauty truth. Norton and Lytton took up the attack and even James and Gerald . . . stabbed him in the back. Finally Lytton, enraged at Rupert's defences, thoroughly lost his temper and delivered a violent personal attack.'[28]

Nonetheless, by using 'states of mind' as a touchstone Rupert was defining politics much more widely than the Webbs would have done. 'Every action', he wrote, 'which leads on the whole to good, is "*frightfully*" important. . . . It is not a question of either getting to Utopia in the year 2,000 or not. There'll be so much good then, and so much evil. And we can affect it.'[29] The key word here was 'Every'. Why shouldn't a Sunday breakfast under the apple boughs contribute as much good, in the long run, as organising transport to the polls in a General Election? Private life had no shortage of attractive projects, while a deeper political commitment would require submission to large and menacing powers: first the Webbs, and behind them what Rupert called 'Modern Industry'. When he invited Keeling to visit Grantchester and sample 'the bovine existence of a farmer', there was a true word in the jest. Rupert had no intention of leaving his rural Arcadia for the gritty world of factories and workhouses. The North of England would remain for him what it was for most people of his kind: what you passed through on your way to the Lake District or the Highlands.

'Some Kind of Ritual?'

After *Faustus*, Jacques Raverat returned to France to join in another attempt to build a new form of life. A family friend called Paul Desjardins, professor of literature at Sèvres, had bought an ancient Cistercian abbey at Pontigny. He restored it, and in August 1910 held the first of a series of intellectual assemblies there. The aim of Pontigny, as Jacques understood it, was to become 'the stronghold of European *Culture* against all barbarian invasions: americans, utilitarians, fanatics and all other materialistic incarnations of Evil; and it is to combine a revival of craftsmanship and scholarship working as it were hand in hand. And it is to be international and open to men and women equally.' The first participants were a mixture of socialist politi- cians and intellectuals. But coming from Beaulieu River and Cambridge, Jacques found them disappointing:

> They are all admirable men, for intelligence and their devotion to truth and the true nobleness of their minds. But alas, they are old men, have forgotten the earth and the smell of the woods after rain and the radiance of midsummer nights and their bodies are shrivelled and weak. (Where are the young gods I knew?) And I cannot choose but pity them. . . . Yet they are wise, and their minds are free – free from passion and desire and all but love . . . of an idea.[30]

In the event, Pontigny became a successful 'talking shop' for French and British intellectuals in the twenties and thirties. André Gide was its most prominent supporter.

More inspiring for Jacques was a gathering of his English friends at his family home at Prunoy, on the northern fringe of Burgundy. Frances and Francis Cornford were invited to come in September, along with Bryn, Noel and Ka. Rupert asked Ka if he should try to escape from Bilton Road and come himself, to harmonise the clash of sensibilities:

> it will be splendid for both parties – and for everyone else – if Brynnoel and France/is love each other. But that sort of joining-up is made easier by an extra person who knows and loves both lots and has a calmer, more intriguing and far- seeing mind than the romantic dreamer Jacques. So that I felt, though they of course *would* join, Francis' brooding and Frances' energy and Brynnoel's shyness and partly affected stupidity might *just* possibly make it less complete and happy than it would be under the benign encourage- ment of one so wise and so competent in *both* the languages and natures as (I was perfectly confident!) myself. . . .
> (No, I'm not pretending, even to myself, that I imagine you hadn't thought of it just as much as I; having seen, as you did, for instance, the frightened gleaming silence of Bryn and Noel at Faustus' time – in company.)[31]

In part, Rupert just wanted to bridge a cultural gap. Francis

Cornford was a thirty-six-year-old don with a brilliant book on Thucydides, Frances an offshoot of the Cambridge aristocracy even if she had not herself gone to university. Bryn, on the other hand, had never sought an intellectual career; at this time she was trying her hand at making jewelry, with frequent interruptions for country outings or going to London theatres. Noel was aiming at medical school rather than university. One can see how both sisters might have been intimidated by the bantering intellectual style of Cambridge – and also how they might hold defensively on to their own powers of beauty, vigour and tribal solidarity. A gap could be seen opening between those Neo-pagans who held by the examined or the unexamined life – or so Jacques explained it to Ka after his reunion with Justin in July:

> He certainly has thought a good deal about more general things than he had ever done before – a little confusedly, but still a beginning. But it does not seem to me that emotionally – if I may use the word – he has progressed at all. I wonder whether he ever will? There is an essay of Walter Pater called 'Diaphaneite' in 'Miscellaneous Studies', I think; which is all about such as he and Bryn. You see, I think the matter is that they are 'good as ends' – well nigh perfect and therefore imperfectible.[32]

What had been overlooked in all this anxious anticipation was the effect of the place where they were to gather. Probably his English friends joked about Jacques' château, imagining it as an oversized country house; when they arrived, they would find a combination of domestic charm and grandeur. Georges Raverat, its first bourgeois proprietor, had bought the Château de Vienne in 1901 from the impoverished Comte de Goyon. It had been built between 1710 and 1725 by the Lalive family, favourites of Louis XIV, after they had razed the medieval château that stood on the site. Used mainly in the summer, for hunting, the château was not built for warmth, but for light. The main block had great windows that gave a clear view right through the building. There were scores of rooms of all shapes and sizes, towers with conical roofs, huge chimneys for the wood-burning stoves in the cellars, stables, a walled kitchen-garden, and some seven hundred acres of woods and tenant farms. Best of all, for these particular guests, was the sweeping park behind the house that led to a large and secluded artificial lake.

It was a place to enchant its visitors – and to dispel the nervousness and uncertainty that often put Jacques in the shade in England. He went for long walks with Bryn and found her 'more marvellous than ever . . . radiant and wild rose like'.[33] With his romantic sensibility, he dreamed of some charm to preserve the golden friendships he had enjoyed since his recovery in 1909. When he had seen Justin off to America nine months earlier, they were already planning a ceremony for his return:

> on midsummer day, at night, we'll make a solemn sacrifice again to the Gods of perpetual youth, to close the cycle and celebrate most worthily his deliverance and birth. I am pondering over the ritual even now: there must be fire; and water, clear spring water poured at sunrise out of a cup of virgin crystal; and wreaths of dog roses and honeysuckle; and there should be a bird in a cage to set free at dawn and a fair prayer to sing as we dance hand in hand round the leaping fire. . . .[34]

After Ka left Prunoy, the rest of them took up the idea of composing a Neo-pagan rite:

> We had some fair days even after you went – for all that I was a little sad. And we invented fires, after bathing, between tea and suppertime. I wish we had thought of that before. We talked a great deal of the urgency of some kind of ritual, mystery, initiation, symbolism and we planned a great litany of the four elements. But I doubt whether it will ever come to anything. As Francis says, we are all much too rational and self-conscious – all except Frances perhaps, that child.[35]

Francis Cornford was steeped in Cambridge anthropology and well able to design a modern ritual for his friends. Nonetheless, they were right to doubt their power to be real, rather than Neo-pagans. It was not just that they were too rational. The ancient world had a philosophy founded on the cycle of youth, maturity and decay; the Edwardians, however, were obsessed with these themes precisely because modern thought found it so hard to deal with them coherently. Their best hope lay in poetry, that attenuated modern substitute for living myth. In poems like 'Dining-room Tea' and 'Grantchester' Brooke would come as close as any of them did to settling their quarrel with Time and Change.

VI

Foreign Affairs

Still to Be Enjoyed

When Jacques, Bryn and the Cornfords bathed in the lake at Prunoy and then built fires to dry themselves, they had all the symbolism they needed to define their situation. The naked swimmers were children of summer; the fires of that September a reminder that summer was coming to an end. For all their cult of perpetual youth and comradeship, the Neo-pagans were now in their mid-twenties. They had to think more insistently about sexual fulfilment and about claiming a place in the world through marriage and work.

Except for the Cornfords, they had up to now kept their private loves separate from the affections in which they all had an equal share. Because the young women of the group still expected to remain chaste until they married, the collective spirit of the Neo-pagans kept sexuality in the background, or even tried to deny it altogether. But the young men were becoming impatient with this sexual moratorium. How long could the girls they loved go on hinting that they would embrace sensuality some day – but not yet? For the men, friendship opposed itself to sex, love of comrades to love for a wife or husband. Either their love had to be followed through to its logical consummation or they would pursue sex outside the group, as Rupert had already done surreptitiously with Denham Russell-Smith.

Godwin Baynes was one such frustrated suitor. He was twenty-eight in 1910, amorously inclined, and already launched on his medical career. Bryn was fond of him, it seems, but not fond enough to commit herself to marrying him. Baynes was not willing to be put off indefinitely, so when climbing in Wales at Easter 1910 he proposed to one of Bryn's cousins, Rosalind Thornycroft, and was accepted.[1] Rupert and Jacques had tea with the happy couple, and left feeling melancholy.[2] Proud self-sufficiency was their public line, but they were both feeling the strain of their bachelorhood.

It is possible that Baynes's engagement to her cousin contributed to Bryn's unsettled feelings during the year. She had never gone to school, much less university and it seemed time to find herself a vocation, now that she was twenty-three and with no immediate prospect of marriage. She had done some painting, and an art jeweller named Wilson agreed to take her as a live-in apprentice. Bryn worked with him for some months at Platt, in Kent, and dreamed of having her own jewelry studio in an 'old red house with the long rooms' that had struck her fancy in Essex.[3] But the close work caused problems with her eyes; and the summer's excursions kept calling her away from her workbench.

Bryn's mother was always trying to keep her daughters by her in Jamaica, and Bryn agreed that when Margery and Daphne came back to England in October she would take their place for several months.[4] Before leaving, unhappy with the empty months that stretched ahead, she unburdened herself to Hugh Popham while they were on a train together. Hugh jumped to the conclusion that she was in love with him – as, he confessed, he already was with her:

> I have been very attracted to you since last Easter. I did not definitely call it love to myself, but now I know it is. . . . I wondered always what your relations were with other men you knew, whether you had an extraordinary facility for being friends, whether you realized that others – and I – must feel more for you. Of course I knew you really must know. Then at times I thought you must be without heart, that you realized and would not see because it gave you pleasure.[5]

Like many beautiful women, Bryn had cultivated the arts of vagueness and evasion to shield herself from importunate admirers. The problem, at this stage of her life, was to avoid vagueness in what she wanted for herself. Her response to Hugh was designed to cut off his hopes, yet one senses that she was sincere in speaking of her own unhappiness and confusion:

> You made a person who was very fond of you and who had during the last few days gone through too many excitements and emotions for her nerves to be quite steady absolutely unbearably sorry for you too. Perhaps you did not know I could mind things. But I think you knew a little what I felt about you – and *that* I still feel.
>
> It was very well as it was, and now I suppose, for you, it is just all wrong. . . . I meant once, quite a long time ago, to warn you against myself – but it seemed altogether too silly and impossibly presumptuous. . . . I am *not* sorry yet, and please, *please* don't let me be, at any rate not now – when everything else is almost unbearably difficult. . . . you must not make me hate myself any more.[6]

It is hard to reconcile Jacques' image of Bryn's flawless calm with her own sense of desperation. Perhaps she did not know herself what her trouble was, but surely it was not going to be resolved by someone who was two years younger than herself and still an undergraduate. Hugh was a cousin of Maitland and Evelyn Radford. He came from a well-established family of Hampshire brewers, and he was known for such Neo-pagan feats as diving into a hole in the ice and coming up at another hole. Although Bryn was beginning to think that marriage and having children was the best thing for her to do, Hugh, at this time anyway, was not a credible husband. When she came back from Jamaica after six months she refused his invitation to May Week and generally avoided his company. But Hugh bided his time, and at last carried off the prize.

Towards the end of June 1910, while Rupert was on the Broads with Bryn and Noel, Jacques also found his chance of living a more serious and committed life. He went walking with Ka Cox and the Cornfords in the Lake District. Somewhere near Ullswater, love, as he put it, sat down between him and Ka like a 'rude, unbidden guest'.[7] In fact, this was the natural culmination of an intimacy that had already lasted three years. But their relations had always been lopsided. Although he was two years older than Ka, Jacques felt her to be more mature, more 'wise and good' than himself. His ill-health made him long to be mothered and protected. 'Think of me but as a wild and wayward child,' he wrote to her, 'and sometimes lay your cool hand on my head.'[8] Yet in reaction against his own loneliness and dependency he had often denounced love, seeing it as a snare that had humbled too many of his friends. Whatever happened, he told Ka, his pride would not allow him to ask anything at all of her. 'To love and yet to be *perfectly free*,' he wrote her, 'is not that an ideal?'[9]

In Gwen Raverat's novel, Ka is asked why she won't agree to marry Jacques. 'He doesn't seem enough of a person somehow,' she replies, 'he's such a baby. He doesn't seem worth marrying.' Jacques was full of grandiose plans, but he was also pathetically nervous and fragile, with sores along his wrists.[10] He kept pouring out his heart to Ka; for whatever reason, she would only return him friendship for love. From the Lake District Jacques went off by himself to climb in Corsica. Justin persuaded him to return to take on the role of Mephistophilis in *Faustus*, which also allowed him to see Ka again at the Bucklers Hard camp. After two months at Prunoy, where Ka visited him with Bryn and the Cornfords, Jacques came back to the Slade in October.

Ka's four years at Newnham were now over, and she was living either with Hester in London or at her own cottage in Woking. She wanted a vocation, but had no financial need for one, and no firm idea of what it should be. 'There were several Darwins and a young Frenchman named Raverat,' observed one exasperated biographer of Rupert Brooke, 'none of whom had anything to do, or who did anything.'[11] One sympathises a little with his impatience, but it is inaccurate as well as unfair. Jacques and Gwen were both working hard and professionally at the Slade. Ka's hopes of becoming a writer were more vague, and she was too shy to show anyone her efforts. But she was active in several Fabian causes and also lectured at Morley College for working men and women, as Virginia Stephen had done a few years before.

Ka and Jacques saw each other constantly, and he proposed to her several times during the autumn. She would neither accept him, nor send him away. He complained of 'the whip of Eros', stormed at her and kept trying to win her over. To progress from sentimental attachment to emotional and sexual intimacy was a move they seemed unable to make.

Rupert, meanwhile, was very much in the same boat. After *Faustus*, in August, Noel again told him that he was too disturbing and made herself unavailable.[12] Two months later she granted him one of those hurried and semi-clandestine meetings at Edward Thomas's. It was becoming clear that in agreeing to be 'engaged' to him at Bucklers Hard she had actually committed herself to very little. And for Rupert the engagement had frozen his emotional development instead of advancing it. In several poems of this time, he imagined his love for Noel as no more than a death-in-life.[13]

At the end of November, Rupert formed a plan to break out of his impasse. He had already decided to spend the spring term in Germany. Before he went, he would go for a quiet holiday in England with Jacques (rather than a riotous one in Switzerland) and settle things calmly with Noel. Margery and Daphne were going to the Alps with Hugh Popham and others, so Noel would be at a loose end for her Christmas break from Bedales. She would have to be chaperoned, of course, but Ka agreed to come and watch over her. The holiday would start the day after Christmas, at Lulworth Cove. 'You'll have to arrange about Noel,' Rupert told Ka, '– unless you think she'd be a nuisance, and the conversation *too* much above her head. You'd be responsible (to Margery!) that that very delicate young flower keeps her pale innocence, and her simple trust in God unshaken by the world-worn scepticism of Jacques and me. You *appear* (which is the point) equal to *that* responsibility.'[14]

Then, at the beginning of December, Noel wrote to tell Rupert that she would not come, but was going to Switzerland with Margery instead. Jacques went down to Limpsfield, and reported that Noel was 'oppressed with a sense of responsibility to that woman her mother'.[15] If Noel went on holiday with two young men, might not Ka's presence make things look, if anything, worse? But Rupert believed this was just a pretext. Once again, Noel was using a conventional excuse to avoid an honest encounter with him. 'What hurts', he told Ka, 'is thinking her wicked. I do, you see. Not very judicially, but I do. And what's to be done if you think a person you know so well is wicked? I don't see what I'm ever to do about Margery.'[16]

Ever since Margery had flatly told Rupert to call off his stubborn pursuit of Noel he had made her the villain of the affair, wantonly cramping her youngest sister's emotional life. But Margery had been in Jamaica from January to October, and Rupert should have realised that it made little sense to blame her for Noel's continued evasiveness. It was plain now, anyway, that Noel had been pulling her own strings all the time. 'I find I've been a devil to Margery,' Rupert confessed to Ka, 'as well as in every other way. She says she never interfered (after a momentary impulse). Noel agrees. Ecco! Where am I? . . . I *am* a beast, after all. Worse than ever. But apologizing to Margery is a little thing; finding oneself in a mere Chaos of disconnexions is the horror.'[17] As he planned his holiday with Ka and Jacques, Rupert must have felt that his relations with Noel had reached, after two and a half years, a complete dead end.

Lulworth 1910: Second Bests?

Lulworth Cove had taken Rupert's fancy in April, when he had stayed there with James and Lytton Strachey.[18] The village itself was a single row of cottages, tucked cosily between the downs and the sea. From it you could sally out for strenuous walks along the cliffs around the miniature harbour. In those days before rural bus services Lulworth was well off the beaten track. Its remoteness and its layout (a bit like an ocean liner) made for an intense emotional atmosphere – as if the assembled intellectuals had slipped their moorings in everyday life.

After three raucous Christmases in Switzerland the party at Lulworth was there to take stock, rather than to celebrate. Gwen had wanted to come, but her family frowned on her going away without a married woman as chaperone. So there were only four of them at Churchfield House: Rupert, Jacques, Ka and Justin.[19] By day they rambled and picnicked up on the downs; in the evening they read *Prometheus Unbound* aloud. Justin was, as usual, the observer and the sympathetic ear, but between the other three the atmosphere was tense. They were each shifting their emotional investment. Jacques again asked Ka to marry him, and was again given the half-serious answer: 'You're too much of a baby.'[20] Rupert was broody, and went for long walks alone. He wrote to Bryn in Jamaica, telling her that he was tired of letting things slide; it was time to seize opportunities and stop worrying about what people might say. He was working himself up to a decision.

In her novel Gwen Raverat shows the tip of the iceberg emerging, when Rupert and Jacques return to Ka's flat after the journey from Lulworth:

> they sat like mummies on the sofa while she lit the fire. George [Jacques] thought there was something terribly feminine about her heavy form, as she squatted on the hearth, puffing with round cheeks; something eternally servile and domestic, utilitarian. . . .
>
> 'She's a good *woman*,' said George to Hubert [Rupert]. 'A good *squaw*,' said Hubert. These were almost the only words that were said. . . . The fire and the tea melted them a little, but they would not talk; and directly afterwards Hubert said:
>
> 'Come on George,' and with a couple of gloomy goodbyes they left. In the street Hubert's arm came through George's.
>
> 'I like *men*,' he said.[21]

At Lulworth, Rupert had decided to turn towards Ka in reaction against Noel. Noel held aloof and always denied, whereas Ka served and accepted. But her acceptance stirred up cross-currents of emotion in Rupert: a mixture of desire, contempt, repulsion and the wish to reaffirm male comradeship against the world of women. Under all of these was a powerful sense of guilt for his own lack of integrity. 'I'm red and sick with anger at myself,' he told Ka after Lulworth, 'for my devilry and degradation and stupidity. . . . I was mean and selfish, and you're, I think, of the most clear and most splendid people in the world.'[22] He was falling in love with Ka, but doing so in a way that was bound to cause trouble for her, for himself and for Noel.

With all the festivities of 1910, Rupert had lagged far behind schedule with his fellowship thesis for King's, on the Elizabethan dramatists. By September he had decided that he would have to submit it a year late, at the end of 1911. Four months of study in Germany were supposed to make him into an expert philologist; but his real reason for going was to escape the frustrations of his personal life in England and sort out his conflicting emotions about Noel and Ka. He went down to Limpsfield early in January for a couple of days, to try and clear the air with Margery and Noel before he left. 'I shall be glad', he told Ka, 'to be in Germany, at peace. Rest means being where no one knows you.'[23] The stay in Germany was meant to disentangle him from his undergraduate follies, and launch him into a more sober adulthood and career. In the event, the outcome was more the reverse. During his year and a half at the Orchard Rupert had come as close as he ever would to having a stable home, a single beloved, a cohesive group of friends, and even a coherent personality. When he left for Munich on 9 January 1911 he had four years and a few months left to live, and was heading towards a crisis that would last until his death.

Part of Rupert's confusion lay in having made an implicit declaration of love to Ka, heedless of her long and intimate involvement with Jacques. But while he was in Germany that relation quickly unravelled. At the same time as she dampened Jacques' ardour, Ka had kept hinting that he might be more warmly received by Gwen, who was probably her closest friend. Gwen was now twenty-five, the same age as Jacques, and had been with him at the Slade for a year. Two weeks before the Lulworth party she had gone walking with him in Dorset, accompanied by the Cornfords. Next to someone like Bryn she might seem plump and plain, but she had wit, a keen eye for character and a real, if small-scale, artistic talent. This last gift was the strongest bond between her and Jacques. Both were exhilarated by the great Post-Impressionist Exhibition in London during November, and both had an almost fanatical devotion to their artistic work. They knew what they wanted, and they wanted the same thing. In the right circumstances, it could be enough to kindle love between them.

Whatever sexual difficulties he may have had, Jacques was not a self-divided puritan like Rupert. He considered it long overdue that he should have a regular sexual fulfilment, and fiercely denounced the chastity of middle-class girls – especially English ones. Gwen recreated one of these battles in her novel:

> 'It's all this sex business. It's you and such as you that help to make it so bad. You think about your virginity and nothing else –'
>
> 'I *don't*,' interrupted Sophy [Gwen], 'but I'm not going to give myself until I love someone.'
>
> 'Pooh,' said George, 'you're just an English lady, you'll be *safe* first. Prudence and prudishness covered with a smear of sentiment. Ugh. I despise you.'
>
> 'O! you *are* unfair,' cried Sophy, 'it's not that. It's not that at all.'[24]

Jacques was not really the rampant immoralist he claimed to be, but he did know that sexual convention was putting him under an unbearable strain. 'I wish you could once see right into me,' he wrote to Ka after one confrontation, 'you would know that I am not wise, but most feeble, most fond and foolish, lustful, vain, ambitious, cruel – my only grace, love. . . . And between these two I am torn and buffetted [*sic*]: my love and my desire: my wild and passionate desire to try and *make* you love me; and the fear I have that you *should* love me; because I love you and because I know myself so vile a thing.'[25]

After Lulworth, Jacques apparently decided to go from push to shove. In Gwen's novel, George bluntly tells Barbara (Ka) that it is time she 'had him', with or without marriage:

> 'But supposing I had a baby?' said Barbara, 'I mustn't harm you, you know.'
>
> 'Why on earth should it harm me?' said George, '. . . It's *you* it would be supposed to harm. . . . of course we could be married before it was born if you wanted to.'
>
> 'I don't know that I do want to,' said Barbara.
>
> 'As you please,' said George exasperated, 'that's your business. I'll provide for the child if there is one. Or if you want to be *prudent*' (with a sneer at the word) 'we won't have one. We can take precautions; though I should like to have a son. . . . Only for God's sake make up your mind.'[26]

Barbara's response was to say she *would* have him – but not yet. To George this meant that she was playing a game, like a hen running from a cock. It was his cue, he realised, to sweep her off her feet:

But his anger rose steadily: why couldn't she confess what she wanted? What a liar she was. Well, if she could be obstinate, he could be obstinate too. No, he would not take her as she wanted 'so that she can say afterwards she couldn't help it'; not though he died with the effort to restrain himself.[27]

In the novel, George flings Barbara back into her chair, storms out and takes the night train to Paris. After ten days of debauchery, he comes back 'knowing women'. He snubs Barbara when he sees her, tells Sophy what he has done and asks her to marry him. She goes off to Barbara, who tells her that she fell in love for the first time at Lulworth – but with Hubert: 'One night when the others were all out, I was sitting by the fire with him. And suddenly I found I was shaking all over and I wanted to take his hand. And he was shaking too. . . . But, you see, Sophy, he really loves Nancy [Noel]. So he can't care for me like that.'[28] Barbara cannot decide whether or not she wants George. They both stand on their pride, while Sophy admits she loves George without reserve. Next day they are engaged, while Barbara dithers. In the evening George comes to her, and tells her, 'it seems simpler to marry Sophy. I like Sophy. She's got bones in her mind. We understand each other. It's rather like marrying yourself in a way; but it's all right. Anyhow it's settled.'[29]

All this, or something like it, happened in January and February 1911. Soon Jacques' and Gwen's engagement was announced, to the general approval of their friends. By April, however, Virginia Stephen was regaling her sister Vanessa with stories of how Jacques' emotions were wilder than ever:

> [Jacques] says now that he is in love with them both; and asks Ka to be his mistress, and Gwen to satisfy his mind. Gwen is made very jealous; Ka evidently cares a good deal for Jacques.
>
> Obviously (in my view) J. is very much in love with K: and not much, if at all, with Gwen. Ought they to break off the engagement? J. has doubts, occasionally; Ka sometimes thinks she could marry him; Gwen alternately grows desperate, and then, accepting J's advanced views, suggests that Ka shall live with them, and bear children, while she paints.[30]

As Virginia saw it, Jacques had 'muddied their minds with talk of the unchastity of chastity'. He was certainly bombarding Ka with immoralist orations: 'Chastity is criminal. Particularly in women. The more I think of it, the worse I think it. It's much worse than prostitution and equivalent to murder, suicide, abortion or self abuse. A society where it is not only tolerated but encouraged is rotten, rotten, rotten . . . [etc.].'[31]

It was Gwen, the most mature and sensible of the three, who called them to order. For a while she was ready to give up Jacques, or even to share him with Ka, but at last she gave her rival her marching papers:

> I would never have consented to marry Jacques, if I had thought you loved him like that. I now think that it is possible you will find you do, when you face up to things. Which *you must do* Ka. But now I think things have changed and I think Jacques loves me more than he does you (I hate being so brutal). If either you or J. have the *least* doubt of this, I absolutely refuse to go any further in the matter.
>
> But if things are as I think, I am sure that for *your own sake* all such relations must stop between you and Jacques; and that it will be better if you don't see Jacques at all for a longish time.[32]

Jacques chimed in with a recantation of his polygamous hopes:

> The truth – it's hard – is that since the beginning of this year, I've not really wanted you except 'in the common way of lust – and friendship'. The difficulty was that no one knew – not yourself even – what you felt about me. It seemed that as I ceased to *need* you, you began to need me. And I was afraid of being cruel and truthful – so much so that I sometimes deceived myself. Now I am *sure* that I am in love with Gwen and not with you. You see I'm very honest and brutal about it.[33]

With these ungracious farewells, the door was firmly shut in Ka's face. Jacques had been reading *Les Liaisons Dangereuses*, and trying to follow its example of sexual sophistication. But the Neo-pagans were, at heart, nothing like the jaded aristocrats of Laclos. Although Gwen had started with a weak hand, she had known what she wanted and managed to get it. The marriage was set for early June, followed by a month-long painting honeymoon at – Churchfield House, Lulworth! For the rest of the summer they would go to France. Their 'Moment of Transfiguration' – as Rupert sardonically called it, borrowing Jane Harrison's phrase – would now be a strictly private affair, with Ka written out of the script.

Faschingsbraut

To study in Germany was a natural move, in 1911, for any aspiring academic; but to go to Munich showed the particular Germany that attracted Rupert. The academic centre of the country was Heidelberg and the political one Berlin. Munich promised a warmer and softer life than either: as D. H. Lawrence put it, on his first visit a year and a half later, 'a lovely town, all artists, pictures galore'.[34] The artists lived, if they could, in Schwabing, the headquarters of German bohemianism. By going to Munich, Rupert was looking for sensual adventure rather than mere academic improvement (in fact, he did no serious studying while he was there). Adventure he found; but he recoiled from the experience and left Munich without having accepted the spirit of the city. The full-blooded pagan revival that was going on there made Rupert hesitant and uneasy, and his return a year later was largely an attempt to redeem the disappointment of his first visit.

In 1908 the Kaiser had dismissed Hugo von Tschudi, director of the National Gallery in Berlin, for being too sympathetic to modern art. Tschudi left for the friendlier climate of Bavaria, where in 1909 he became general director of the state museums. He stood as friend and patron to the avant-garde artists of Munich, who organised themselves first as the *Neue Künstlervereinigung München*, later as the *Blaue Reiter* group. Their leading spirit was the Russian émigré Wassily Kandinsky, allied with Franz Marc, Hans Arp, Paul Klee and the musician Arnold Schönberg. Somewhere on the fringes of bohemia, at once sympathetic and ironic, was Thomas Mann. At the time of Rupert's stay he was writing his own meditation on paganism, beauty and transience, *Death in Venice*. In September 1910, just before the London Post-Impressionist show, Kandinsky's group put on a show with works by Braque, Picasso, Rouault, Derain, Vlaminck and Van Dongen. As in London, these paintings set off a furore. 'Either the majority of the members and guests of the Association are incurably insane,' said one newspaper, 'or they are shameless bluffers who are not unfamiliar with the age's demand for sensation, and who are capitalizing on it.'[35]

Into this crucible of modernism drifted Rupert – armed with a few scraps of German and a passion for the drawings of Augustus John:

> I move among the München P[ost] I[mpressionist]s. They got up an exhibition of their French masters here last year; and go pilgrimages to all the places where Van Gogh went dotty or cut his ears off or did any of the other climactic actions of his life. They are young and beetle browed and serious. Every now and then they paint something – often a house, a simple square bordered by four very thick black lines. The square is then coloured blue or green. That is all. Then they go on talking. . . . It is all very queer and important.[36]

This report was for Jacques, so that he could compare the artist's life in Munich with the Slade. The aim of Rupert's account, it seems fair to say, was to render the 'queer and important' familiar and *un*important: Cambridge looking down its nose at the Continental avant-garde. After Munich, Rupert would be equally unimpressed by Vienna. In time, his most famous poem would take insularity to its logical extreme by vowing to turn a foreign field into British soil.

Insularity was reinforced, in Rupert's case, by the fear and self-doubt that threatened him whenever he was left to his own devices. When asked what experiences he was having, he said he had come to Munich '*exactly* to escape "experiences". I'd been having too damned many! . . . "Experiences" – one stays in England for *that*.'[37] Was he just going through the motions of foreign travel from a sense of duty, like the revellers who filled the streets for Fasching, the carnival of Lent? Rupert was left with his eternal fear of losing himself in spontaneous action. The worm of self-consciousness had turned his affair with Denham Russell-Smith from an experience into an experiment; now, when opportunity with a woman came his way, he would find himself in a similar plight.

On the 'Bacchus-fest' night of Fasching everyone roamed around dressed, as scantily as possible, like ancient Greeks. Each man was looking for his *Faschingsbraut* – his carnival bride for a day, or a week. 'I found', Rupert told Jacques, 'a round damp young sculptress, a little like Lord Rosebery to look on. We curled passionate limbs round each other in a perfunctory manner and lay in a corner, sipping each other and beer in polite alternation.' The evening progressed well along ancient Greek lines, but when it came to the crunch both Rupert and the sculptress found that they were 'conscious, sensible intellectuals' rather than devotees of Bacchus.[38] The girl went home with her mother and Rupert slunk back to his lodgings at dawn, naked, cold and ridiculous.

Elisabeth van Rysselberghe was a more serious proposition. Rupert met her briefly around the beginning of February, prob- ably through the painter Frau van Ewald, who had taken him under her wing. Unlike most of the other young ladies that he met in Munich, Elisabeth spoke fluent English. Three years younger than Rupert, she was the daughter of the Belgian neo- Impressionist painter Theo van Rysselberghe. The Flemish poet Emile Verhaeren was her godfather. She was visiting Munich with her mother Maria, a writer who travelled widely and was an intimate of André Gide's literary circle. At the beginning of March Elisabeth came back to Munich by herself, giving Rupert a chance to 'snatch the opportunity' of an affair, as he had told Bryn he was now determined to do. Elisabeth was an ardent and impulsive soul who had fallen head over heels in love with Rupert. She was dark-skinned, with large sad eyes and aquiline features – a bit like Noel in appearance, though Elisabeth's looks were more strong than pretty. She was attracted to men who were weaker than herself, with a feminine side to their nature. One sees a lot in common between her and Ka Cox, qualities of devotion and integrity that would reassure Rupert – but also, unfortunately, make him skittish. Here was a free-spirited young woman, alone with him in a foreign city, making it plain that she was in love with him. All he had to do, it seemed, was plunge into the waves of passion.

In his sonnet 'Lust' Rupert tells how he 'starved' for Elisabeth, how 'the enormous wheels of will / Drove [him] cold-eyed' in her pursuit.[39] But when she actually responds to his desire, he pulls up short of his goal:

Love wakens love! I felt your hot wrist shiver,
    And suddenly the mad victory I planned
        Flashed real, in your burning bending head. . . .
My conqueror's blood was cool as a deep river
    In shadow; and my heart beneath your hand
        Quieter than a dead man on a bed.

One suspects that it was not the heart, but another organ that failed him. Soon Rupert was complaining to Ka that he was 'in a state of collapse – from disease and Elizabeth. She is a Rat.'[40]

When it came to sex Rupert could always 'talk a good game', as the saying goes. Recoiling from his difficulties with Elisabeth, he went off to Vienna to stay with E. P. Goldschmidt, a Cambridge friend. When he got there, Elisabeth wrote agreeing to spend a couple of days with him at Venice, later in April. Would he desire her, there, she asked wistfully? Of course he would, Rupert vowed, in the middle of a roundabout disquisition on the dangers of pregnancy. He had written to James Strachey, asking about contraception. James regaled him with a scabrous description of French letters, pessaries and syringes. The syringe was best, he said, with a mixture of quinine and *cold* water; but it was a filthy business at best, and Rupert would be better off coming back to take up James on his standing offer. There was also, he added, Henry Lamb's method – to withdraw in the nick of time – but that was risky, and called for iron nerves.[41]

Unfortunately for Rupert, Elisabeth promptly wrote back to tell him that she was not prepared to 'give herself' to him in Venice. He told her that she should expect to take 'Life', and the sooner the better – Life meaning a brief affair, with a clear understanding that there would be no strings afterwards. Rupert was bitter at the lesson he had just learned, that honesty about one's intentions was not the best policy when dealing with romantic young ladies. 'I can't help believing (am I right?)', he told her, 'that if we'd met in Venice, that *there*, touching your

hands, looking into your eyes, I could have made you understand, and agree. But I preferred to be honest. And so perhaps
one of the best things in my life, or yours, is lost – for a time –
through a desire for honesty!'[42]

Rupert now had to go to the aid of his old classics master, Bob
Whitelaw, who had been taken ill in Florence. Before going, he
returned to Munich for a melodramatic settling of accounts with
Elisabeth. After having fled from the emotional complications of
England, Rupert found himself fleeing the worse complications
he had stirred up in Germany:

> The parting with Elizabeth was most painful. I felt an awful
> snake. Especially when she said she would kill herself, and I
> felt frightened of the police. She's quite come round, and
> apologised for her telegram; and, it appears, we're to have a
> week at Marseilles in August. I am very bitter with myself,
> and frightened of England. . . . the maid-servant suddenly
> brought two students to see the room, and found her with
> her hair down weeping, at full length, on that *plateau* of a
> sofa, and me in great pain on one leg in the middle of the
> room, saying 'Yes . . . yes . . . yes . . .' But, anyhow, do assure
> me that one *ought* to tell the truth: and that it's not honest to
> want to be raped.[43]

Elisabeth, Rupert felt, wanted to be promised eternal love and
then swept off her feet; whereas he wanted her to copulate with
him on fixed terms, having first carefully read the directions that
came with the syringe. Both of them were by now thoroughly
confused, guilty and unsatisfied. But Elisabeth would soon rally
and make another attempt to win his love.

Rupert went to a string of Ibsen plays in Munich, of which
John Gabriel Borkman made by far the strongest impression on
him. Mrs Borkman is an ice queen who wants to make her son,
Erhardt, as deathly as she is. Erhardt mopes around the house
complaining 'Ich muss leben, Mutter! Ich muss leben!' Finally he
escapes to the south with Mrs Wilton, a divorced woman seven
years older than himself. Rupert identified with Erhardt, though
he could not order his own affairs so decisively. He had not
encountered the vanguard of Schwabing, figures like Ludwig
Klages, Fanny zu Reventlow and Otto Gross who had declared
war on bourgeois convention.[44] But when he heard from Gwen

Darwin about her tangled relations with Jacques and Ka he affected the Ibsenite stance that we can always seize our Fate by the neck:

> You said you'd all three felt, that week, as if you were in the hands of some external power, rushing you on. External Power? What? God? The Life-Force? Oh, my Gwen, be clean, be clean! It is a monstrosity. There is no power. Things happen: and we pick our way among them. That is all. If only you'd been at Camp last year, you'd have learnt that one can sail eight points *into* the wind. To be certain of it is the beginning and end of good behaviour.[45]

What did Rupert's nautical metaphor mean? Apparently that the Neo-pagans were free to ignore convention, and that telling the truth about one's emotions was guaranteed to keep any love affair on a steady course. But since that camp Rupert had done more drifting than sailing, whatever he claimed to Gwen.

Clearly, however, that drift was carrying him away from Noel and towards Ka. Rupert told her to make a clean break with both Jacques and Gwen – good advice, perhaps, but not quite disinterested:

> Why are you sad? . . . Lust. But that's absurd. You'd never have gratified that anyway. . . . even if, as I'll grant, a sort of lust–jealousy may plague you (an infinitely pale reflection of part of that plagues me every time I hear of anyone getting married!), that doesn't come to much. Tragedy – much pain – doesn't come from that, for any creature.

The heaviest blows to Ka were her wounded vanity, and the fear of losing both Jacques and Gwen as friends. Rupert, however, told her to cheer the engaged couple on:

> Jacques and Gwen are in love and are going to marry. That is very fine. . . . It is a risky business, as they're both so dotty. I hope Gwen won't hurt her wood-cuts with babies, or Jacques get domesticated. It's very splendid. They'll be in love for a couple of years. I hope they'll do it more gracefully than most.[46]

His agenda, as soon as he got back to England, was clear: to catch

Ka on the rebound, and succeed with her where he had failed with Elisabeth.

One definite result of going to Germany was to harden Rupert's politics. The Jewish milieu of Vienna in which Goldschmidt lived provoked some nasty racial sneers in Rupert's letters, but he found the Aryans even more repellent:

> I have sampled and sought out German culture. It has changed all my political views. I am wildly in favour of nineteen new Dreadnoughts. German culture must never, never, prevail. The Germans are nice, and well-meaning, and they try; but they are SOFT. Oh! They ARE soft. The only good things (outside music perhaps) are the writings of Jews who live in Vienna.[47]

This bulletin went to Eddie Marsh, now Private Secretary to Winston Churchill at the Admiralty. Rupert was not just unveiling a visceral chauvinism, he was trying to get it high on his country's agenda. The naval rivalry between Britain and Germany had been getting more intense for some years, coinciding with a rash of small colonial wars and crises on the periphery of Europe. Rupert came back from Munich convinced that Britain should keep Germany in check, and fight her if necessary. Along with his anti-semitism, this nascent imperialism exposed the shallow roots of his professed Fabian beliefs. He, and all Europe with him, was now only a short step away from the catastrophes of 1914; a step that was fatally easy to take when no one realised what 1914 would come to stand for.

VII

Combined Operations

Virginia Takes an Interest

What might be called a collective 'affair' between Bloomsbury and the Neo-pagans began near the end of January 1911, when Virginia Stephen met Ka Cox at Bertrand Russell's house near Oxford. Like individual affairs, this one moved quickly into excitement and mutual admiration; began to be plagued by rival commitments after a few months; and ended a year or so later in crisis and a good measure of rudeness and dislike. Later some friendship survived, and after both sides had suffered their share of death and disaster the affair reached its final stage: nostalgia. But why should relations between these two groups follow such an erratic course? Superficially alike, Bloomsbury and the Neo-pagans had crucial differences of style, beliefs and morals. They might still have made peace with each other, but Rupert's vagaries in 1911, and his truculent philistinism in 1912, opened a breach that had become an abyss by the time of his death three years later.

In March 1910 Rupert was sorting through drawers at School Field, getting ready to move out after his father's death. He came across 'two old photographs, 1893 perhaps, of me, Dick, Adrian Virginia Vanessa Toby Leslie – – – all very sporting and odd. Virginia and Vanessa are incredibly old in it: a little gawky: Virginia very fat faced.'[1] This would be the Brookes and Stephens playing cricket on the sands at St Ives, when Rupert was six and Virginia eleven. When he was ten, Rupert met Duncan Grant and James Strachey at Hillbrow School; at fourteen, Geoffrey Keynes

joined him at School Field. After James fell in love with him and
got him into the Society, Rupert knew all that went on in
Bloomsbury. But Bloomsbury, he took care, knew much less of
what went on with him. 'He lived a kind of double life,' Jacques
recalled,

> he had two sets of friends that he was not interested in
> bringing together; for a long time, he even tried to keep them
> apart. Was this because of his natural love of mystery, from
> fear of too great an incompatibility and mutual disdain, or
> did he fear a rapprochement at his own expense – that both
> sides might be exposed to a dangerous influence?[2]

Why did the wall between the two groups break down in
1911? In the first instance, because Virginia took a fancy to Ka,
just after Rupert had gone off to Germany for four months. They
met through a mutual friend, Ray Costelloe, a Newnham student
and niece of Bertrand Russell's wife Alys.[3] Having missed going
to Cambridge herself, Virginia was intrigued by the new generation of women students. She found Ka, who was five years her
junior, 'a bright, intelligent, nice creature; who has, she says, very
few emotions, but thinks so highly of Gwen that she even copies
her way of speech'.[4] Soon they were firm friends. Virginia was in
a phase of feeling inadequate: 'To be 29 and unmarried – to be a
failure – childless – insane too, no writer.'[5] She compared her
gloomy isolation with Ka's Cambridge career, her vigorous
hikes, her political work with the Fabians. These young people
had a style of their own, Virginia decided, and deserved a
nickname: the 'Neo-pagans'.

'Neo-paganism' had been current since the 1880s, as a label
pinned on the Pre-Raphaelites.[6] A few years before Virginia
picked up the idea, Edward Carpenter had been lecturing on
'Neo-paganism' as a modern ideal. In April 1911 Rupert heard
from James Strachey that 'Virginia had become a . . . what is it?
"Neo-Pagan"? . . . Lord! Lord!'[7] James had stayed with Virginia
in the middle of March, so we can assume that she began using
the term around then – and that Rupert greeted it with surprise
and derision. Nevertheless, it stuck, though without spreading
beyond Bloomsbury and environs. It was a private joke; but also
something more, especially for Virginia.

When she first imagined Ka, Rupert and their friends as Neo-pagans, Virginia did so almost wistfully. They were only a few years younger than her own generation, but they seemed to have a much firmer hold on the strings of life. The Bloomsbury style of exclusive other-worldliness could easily be seen as a form of invalidism: physical with Lytton and James Strachey, social with E. M. Forster and Saxon Sydney-Turner, psychological with Virginia. Except for the Bells and the McCarthys, Bloomsbury seemed unable even to have children. Virginia and Lytton were brilliant in conversation, but slow and uncertain writers; around 1911 they often wondered if they could ever bring a substantial work to completion.

Virginia saw the Neo-pagans as capable of a clean start, free from the Victorian gloom and debility that had shadowed the youth of herself and her friends. They also stood for a move from town to country. Nineteen-ten had been for Virginia a year of nervous breakdowns and long rest-cures away from London. She found these retreats so agreeable that she decided, at the end of the year, to rent a modest house at Firle, Sussex. 'Another side of life reveals itself in the country,' she explained to Clive Bell, 'which I can't help thinking of amazing interest. It is precisely as though one clapped on a solid half-globe to one's London life, and had hitherto always walked on a strip of pavement.'[8] Perhaps she could recapture some of the glory of her childhood summers in Cornwall, rudely interrupted when her mother died in 1895.

Such were the overtones of her plan to go on holiday to France with Ka, in April: 'I mean to throw myself into youth, sunshine, nature, primitive art. Cakes with sugar on the top, love, lust, paganism, general bawdiness, for a fortnight at least; and not write a line.'[9] Behind the high spirits, we sense that Virginia found Ka very appealing physically. This is not to say that 'general bawdiness' would mean a real affair with her. Virginia's passions – for Madge Vaughan and Violet Dickinson – had been unconsummated, girlish crushes. But she gave Ka a pet name, 'Bruin', that suggested the mixture of affection and sexual interest she felt for her.

The trip to France fell through when Virginia had to rush to Turkey to help her sister, victim of a miscarriage in a remote village. But Virginia's plan was clearly to take up the Neo-pagans, and to sound them out. She expected to renew her acquaintance with Rupert when he returned from Munich. Meanwhile she invited Jacques in March to stay at Firle for a weekend. They too became friends – though each found the other somewhat intimidating – and Jacques urged her to make the step from country house to living in a tent, at the Neo-pagan camp in August.

Looking back at this time, Virginia spoke of Jacques as an 'adorable' young man. Bertrand Russell was less impressed:

> I went to Grantchester . . . to tea with Jacques Raverat who is to marry Gwen Darwin. He has immense charm, but like all people who have superficial and obvious charm, I think he is weak and has no firm purpose. He is staying with Rupert Brooke whom I dislike. I find there Keynes and Miss Olivier (daughter of Jamaica Olivier) and Olwyn Ward, daughter of Prof. James Ward. Young people now-a-days are odd – Xtian names and great familiarity, rendered easy by a complete freedom from passion on the side of the men.[10]

Russell was in the throes of separating from his wife Alys in order to pursue his affair with Ottoline Morrell. Perhaps he was annoyed by the offhand way the male and female Neo-pagans treated each other, and he certainly loathed Rupert's breezy, schoolboy-hero manner. But Jacques' engagement had scarcely been settled so casually as Russell imagined. After staying with Virginia at Firle Jacques had gone off for a walking tour in Cornwall with Dudley Ward, to make up his mind about his love triangle with Ka and Gwen. Virginia at this point knew only about his engagement to Gwen, which struck her as too self-consciously lusty. Jacques 'is quite red, quite unshaven, hatless', she told Clive, 'with only one book – Rabelais; in two months, he says, . . . That I take to mean, bed with Gwen. It is portentous; I think the dots give the feeling rather well. How malicious we are about them! But I suppose they have their own brand of malice.'[11]

Soon afterwards, Ka took her out on the downs and confided the whole story. No doubt Virginia showed concern and sympathy, though to her sister she gave an acid survey of the future of Neo-paganism:

cynically considering the infantine natures of all concerned, I predict nothing serious. Ka will marry a Brooke next year, I expect. J. will always be a Volatile Frog. Gwen will bear children, and paint pictures; clearly though, J. and K. would be the proper match. . . . I'm sure J. will always be susceptible; and as Gwen will grow stout, he will roam widely.[12]

By involving herself with the loves of Ka, Jacques and Gwen, Virginia was serving two of her own interests. First, she loved intrigue for its own sake; then, she was trying out at second hand the possibilities of heterosexual love for herself. Until now, she had been interested mainly in her own sex, and her male friends had been largely homosexual. But she was nearly thirty, and becoming reconciled to the idea that the sensible thing for her to do was to marry. The Neo-pagans were to her an intriguing new society, in which young men and women mingled freely and tried out a series of sentimental attachments before settling down. She hoped to be both entertained and guided by observing them.

Merger Talks

Rupert arrived back from Florence early in May. The immediate task he faced was to write his fellowship dissertation, on John Webster and the Elizabethan drama. He had less than eight months to do it, and this time he could not hope to get through by skimping and bluffing – as he had done too often before in his academic career. For the balance of the year, he had to stay in England and try to put work before pleasure.

At Grantchester, he began by moving house. The Stevensons, his landlords at the Orchard, had had enough of the free and easy ways of Rupert and his friends. Bare feet were apparently the last straw, and when Dudley Ward came to stay at the Orchard with two German girls Rupert warned him that they would have to keep their boots on at all times.[13] Fortunately Mrs Neeve at the Old Vicarage next door was willing to give Rupert room and board, including the famous honey from her husband's bees. The house was a bit decrepit but had a pleasant garden, and was so close to the river that its sounds and smells filled the three rooms where Rupert lived. He described it to Elisabeth van Rysselberghe as one of the loveliest but also one of the unhealthiest houses one could imagine. It was infested with fleas and woodlice, against which Mrs Neeve waged ineffectual war with a yellow powder. Not surprisingly, Rupert took to sleeping out on the lawn. The birds woke him up at 2.30 a.m.; he would curse them, and finally get back to sleep, and wake with his hair wet with dew.[14]

A month after his return Jacques and Gwen got married in Cambridge.[15] There was a dinner a week before at Gwen's house, where Rupert met Monsieur Raverat and renewed his acquaintance with Virginia. 'I'd a bad touch', he reported to Ka, 'of that disease you too'll have known. The ignoblest jealousy mixed with loneliness to make me flog my pillow with an umbrella till I was exhausted, when I was shut into my lonely room to read myself to sleep, and they went roaming off to tell each other truths. ... But we might convalesce together.'[16] He was not jealous of Jacques' possession of Gwen, since on the sexual plane she was never anything more to Rupert than 'a square-headed woman who cuts wood'.[17] His jealousy was of the married state itself, mixed with fear of losing his closest male friend, and the first one to marry.

This fear turned out to be largely justified. Gwen and Jacques were married equally to each other and to art; from now on, friends would play a lesser role in their lives. Rupert, full of romantic idealism, did not think of marriage as a partnership based on a common interest. But Gwen had taken warning from the way her cousin Eily's artistic ambitions had been swallowed up by marriage: 'You know all the artists in the world feel like that when they're married – except for J. and me. Particularly the women. For they are quite clean cut in 1/2. There never was anything in the world like us before – except Mr and Mrs Browning only for some reason my fiance does not like me to say this.'[18] Before her engagement Gwen believed that she valued her work more than people, but with Jacques she discovered the power of her 'dreadful feminine craving for someone to love and pity'.[19] The solution, once she was married to him, was for both of them to submerge themselves in work and cut themselves off from the overcharged emotional atmosphere that Ka had created. It may seem unkind to note that Gwen suffered as the 'Plain Jane' of the group and that she may have had a residue of hurt feelings over this status. Certainly she was frank enough about the jealousy and exclusiveness she felt towards Jacques, once she had won him.

Ka thus had no rival claims when Rupert, once installed at Grantchester, began sending her plaintive letters asking her to visit and hinting that he was falling in love with her. But she must have been uneasily aware that when he got back from Munich he was somehow too busy to join her in Yorkshire for a walking tour. Instead, he made the rounds of his friends and went down to Limpsfield when Bryn returned from Jamaica, with Sir Sydney, on 14 May. She had written to Rupert affectionately from the boat and mentioned that it was time she got married – a hint that deserved investigation, presumably.

Having been shut out by Jacques and Gwen, Ka needed sympathy and trustworthiness from Rupert. What she got instead was an all-too-Apostolic frankness about his confused emotions. When Geoffrey Keynes asked for a portrait Duncan Grant had painted of her, Rupert lectured her on the Neo-pagan code:

> Oh, come. The group of people we're part of may be awfully honest and genteel and chaste and self-controlled and nice – but at least we're far enough ahead for that. We don't copulate without marriage, but we *do* meet in cafes, talk on buses, go unchaperoned walks, stay with each other, give each other books, without marriage. Can't we even have each other's pictures?[20]

That seemed to draw the lines clearly enough; as did Rupert's vow that he wanted to be *damned* intimate with Ka. But she would have done well to heed the warning that went with it: 'I'll try to cut off all the outside, and tell you truths. Have I ever seemed to you honest? That was when I got one layer away. There are nineteen to come – and when they're off what?'[21]

Rupert was indeed jealous of other people's marriages, but he was also extremely wary about the prospect of his own. When Dudley got engaged that autumn, Rupert told him he hoped he would 'cohabit in spells first'.[22] In the middle of July Elisabeth van Rysselberghe suddenly turned up in England. Rupert arranged to meet her in the Italian Room at the National Gallery, and said he was glad to see her, but in fact he would be glad only if a spell of cohabitation could be arranged. He told Ka later that he felt a 'horrible mixture of lust and dislike' for Elisabeth at this time.[23] She was staying, unhappily, with the family of a clergyman at Teddington. Rupert told her to go and engage rooms at a nearby town, after which he would join her; then he said he was tired and confused and didn't really know what he wanted. It was simple enough, really: he wanted to hide her from his other friends, to go away with her for a week of passion when he could find the time, and then be free to move on.[24] Elisabeth loved him, but would not have him on those terms. They met occasionally and secretly until the autumn, when Elisabeth went back to Paris.

Rupert was working his way around to getting Ka on the same basis, if he could. The idealistic side of his nature remained faithful to Noel, however awkward it might be actually to carry on any connection with her. From Ka he wanted sensuality, when he was feeling lustful, or somewhere to lay his head, when his strenuous and complex activities brought him to the point of nervous collapse. Since Ka was above all someone who needed to be needed, they were in a way well matched. But neither their friends, nor society at large, nor their own consciences, would allow them to be peaceably together on any such terms.

Virginia's interest in the Neo-pagans revealed her desire to move from loving her own sex towards the heterosexual mainstream. Similar impulses were at work among some of the Bloomsbury men. The Society was at a low ebb in 1911, and its members inclined to seek new horizons. After James Strachey moved to London to work on the *Spectator* in 1909, only three of the younger Apostles were left at Cambridge: Rupert, H. T. J. Norton and Gerald Shove. From Shove's election in January 1909 nearly two years passed without the election of a new member. There was an uneasy balance between Fabians and Liberals, and between those who were homosexual and those who were not. Bill Hubback, Frankie Birrell and others were looked over, but none aroused general enthusiasm. In November 1910 J. T. Sheppard, Rupert's former tutor at King's, pushed through the election of his 'special friend' Cecil Taylor. It was a blatant case of sexual favouritism, like the election of Hobhouse five years before, and had no better result. Taylor's main claim to fame was the unfortunate one of having three balls. There was a tendency in the Society to jeer at him behind his back; he was nicknamed 'the squitter-squatter', and Rupert never took him seriously.[25] It would be fifteen months before the next election. Though Rupert still attended on Saturday nights and read several papers, the Society at this period claimed only a modest share of his interest and energy.

For two years after he joined the Society, Rupert deliberately kept Apostles and Neo-pagans apart. The Neo-pagans knew little or nothing about the Apostles. They could see why James constantly hung around Rupert, but why did Rupert tolerate him? James had a nervous dislike of women; he was sensitive about his ailments and his physical awkwardness, but could be cuttingly sarcastic to people who threatened him. 'He felt for our group, and perhaps especially for Ka, a kind of jealousy,' wrote Jacques. 'He had the face of a baby and the expression of an old man; he seemed to take no pleasure or interest in material life or the physical world, and to exist only in the realms of pure intellect.'[26] But jealousy is also a bond. Two quite different groups of friends wanted to claim Rupert. In the long run they were bound to find a way to share him – and to discover, in the process, other things they had in common.

To Rupert's divided and compulsively secretive nature, such a merger was deeply threatening. 'He did everything he could to hold off a rapprochement,' recalled Jacques.

> He may have been right, but despite all his efforts he couldn't prevent it. Finally James, whom he could not keep away, made the treaty of union between these two milieux, which had become too curious about each other, but which were deeply incompatible. The results were sometimes comic; but the rapprochement led Rupert into an ordeal that was sufficiently cruel and tragic to justify fully the instinctive fear he had of it.[27]

A good index of relations between the two groups was the connection between James and Noel. James first became interested in her because she was loved by the person he loved. In

Rupert's room there was a picture of Noel; in James's a picture of Rupert. If James could get close to Noel, the triangle would be closed and he would be less of a yearning hanger-on in Rupert's life. After putting him off for two years, Rupert arranged for James to meet Bryn and Noel while they were staying at the Old Vicarage during the production of *Faustus*, in the summer of 1910. But James for some reason failed to keep the appointment. 'Bryn was especially eager,' Rupert told him. 'And I'd very carefully brought Noel up to the point at which she could and must meet an Apostle. So there's a year or so lost for *her* education. And even you might have Widened a little.'[28] If he did not actually meet them, James had discovered by going to the play how attractive the Neo-pagan ladies could be:

> The beauty of the evening was of course Bryn as Helen of Troy – though chorus [Rupert] was also admired in some quarters. . . . I had the pleasure of seeing Noel Olivier in the audience. She certainly looks intelligent as well as beautiful. I expect you'll hear more of her before you die.[29]

Lytton did not get to know Noel and Bryn until three years later, when he shared a holiday cottage with them in Scotland. 'Noel is of course more interesting,' he then observed, 'but difficult to make out: very youthful, incredibly firm of flesh, agreeably bouncing and cheerful – and with some sort of prestige.'[30] Firmness of flesh seems to have been James's fancy, for two weeks after seeing Noel he was struck at the Fabian Summer School by another 'delightful Bedalian . . . an absolute boy'.[31] This was Alix Sargant-Florence, the only girl to play cricket for the boys' First XI. 'Very handsome, built like one of the Medici tombs,' was Mary Newbery's memory of her. Ten years later she would become James's wife.

It took until the summer of 1911 for the fences between the Neo-pagans and Bloomsbury to come down altogether. Rupert kept shuttling between London, Grantchester, Rugby and Limpsfield, often with two or more Oliviers in tow. Diaghilev's Russian Ballet, in its first astounding London season, was a magnet for him and for them all. After one performance, Lytton claimed that 'the audience for it contained everyone I knew in Europe'.[32] At the end of July, Rupert was going to *Schéhérazade* for the third time. James had sent him a note asking if he could meet Noel there, to see if she was as amazing as he imagined.[33] Rupert did better: he invited James to dine with Margery and Noel before the performance at one of his favourite haunts, Eustace Miles's vegetarian restaurant. James was as far removed from the Bedales type as one can imagine, and Noel gave short shrift to his finicky intellectualism. Nonetheless, a friendship was launched which would have great consequences for all three of them.

Having given the Neo-pagans a name, Bloomsbury now drew them into its androgynous embrace. Duncan Grant came to Grantchester to paint; Lytton took lodgings in Cambridge for June; and a troop of friends came up for the end-of-term festivities. James Strachey reported to Rupert that Maynard Keynes had buggered Justin in the middle of one garden party, to the embarrassment of the Neo-pagan onlookers. Translated from Apostolic hyperbole, this meant that Keynes had tried to fondle Justin — whom he fancied as a 'faun or creature of the wood' — and was sent off empty-handed.[34] In fact, the sexual currents were flowing in the opposite direction. Their revels with the Neo-pagans showed how the 'Bloomsbuggers', as Virginia called them, were being converted to the pleasures of mixed company. Many of them would marry, in due course — or at least, like Duncan Grant and Lytton Strachey, set up house with a woman. And Virginia, who up to now had felt little sexual interest in men, decided that it would be an interesting experiment to stay with Rupert for five days at the Old Vicarage.

Virginia had kept an eye on Rupert's career through her friends in the Apostles and in spring 1909 they had become casual friends, going to Ottoline Morrell's for tea and meeting at James Strachey's rooms in Cambridge. On the latter occasion, however, Virginia decided that Rupert's silence meant disapproval of her presence, and the friendship languished until her interest in Ka revived it.[35] She went to the Old Vicarage in part to see how Rupert's version of 'Life in the Country' compared with her own, in part to see how much of his charm might rub off on her at close quarters. Not too close, we may be sure — they slept on opposite sides of the house — though both might relish spreading some whiffs of scandal among the curious onlookers.

Mostly they ran a joint literary workshop: Rupert with his thesis and forthcoming collection of poems, Virginia at her endless revisions of her first novel.[36] The climax of the visit, if legend be true, came when he got her to bathe naked at Byron's Pool and showed off his party trick – jumping in and emerging with an instant erection.[37] Virginia, who prided herself on knowledge of earth closets and 'the female inside', presumably took it in her stride. More nymph than maenad, she was not to be bowled over by Brooke's caperings.[38] Perhaps, like many beauties, they were also relatively immune to each other.

When Virginia left, Rupert came with her for a short visit to Firle. They made their way through London despite a railway strike at Victoria – where Rupert, Virginia reported, 'tried to work up some Socialist enthusiasm'. Whether it was in Virginia, the passengers, the workers or Rupert himself is left unclear. Some scepticism about Neo-pagan politics is surely apparent, and also in Virginia's further comment that 'He does not eat meat, except when he stays here, and lives very cheaply.'[39] Rupert did boast at this time that he dressed himself on three pounds a year; this may not have been too far off the mark, since when not naked he was at least barefoot, and most of his eye-catching open-necked shirts were made by Ka. His role as the Noble Savage of the Cam was relished as much by Virginia as it was by him – so long as the good humour of it lasted.

Clifford Bridge

During Virginia's visit Rupert was already planning a more ambitious venture. This was to be 'Bloomsbury under Canvas', a joint camp with the Neo-pagans. Jacques had first proposed this to Virginia in April; since then Maynard Keynes had met the Oliviers (through Mary Berenson) and other new links had been made. 'The company going to Camp', Rupert told Maynard, 'is quite select and possible company for such delicate blooms as Virginia and Duncan; and Bryn is white with desire that they should come.'[40] The chosen spot was Clifford Bridge at the edge of Dartmoor, where a long meadow bordered the River Teign as it ran through wooded hills. Earlier in August the Old Bedalian camp had been set up there; Justin Brooke arranged for the Neo-pagans to take over their gear on 24 August. Lytton was installed beforehand at nearby Manaton, where Rupert had discovered an attractive guesthouse in a rocky valley. At Becky House Lytton could work on his first book – *Landmarks in French Literature* – and walk on the moors with a series of Apostolic visitors: G. E. Moore, Gerald Shove and Leonard Woolf (who had just returned from five years in Ceylon).

The 'select and possible company' for Bloomsbury included the Olivier sisters (except Margery), Justin, Geoffrey Keynes and an old Bedalian named Paulie Montague. Paulie was a devotee of Elizabethan music who made his own instruments – both very Bedalian hobbies. He was killed in the war. Maitland Radford also turned up, and made Bryn nervous by falling in love with her. The surviving photographs show the Neo-pagans all dressed for the part, while Gerald Shove lies on the ground in a suit and a trilby hat.[41] He lasted only one night, though this was enough time, according to Ka, for him to fall in love with Bryn too.

Hovering at the fringes were James Strachey and Maynard, both more at home in the drawing room than with a canoe or sleeping-bag. James turned up late and spent a miserable night under a bush, wrapped in a blanket. For a confirmed hypochondriac this was pretty game, but he went back to the comforts of Becky House after being lampooned by Rupert:

In the late evening he was out of place
And utterly irrelevant at dawn.[42]

Lytton wisely stayed away altogether, pointing out to Rupert that the ground was rather an awkward shape for sitting on.

Maynard, however, more than held his own. 'Camp life suits me very well,' he told his father. 'The hard ground, a morning bathe, the absence of flesh food, and no chairs, don't make one nearly so ill as one would suppose.' With his usual competence he passed the threefold ordeal that made one an honorary Neo-pagan: 'sleeping on the ground, waking at dawn, and swimming in a river'.[43] Virginia, too, did nobly. Ka brought her down two days after the camp had begun. On her first evening she walked eight miles from the station with Ka, found no one there on arrival, and ate rotten blackberry pudding by mistake in the dark. A picture shows her sitting on the ground with Rupert, Noel and Maitland Radford in front of a five-barred gate; her hair is tied in the approved Neo-pagan gypsy scarf and her expression is, reasonably enough, quizzical.[44]

She must surely have been amused by the Neo-pagan cult of nudity. Someone at Clifford Bridge tried to immortalise the occasion by taking nude photographs of the campers. Maynard Keynes had taken such pictures of Duncan Grant when they were on holiday in Greece the year before, and he had told Duncan that 'when I'm at Burford everyone who stays with me will be forced to have their photographs taken naked.'[45] Whether Keynes was the one with a camera at Clifford Bridge is not known; two sets at least of the photographs seem to have survived, but they are not now to be found.

The camp lasted for eighteen days, and by the end nerves were strung tight. Bryn, who was in charge of cooking and finances, took a dislike to Justin. 'Poor old Bryn, what are we to do with her?' Rupert asked Ka; but he didn't know what to do with himself either. Finally he lost his temper and went off by himself, and lay out all night, crying, on a hill by Drewsteignton.[46] Ka had left by then, so it must have been Noel who drove him to fury and despair, as she so often did. He went from Clifford Bridge to stay five days with James and Lytton at Becky, to get over it. They roamed the moors laughing and arguing – Lytton, with his knickerbockers and tam-o'-shanter looking like 'a mechanical Scotch Christ on a walking-tour'.[47]

When the camp was just beginning, Rupert was already musing on how to save it from time and oblivion. On the day Virginia and Ka arrived, the others had walked over to Crediton to see Paulie Montague's parents. During the camp Rupert wrote 'Dining-Room Tea' about that visit. The poem is a tribute both to Noel and to the whole group that formed the setting for Rupert's love. One might keep an individual friend for life, but these gatherings of ten or twelve were like a moment in the play of a fountain: a combination of people, place and emotion that was lit up for a moment, then gone forever:

they and we
Flung all the dancing moments by
With jest and glitter. Lip and eye
Flashed on the glory, shone and cried,
Improvident, unmemoried;
And fitfully and like a flame
The light of laughter went and came.
Proud in their careless transience moved
The changing faces that I loved.

Then the poet seizes on a single face in the crowd – surely Noel's
– and the flow is arrested:

Till suddenly, and otherwhence,
I looked upon your innocence.
For lifted clear and still and strange
From the dark woven flow of change
Under a vast and starless sky
I saw the immortal moment lie. . . .
I saw the stillness and the light,
And you, august, immortal, white,
Holy and strange; and every glint
Posture and jest and thought and tint
Freed from the mask of transiency. . . .

The lover, the beloved and Time are the eternal triangle of lyric
poetry. What is special about Rupert's love poems is the lack of
reciprocity between the poet and his beloved. The woman gives
him a glimpse of transfiguration, but never knows what she has
given:

How could I cloud, or how distress,
The heaven of your unconsciousness? . . .
The eternal holiness of you,
The timeless end, you never knew. . . .

While the laughter plays around the table, the poet goes 'a
million miles away' – then comes back to this single summer
evening in Devon.

His beloved's unconsciousness was an old story with Rupert by now, and had become a self-serving myth that did little justice to Noel's sense of her own personality and interests. What saves 'Dining-Room Tea' is how the poet makes the beloved's unconsciousness stand for that of the whole group. In their spontaneous joy, they are unaware of the party's aesthetic value. Only the poet, from his position of detachment, can see it and capture it. Virginia Woolf would make a similar event, Mrs Ramsay's dinner party, the centrepiece of *To the Lighthouse*. But there the radiant moment is kindled by Mrs Ramsay's labours as hostess and mother. The success of that party comes from her nurturing; Rupert, in his, is either carried along with the others' joy or stands above it with a superior vision.

To the Lighthouse epitomised Bloomsbury's struggle against transience and loss. They remained a group for so long because they had such solid foundations of tolerance and mutual affection. The Neo-pagans, on the other hand, were facing disintegration after only a few years together. Part of their fragility as a group derived from a simple inferiority of character and talent, compared with Bloomsbury; in the long run, they had less to build on. But sexual dynamics had a part in it too. Most members of Bloomsbury were either homosexual or married late. In their twenties they were relatively promiscuous. These love affairs caused turmoil and jealousy but when they burned out friendship reasserted itself, and was often strengthened by the ordeal. The Neo-pagans, despite being younger, suffered more from the legacy of Victorianism. So long as their young ladies, at least, did not 'copulate before marriage', they were all caught between the millstones of chastity before marriage, monogamous domesticity after it. Their sexual choices weighed more heavily, because they were thought to be 'once and for all'; and, under the pressure of those choices, the vision of unity in 'Dining-Room Tea' would quickly fade.

Autumn in Fitzrovia

Returning to London from Dartmoor, Rupert learned that Dudley Ward was engaged to Annemarie von der Planitz.[48] Their engagement, coming three months after Jacques' marriage, seemed to Rupert another nail in the coffin of his youth. 'Luckily it's not very definite,' he told Ka. 'Dudley won't give up his freedom for some years yet. But I'd so idolized him. . . . I felt so awfully lonely.'[49] Dudley was too stiff and sober and reticent to count as a true Neo-pagan, but Rupert found his conventionality reassuring. Once married, which he was within months rather than years, Dudley became for Rupert the male counterpart of Frances Cornford: a refuge in times of trouble.

Having met the engaged couple, Rupert congratulated them on not appearing *too* engaged: 'You live in the present; like me (an Infantile Paralytic) and Mr George Meredith (now, alas! dead).'[50] But calling himself an Infantile Paralytic was rather too good a joke at his own expense. Was he really, like Peter Pan, a 'boy who would not grow up'? And was he using Noel's unattainability as an excuse to avoid following his friends into marriage and maturity? If so, an obvious cure was at hand. For three years he had kept up both his soulful love of Noel and his twilight affairs with Denham, Elisabeth or Ka. Why not combine soul and sense at last, by turning wholeheartedly to Ka? After his nervous breakdown he blamed himself to Ka for failing to make that, or any other choice, during 1911:

> For a year you loved me, and I loved Noel and you – Oh I was a youthful fool, and I wronged you, I see, both of you, a great deal. I plead innocence and youth. But I *did* love, both of you, – with a growing uneasiness that if I gave either all I could give I'd scarcely be worthy, but that as it *was* – I was a beast to both. I loved you a great deal; more as the year went on, I think – Once or twice I felt your kindness and loveliness creeping over me, and loyalty to Noel made me kick. And in the autumn occasionally I was tired and cross and worried about Noel, and a little dead to you.[51]

Through the summer and autumn of 1911 the word 'tired' becomes more and more frequent in Rupert's letters. Certainly he was trying to cram a great deal of research and writing into six months. But the underlying cause of his fatigue, and eventually of his collapse, was his inability to choose between Noel and Ka. Instead of resolving the dilemma he tried to ignore its pressure. 'I'm determined to live like a motor-car,' he told Ka, 'or a needle, or Mr Bennett, or a planetary system, or whatever else is always at the keenest and wildest pitch of activity. . . . I am not tired! I am as lively as God, and working like an engine.'[52] His manic side drove him to pack each day with activity, but he was living beyond his emotional means, and the bill would soon fall due.

Early in October Rupert decided that he would start spending weekdays in London and returning to Grantchester at weekends. The ostensible reason was that he needed to use the British Museum Library for his thesis, but he was probably finding the Old Vicarage lonely now that the fine weather was past, and he wanted to be closer to Ka. At Grantchester he was too well known to have any regular intimacy with an unmarried young lady, whereas in London the main hazard would be running the gauntlet of Bloomsbury gossip:

> If you only knew what James said Virginia said So and So said. . . . But your repper, my dear, is going. Oh, among the quite Advanced. I, it is thought, am rather beastly; you rather pitiable. . . .
> All the worst things drive them on. The furtive craving to interfere in the other people's lusts, the fear of unusual events, and the rest. The mother and the clergyman are at one in these kind hearts. . . . Is there no SIGN to give them, that each minute is final, and each heart alone?[53]

This was really a message in code to Ka: that Rupert didn't want her to be afraid of having an affair, but also that he didn't want to be manoeuvred into marrying her. Bloomsbury, of course, had little to do with the values of mothers or clergymen, and was just coming up with its own remarkable designs for living. Virginia had been sharing rooms with her brother Adrian at 29 Fitzroy Square; the lease ended in November 1911 and she decided to set up a communal household at 38 Brunswick Square. Besides herself and Adrian, there would be quarters for Maynard Keynes, Duncan Grant and Leonard Woolf on the top floor. It looked much more improper than it really was, but friends and relatives were shocked, while Vanessa helpfully pointed out that it was just across the road from the Foundling Hospital.

Ka's friendship with Virginia was making her a part of this milieu. Its sexual heresies, along with her failed affair with

Jacques and Rupert's solicitings, threw Ka's morals into confusion. The rules of Neo-pagan sex were that the women should
appear fast but remain chaste, while the men should practise
chastity within the Neo-pagan circle and, if they could manage it,
enjoy a surreptitious licence outside. By proposing that he and Ka
should have an affair, Rupert was radically changing the game as
it had been played up to now. His opening gambit was to settle in
the studio at 21 Fitzroy Square that was shared by Maynard
Keynes and Duncan Grant. Grant was away, and Keynes lived
mostly at Cambridge. Rupert complained to Jacques that his
quarters were 'inconceivably disgusting', but they were handy to
the British Museum, and allowed him to be alone with Ka
whenever he wished.[54] Whatever his professed beliefs or his
commitment to Noel, he had now strung himself up to try and
make Ka his mistress.

Rupert's impatience may even have led him into another brief
homosexual affair as soon as he arrived in London. In her
memoir *Old Bloomsbury*, Virginia Woolf recalls an exchange
with her sister: '"Norton tells me", Vanessa would say, "that
James is in utter despair. Rupert has been twice to bed with
Hobhouse" and I would cap her stories with some equally
thrilling piece of gossip; about a divine undergraduate with a
head like a Greek God – but alas his teeth were bad – called
George Mallory.'[55] Describing his affair with Denham Russell-
Smith, Rupert says that he had never gone to bed with anyone
before then (October 1909); the height of the Mallory boom was
around May of the same year. Either the story about Rupert and
Hobhouse was exaggerated, or it happened later. Hobhouse,
once beloved by Maynard Keynes and Lytton, had faded from
the Bloomsbury scene by 1909, but he was still an Apostle, and
the discussions about electing new brothers in the autumn of
1911 could have drawn him briefly back into his old orbit.

A letter from Maynard to James Strachey in October of that
year might refer to James's hurt feelings about an affair between
Rupert and Hobhouse:

> Yes, I should certainly suppose 'nothing', but then that's not
> your theory of life. Nor after the night before does it seem to
> me that last night was really so very unexpected. And
> wouldn't it, if there had been so much as that going on on

both sides, have come to a more palpable longitudinal head before midnight? It seems to me that you've now learnt to sit more firmly, but are not much nearer standing at the end of it. However, we'll see, I suppose. Isn't, perhaps, Covent Garden with Bryn almost out of the propriety?[56]

The reference could also be to James finding Rupert and Ka in a compromising position at Fitzroy Square, but James had never been really jealous of Rupert's 'womanising' – up to now at least. If Rupert slipped into another homosexual affair, in the middle of his entanglement with Ka, he must have been near to complete sexual confusion as 1911 drew to a close.

Unable to tolerate the filthiness of 21 Fitzroy Square – and perhaps wary of Virginia and Adrian at Number 29 – Rupert moved again early in November. Ka had found him rooms nearby at 76 Charlotte Street, and there they had a *demi-vierge* kind of affair that left both of them unhappy and unsettled:

> And then we had those nights – – – I had such lust for your fine body, far more (you *never* understood!) than for Noel. I had passion for you, – and, as you know, other things, other ways of love, (I knew you – ,Ka, – so deeply) as well. I was foolish and wicked, indeed. First, that I didn't chuck everything, turn wholly to you, marry you, if you would. . . .
> Then, I was a fool. . . . I'd baby ideas about 'honour' 'giving you a fair choice' 'not being underhand' 'men (!) and women (!) being equal' – – – I wanted you to fuck. You wouldn't, 'didn't like preventives'. And I respected you! . . . felt guilty and angry with myself when lust made me treat you 'unfairly'! . . .
> I was getting ill and stupid. . . . I was an object for pity – even love; not, of course, lust. You gave me strength, comfort, rest – for a bit. I threw all my affairs – all the mess Noel and I had made – onto you.[57]

When Rupert said that his friends didn't copulate before marriage, he might have added that they hardly knew how to do it. They were in a muddle over contraception for a start, but they were also stuck with the belief that premarital sex was only an overture to the real thing. Although they expected their marriages to be more sensual and companionable than their parents' had been, marriage was still a tremendous rite of passage, with the wife as the high priestess of its mystery. To draw back the veil casually or prematurely would arouse deep guilt. On the other hand, they assumed that the sexual act, by itself, would grant them maturity and strength of will. So long as his relation with Ka remained unconsummated Rupert could hope that, once it was, his emotional confusion would be resolved. He did not foresee how upset he would be when she *did* respond to his sexual needs; and even more, when she responded to someone else's.

In the middle of these intrigues Rupert's *Poems* were published, on 4 December. The volume was divided into two sections: the first decadent and implicitly homosexual, the second, after he met Noel, soulful and Neo-pagan. But Noel refused the dedication – partly, perhaps, because she suspected how deeply Rupert was now involved with Ka. Few of the poems had been written during 1911, but as soon as his thesis was done Rupert wanted to get back to his vocation – to be, he believed, 'a great poet and dramatist'.[58]

He had decided to go back to Munich in the New Year: ostensibly to perfect his German, but mainly because Ka had promised to meet him there, far from Bloomsbury gossip. Before going, though, he wanted a New Year's holiday like the one he had enjoyed the year before, with Ka, Jacques and Justin. He had planned that holiday himself, on the principle of 'four or six or so a good number. Too many, or too vaguely composed, won't do.'[59] This year he was working up to sixteen hours a day on his thesis, so Ka would make the arrangements. Her ideas, however, were different from his. She decided to repeat, at Lulworth, last August's camp. Neo-pagans (including the Oliviers) would mingle with Bloomsbury, some new faces would be blended in, and no longer could the party be counted on one hand. One of the new faces was a painter named Henry Lamb, whom Ka had met at a party and found 'fascinating'. Another could be called the last of the Neo-pagans, Ferenc Békássy.

'Feri' was still only eighteen, three months younger than Noel and a year younger than David Garnett. His parents belonged to the Hungarian landed aristocracy; they sent several of their children to Bedales, probably because brothers and sisters could be together there and because of the school's emphasis on country pursuits. Mary Newbery remembered him at Bedales as gentle, sweet and shy – but not good-looking, because of a weak chin. Though he had fallen in love with Noel at school, when he arrived at King's in October 1911 he soon got into the swim of homosexual Cambridge. Rich, intellectually adventurous and a poet, he at once caught Maynard's eye. Even with such a patron, he must have had unusual charm to be elected an Apostle only three months after his arrival.[60] He was the first foreigner and the first Bedalian to join the Society. His brilliant début indicates how popular Neo-paganism was with Bloomsbury at this point. Békássy soon became a frequent guest at 38 Brunswick Square, and Keynes would visit him in Hungary in the summer of 1912.

However, Békássy was an outsider's idea of a Neo-pagan rather than an established member of the group. Rupert did not like him very much, and not just because he was a rival for Noel's affection. When Békássy was made an Apostle in January Rupert, who was in France, felt that he had been deliberately left in the dark. 'The machinery for not having births till I was out of the way was a bit clumsy,' he complained to James. 'The gloom of Cannes is a trifle lightened for me by the reflection that *gott sei dank* I've done with all that.'[61] Unfortunately, Rupert's letter crossed one from James, containing a campy account of Békássy's successful début at his first Saturday night meeting. Feri had shown great intelligence, James reported, and had also filled Keynes and Gerald Shove with such lust that they wanted to take him right on the ritual hearthrug.[62] Rupert quickly snubbed his enthusiasm for Feri, but by then it was a bit late for James to retract, and say that the Society had taken a wrong turn in electing him.[63]

Rupert's real problem with Békássy, one would guess, was that the younger man's game was too close to his own. Békássy was a disconcertingly fluent bisexual. He loved Noel, but he also aroused lust in the Society, and himself loved a kind of *doppelgänger* for Rupert named Frank Bliss. Bliss entered King's at the same time as Békássy; he came from Rugby and he read classics. He was elected to the Society late in 1912, and was killed in France in 1916. But even James Strachey came to feel that Békássy went over the score when it came to multiple relations:

'Feri' was here on Monday and talked to me for 5 hours. He
came out like so many people – fairly confessed that he was
'in love' with (only guess) cette eternelle Noel. 'It runs on
parallel lines' so he informed me 'with my feelings towards
Bliss.' O God – if there is such a thing as blasphemy. I felt
like Rupert almost inclined for the dagger. . . .[64]

Békássy was probably included in the Lulworth party on
Noel's recommendation. Then Rupert suddenly announced to
Maynard that there would be 'no Oliviers'.[65] Perhaps Ka had put
her foot down: after her nights with Rupert at Charlotte Street
she cannot have relished the idea of spending two weeks at close
quarters with his 'fiancée'. But it is just as likely that Noel had
used what had become her standard tactic: to agree to something
with Rupert in order to avoid a scene, then pull out when she was
safely beyond reach.

With the party set, Rupert sent off his thesis, slept for twenty-
four hours in an armchair, and spent ten days with his mother.
He started a poem on the state he had drifted into in the course of
the past year:

All night I went between a dream and a dream
As one walking between two fires. . . .
The soul, like a thin smoke, is spread
Crying upon the air.[66]

One thing he had not taken into account was that Ka might also
be torn between rival loves, and might inflict on him what he had
inflicted on her and Noel. At Lulworth, he was about to discover
that the knife can cut two ways.

Part Three

Breaking Camp

VIII

The Descent

Lulworth, 1911–12

In 'The Descent', Rupert blamed Ka for having pulled him down into the underworld of sex:

Because you called, I left the mountain height . . .
And from my radiant uplands chose the blind
Nooks of your lost perpetual twilight.

For there your white and hungry hands were gleaming,
Your troublous mouth. And there we found desire . . .
There we found love in little hidden places,
Lost human love between the mist and mire.

At the end of 1911, those 'hungry hands' had thrown Rupert into panic and indecision. His first instinct with sex was to hide it, as he could do with Elisabeth van Rysselberghe and Denham Russell-Smith; but Ka was connected to everyone he knew, and their intimacy was bound to be known. When she embraced Rupert in his room on Charlotte Street, the touch of that warm and desiring body threatened to shatter his whole complex system of evasions and separations. To enter her would break the taboo that had allowed the Neo-pagans to know each other's nakedness – to touch it, even – but never to seize and enjoy it. And with Ka there was a deeper threat: that she might turn into the sexual mother, a woman whose nurturing embrace concealed a predatory lust. As he came to know his old friend in this newly sensual way, Rupert trembled on the brink of consummation. When Frances Cornford said that Ka had 'a frightening amount of sex', she was thinking of the danger to Ka herself, but Rupert was probably more frightened than anyone by the prospect of a real affair with her.[1] Then Ka, through impatience or mere whim, suddenly turned to another man who seemed more capable of meeting her own eagerness for initiation.

Rupert, with his puritanism and over-developed sense of honour, was still a Victorian at heart. Henry Lamb was a modern, a ruthless and mischievous seducer. He was the son of a professor of mathematics and younger brother to the Trinity don Walter Lamb; his sister Dorothy taught at Bedales. He had nearly qualified as a doctor when, in 1905, he decided to throw up his career and turn artist. In 1907 he married Nina ('Euphemia') Forrest, also an art student. They went to Paris to live near Augustus and Dorelia John, which soon did for their marriage. Dorelia took a fancy to Henry, and Augustus to Euphemia. When the dust settled, Henry was left with a life-long attachment to Dorelia, while Euphemia struck out on a lively career as an erotic freelancer.[2] Henry continued to take his cue from John, affecting gypsy ways, sudden changes of address, *louche* morals. Physically, however, he was a very different type. John was swarthy and boisterous, Henry was blond, slender, elusive and prickly. In his own way he was as handsome as Rupert, and his chiselled features and 'evil goat's eyes' appealed forcibly to women.[3]

In the autumn of 1911, somewhere near Fitzroy Square, those eyes fell on Ka Cox. One of the things Henry had taken over from John was an affair with Ottoline Morrell. She fixed Henry up in a studio next to her country house at Peppard, near Henley. But Ottoline was ten years older and a demanding patroness, encumbered with a husband and also, from the spring of 1911, an infatuation with Bertrand Russell. For Henry, Ka represented a target of opportunity. She enjoyed a private income, had vaguely artistic tastes and had a reputation as a soft pillow to lie on. John was rich, and actually liked living in caravans; Henry was hard up, was used to bourgeois comforts, and had few scruples about accepting favours from his friends or mistresses. He was also feeling the nervous strain of his *vie de bohème*, and was seeing the same hypnotist who had treated Jacques Raverat a few years earlier, Dr Bramwell. Marriage to Ka was more appealing than having to scratch out a living in Chelsea and environs. Even Lytton Strachey, weary of his makeshift life, had half-seriously thought of marrying a 'soothing woman' like Ka.[4]

Lytton was not really serious about marrying her, but he rather liked the idea that Henry might. For the past year he had been desperately in love with Henry, but he knew that such a confirmed 'womaniser' would not respond to his physical needs. All he could hope for was Henry's company in society, or for long stays at country hotels. In return Lytton would entertain him with scurrilous wit, pay his bills and accommodate his love affairs. He had to be careful, however, that Henry did not take up with the kind of woman who might try to cut Lytton out. Ka had no establishment of her own, and was accepted in Bloomsbury because she was both likeable and biddable. She could not expect to remove Henry from his usual orbit, and she was soon too besotted by him to object to his whims – or his friends.

Why should Ka have fallen so hard for Henry, just when her affair with Rupert was coming to a head? In Rupert's view, his 'baby ideas about "honour"' and his weak nerves left Ka susceptible to a more aggressive style of courtship:

> Someone more capable of getting hold of women than me, slightly experienced in bringing them to heel, who didn't fool about with ideas of trust or 'fair treatment', appeared. ... You'd met the creature at some party. I have your account: 'Very unpleasant' you wrote 'but fascinating.' 'Fascinating'!!! I dimly wondered ... and passed on. ...
>
> The swine, one gathers, was looking round. He was tiring of his other women, or they of him. Perhaps he thought there'd be a cheaper and pleasanter way of combining fucking with an income than Ottoline. And his 'friends' had come to the conclusion he might be settled with somebody for a bit. He cast dimly round. Virgins are easy game. Marjorie Strachey, I understand, was the first woman he met. What was her answer? Ka was the second: an obviously finer object for lust, and more controllable. He marked you down.[5]

Rupert took it for granted that Henry had exploited Ka's lust and inexperience. But no external pressure was needed to make her pursue him. In those heady days following the Post-Impressionist Exhibition, Henry enjoyed the glamour of being an artist. He was a bohemian city mouse after the country mice of Cambridge – those earnest but often droopy undergraduates who were Ka's friends before she moved to London. Outshone by Bryn and Noel, cut out by Gwen, Ka now had two dashing young men in pursuit of her. Who could blame her for relishing her power?

Early in December Ka had invited Henry to join the party at Lulworth, and confided to Justin that she planned to 'flirt' with him when he came. Rupert had gone to stay for a week in Eastbourne with his mother, to put the finishing touches on his thesis. Ka came to visit him there on the 9th, with the 'madness in her mind' of her infatuation with Henry.[6] Rupert took the news of Ka's outside interest badly. When he left for Lulworth on Thursday 28 December he was still dazed and upset by it, as well as exhausted by completing his thesis. Once at Churchfield House, he found that the Neo-pagans in the party Ka had arranged were heavily outgunned by Bloomsbury. Gwen and Jacques had come no closer than Studland, fifteen miles off, so that only Justin and Ka were left of the old crowd. The three Oliviers had been replaced by three Stracheys – James, Marjorie and Lytton. Feri Békássy also came, and Maynard Keynes after a few days. Then, in what seemed a major shift of allegiance, Ka announced that when Leonard Woolf returned to Ceylon in May she would move into his room at Bloomsbury's HQ, the communal house at 38 Brunswick Square.[7]

Rupert had expected a soothing week in the company of Ka and a few trusted friends. Instead, he had a houseful of Stracheys. Then, to fill the cup, Lytton drove a carriage to Wool Station on Saturday and returned with Henry Lamb, who had been spending Christmas with Augustus John near Corfe. Lytton and Henry stayed together at the Lulworth Cove Inn, but took their meals with the main party at Churchfield House, which now seethed with intrigues and flirtations. Marjorie Strachey took a shine to Justin, whom she called 'Duckie', while Lytton 'would grope [Henry] under the table at meal-times in view of all the ladies'.[8] Lytton's original plan, according to Rupert, had been to stay with Henry at Corfe and entice Ka to join them. Now Rupert gave them another opening by falling ill, on New Year's Eve:

The creature slimed down to Lulworth; knowing about women, knowing he could possibly get you if he got a few hours alone with you (his knowledge turned out to be justified.)

I was ill. Influenza (or poison in the house) frustrated me that Sunday. I was in the depths, leaning utterly on you. Oh my God! how kind and wonderful you were then; the one thing in the world I had.[9]

But Ka also found time to disappear for a long tête-à-tête with Henry. Later, Rupert told James Strachey that Henry 'nearly seduced' Ka — which meant, presumably, that she drew back short of the final act.[10] But when she came back to Churchfield House, she told Rupert flatly that she was in love with his rival. Henry, she pointed out, was four years older than she (Rupert was a few months younger), and had the same first name as her father, who had died when she was eighteen. Rupert, sick and distraught, cast off his endless vacillation between Ka and Noel and asked Ka to marry him at once. She calmly refused. She intended to go on seeing Henry, she said, and hoped, indeed, to marry *him*.

Two prominent traits in Henry's character were a love of mischief and a dislike of being pinned down. Having played the spoiler between Ka and Rupert, he promptly slipped away. He had a running joke with Lytton about paying tribute to 'the Obelisk', which was Henry's penis (as opposed to the rest of him). Back in London, he reported that 'L'Obélisque m'anéantie, mais je finirais par l'asservir. . . . I may write if I recover but it's clear that a visit to the fillettes must be made first.'[11]

Lytton had decided that Henry's propensity for rows and intrigues was taking both of them into dangerous waters. Henry's best bet was to get a rich and complaisant mistress, so even if Ka wanted to marry *him*, he would be foolish to marry *her*:

I can't believe that you're a well-assorted couple – can you? If she was really your wife, with a home and children, it would mean a great change in your way of living, a lessening of independence – among other things a much dimmer relationship with Ottoline. This might be worth while – probably would be – if she was an eminent creature, who'd give you a great deal; but I don't think she is that. There seems no touch of inspiration in her; it's as if she was made somehow or other on rather a small scale. . . .[12]

In any case, Henry was still formally married to Euphemia. Despite her rich and strange love-life, some quirk of loyalty, or malice, made her refuse to give him a divorce. And Rupert and Ka did seem 'to fit together so naturally – even the Garden-City-ishness'. By this Lytton meant their Neo-paganism, projected into the future – a domesticated Simple Life in one of the new mock-rural satellite towns. Henry relished the mockery; he dubbed Rupert 'The Cauliflower', and asked Lytton to arrange the match. 'As the Garden City is quite near,' he suggested, 'wouldn't I be able to give them a wedding present of great permanence? Then we'ld all be quits.'[13]

Lytton, however, was rapidly trimming his sails. It was one thing to indulge Henry's whims, another to have Ka become a fixture in his own inner circle, even as a mistress:

> I've now seen her fairly often and on an intimate footing, and I can hardly believe that she's suited to the post [of mistress]. I don't see what either of you could really get out of it except the pleasures of the obelisk. With you even these would very likely not last long, while with her they'ld probably become more and more of a necessity, and also be mixed up with all sorts of romantic desires which I don't think you'ld ever satisfy. If this is true it would be worth while making an effort to put things on a merely affectionate basis, wouldn't it? I think there's quite a chance that . . . everything might blow over, and that she might even sink into Rupert's arms. Can you manage this?[14]

To achieve such a happy ending, Ka and Rupert had to be brought down to earth and reconciled to each other. Ka had wanted to follow Henry to London, but Lytton convinced her to stay and minister to Rupert instead. 'Rupert is besieging her,' Lytton told Henry, '– I gather with tears and desperation – and sinking down in the intervals pale and shattered.'[15] By 5 January the Lulworth party had been reshuffled to prop up its invalid member. It now consisted of Rupert, Ka and four other Apostles – Lytton, Maynard, Gerald Shove and Harry Norton. Gwen and Jacques at Studland were also called on for support, Rupert walking over the hills to see them. Everything suggests that

Rupert, in his distress, was looked after in a thoughtful and sympathetic way by his friends. There must have been some feeling, also, that the Society should take Rupert's part against Henry, the outsider. But in spite of everyone's care Rupert kept sliding downhill. When it became plain that he needed professional help, Gwen and Jacques were the ones who took him in charge. After a difficult journey, they delivered him to Dr Maurice Craig in Harley Street.

Getting Stuffed

Two months after it happened, Rupert described his nervous collapse at Lulworth as 'a week or so in the most horrible kind of Hell; without sleeping or eating – doing nothing but suffering the most violent mental tortures. It was purely mental; but it reacted on my body to such an extent that after the week I could barely walk.'[16] Whether he was actually insane in early 1912 is a murky issue. The guardians of his reputation – notably Sir Geoffrey Keynes and Christopher Hassall – believed that he was too disturbed to be held responsible for his actions during this period. This is a defensible view; what is less defensible is their withholding of much of the evidence needed to arrive at a fair judgement of his condition.

Rupert's letters at this time are sprinkled with coarse and morally repellent attacks on women, homosexuals and Jews. For his apologists, such passages proved that he was mentally unbalanced and 'not himself'; they therefore suppressed most of them. By this reasoning, anyone could be absolved from their darker impulses. Throughout 1912 Rupert's letters show him to be overwrought, but able to give a coherent account of his troubled emotions.[17] Why suppress only those passages that show him in a bad light? One might just as well argue that the nasty parts show the 'real' Rupert – the golden boy with the rotten core – and write off his charm and affection as mere hypocrisy. Rupert himself, in giving directions for his papers if he died in battle, said 'let them know the poor truths'.[18] It still seems the best rule for those who propose to 'report him and [his] cause' to the world.

*   *   *

What, then, was wrong with Rupert? Why should a lover's quarrel with Ka push him over the brink into an acute manic–depressive condition that lasted for six months or more? It is surely crucial that Rupert's obsessive jealousy of Henry Lamb included an equally obsessive hatred of Lytton Strachey:

> If I can still, at moments, hate you [Ka] for having, in pitiful sight of a flirtation, invited that creature to Lulworth, and then left the rest of us, to go out walks and out for meals with him; how do you think I hate Lytton, who hadn't even your excuse of ignorance and helplessness, for having worked to get the man down there, and having seen the whole thing being engineered from the beginning, – and obligingly acquiesced in it as one of the creature's whims? You told me – in the first flush of your young romance – of the whole picture – Lytton 'hovering' (your word) with a fond paternal anxiousness in the background, eyeing the two young loves at their sport: – it was the filthiest filthiest part of the most unbearably sickening disgusting blinding nightmare – and then one shrieks with the unceasing pain that it was *true*.[19]

Rupert harped on two things about Lytton: his homosexuality and his love of insinuating himself into other people's emotions. Despite his own dabblings in the homosexual milieu, Rupert could not bear the idea of its escaping its bounds and mingling itself with heterosexual love – the school dormitory invading the family bedroom. He remained trapped in the double life, and double standard, that had guided him since childhood. His peculiar upbringing had made him abnormally sly and secretive; these qualities clashed with Lytton's open-minded and rational approach to sex. Both men had been accustomed to orchestrate the emotions of their friends, but they did so in very different styles, until the merger of Bloomsbury and Neo-paganism made them into rival masters of ceremonies.

In his own eyes, Lytton was a kind of scientist of personal relations, doing battle with the remnants of Victorian prudery and hypocrisy in the cause of a new era of sentiment. Since Henry would not physically respond to him, he chose to advance his beloved's other sexual interests. Lytton saw this as a rational compromise in which he settled for the biggest share in Henry's life that he could get; Rupert saw it as pimping. Perhaps he saw it as something worse and believed that Henry, like Julius Caesar, was Lytton's 'wife' at the same time as he tried to be Ka's 'husband'. That Rupert had his own bisexual history seems to have been exactly what made the Lulworth affair unbearable to him.[20]

What Rupert could not acknowledge was how much he remained his mother's child, even as he thought he was escaping from her. The woman's world held an ideal that he craved, as an antidote to his own moral confusion. Women were innately pure, but also innately weak and corruptible. They had to be protected from people like Henry and Lytton – creatures whom he hated because he knew how close, in some ways, he had been to them. Henry, the practised seducer, embodied a style of masculine predatoriness that Rupert both despised and envied. 'All the women of that circle have been treated so well – too well – by the men they know,' observed Dudley Ward, 'that they're peculiarly at the mercy of the other sort of man when he comes along.'[21] Perhaps so; but it was also true that Henry and Lytton drove Rupert into madness by acting out, without compunction, his own hidden or unsatisfied desires.

Dr Maurice Craig was one of Britain's leading psychiatrists. He was consulted by Leonard Woolf over Virginia's breakdowns, and treated many other intellectuals. But his management of Rupert's breakdown effectively left the mind out of account:

> My nerve specialist's treatment is successful and in a way pleasant, *aber etwas langweilig*. I have to eat as much as I can get down, with all sorts of extra patent foods and pills, milk and stout. I have to have breakfast in bed about 10 every day, go to bed early, never take any exercise, walk never more than two miles, and do no kind of brain-work. After a few weeks of it one feels like Oldham or a sleepy version of the master of Magdalene.[22]

When Daphne Olivier had a breakdown in 1915 she got the same treatment from Sir Henry Head: a course of 'stuffing', as it was called, lasting six weeks.

The 'stuffing' treatment was really no treatment at all. First there would be one or two sessions in Harley Street for the diagnosis: Rupert, for example, was told that he was suffering from a 'seriously introspective condition'! Then the patient would be packed off to the country to follow a regime of absolute tedium, either in the care of a relative or in a nursing home if he threatened violence. Mrs Brooke happened to be in Cannes for an extended holiday, so Rupert was sent there for his cure. He was given a drug to repress sexual desire (though he reported it had the opposite effect), and some tonics and sedatives. It was not out-and-out quackery: the drugs did no real harm, while tranquillity and good food helped many patients to feel better. But neither was it psychotherapy in any modern understanding of the term.

The truly bizarre feature of 'stuffing' was the obsession with the patient's weight as an index of his mental state. Everyone was put on the same regime of inactivity and a fattening diet, regardless of the nature of their distress, and the cure was measured by how many pounds the patient gained each week. Thirty pounds in two months was the usual target. Rupert gained seven and a half pounds in the first twelve days of treatment, then another seven more gradually. When Virginia Woolf broke down after her marriage she was 'stuffed' by Sir Henry Head; she weighed 119 pounds in September 1913 and 179 pounds fifteen months later. The mythology of Leonard Woolf sitting devotedly by her for hours at a time, spoon in hand, appears in a different light when one knows anything about 'stuffing' as the standard – in a sense, the only – treatment for mental illness.[23]

When the patient tried to pour out his troubles, it would be taken as a morbid sign. Instead of responding to the feelings, the doctor would try to get them repressed again as soon as possible. If Rupert's letters to Ka seem obsessive and wild, we must remember that she was the only real therapist he had. Since she was also the main cause of his trouble, he alternately attacked her and cast himself on her mercy – which put her, also, under an almost unbearable strain.

Despite his feeble state Rupert managed, a day or two after returning to London, to go and see Noel at Limpsfield. He cannot have found it easy to explain why he was so upset, and she evidently did not offer him much of a shoulder to cry on – she would speak casually later of how Rupert had 'pretended' to be ill. Ka was more sympathetic, and had now agreed to meet Rupert in Munich. On 9 January she put Rupert on the train to Cannes. She would stay in London for a week, then go directly to Munich; Rupert would join her there as soon as he was fit to travel.

Elisabeth van Rysselberghe undertook to look after Rupert for two nights and a day in Paris, at her parents' villa. 'I find myself so unmoved and kindly with her,' he reassured Ka, '. . . Don't mind my being here a day. I'm not loving Elizabeth.' What he now wanted, he said, was 'to turn altogether to you and forget everything but you, and lose myself in you, and give and take everything – for a time. Afterwards – doesn't matter.'[24] In other words, they should agree to ignore their other commitments – for just so long as their affair lasted. Moved by guilt and concern for Rupert's collapse, Ka accepted his dubious terms.

She had no intention, however, of staying away from Henry. She wrote to him from Lulworth, asking to meet him for dinner in London on 7 January (this may have coincided, appropriately enough, with Rupert's visit to Limpsfield). In the week before she left for Munich she pursued Henry shamelessly, deeply offending Ottoline Morrell (who had taken on Bertrand Russell, but was still clinging to Henry). Having been declared surplus by Jacques and Gwen a year earlier, Ka was not willing to sacrifice herself on the altar of Rupert's jealousy. She would give him all the help she could – short of giving up Henry. This would not be made clear to him, however, until they met face to face.

Rupert, meanwhile, was being 'stuffed' in Cannes, and consoling himself that he had at last cleared a path into the future:

> I'm certainer than ever that I'm, possibly, opening new Heavens, like a boy sliding open the door into a big room; trembling between wonder and certainty. . . . I know now how beastly I was both to you and to Noel; and that one must choose – choose, being human – one thing at a time. . . . I couldn't give to either of two such people what I ought, which is 'all'. Now I've got a sort of peace, I think; because I shall be able.[25]

During the three weeks of their separation he wrote to her daily, some of the letters thousands of words long. His mother was kept

in the dark, though she realised her son was upset over something, and suspected Bryn of being responsible! In choosing Ka
for his confidante and compulsively spilling out his troubles to
her, he was making his own attempt at Dr Freud's new 'talking
cure':

> The pleasure of telling you about things is so extraordinarily
> great. What does it mean? Keeping telling you everything
> would, it seems, make such a wonderful and golden back-
> ground for everything else between us. I've such a longing to
> get out of myself, my tight and dirty self – to put it all out in
> the sun, the fat sun. And it's so hard to tell the truth, to give
> oneself wholly away, even to you. So one wants to chatter
> and pour everything out . . . and then perhaps truth may slip
> out with it. . . . I've never told anyone anything, hardly.
> 'Secretive.'[26]

Rupert believed that his breakdown was caused not by over-
work – the standard Victorian explanation for mental illness in
men – but by sexual frustration:

> I've been half-mad, alone. Oh, it's all mixed up with this
> chastity, and everything's a whirl, and still I'm mad and tiny
> and frightened. . . . Jacques, being Jacques, went mad for
> half a year. I, being tougher and slower, defied chastity a bit
> longer, and then, naturally, would take it worse. . . . It'll be a
> curious comment on civilization or women or something if I
> do go.[27]

His sexual experience was indeed scanty for a man of twenty-
four, consisting mainly of one night with Denham Russell-Smith
and a half-baked affair with Elisabeth van Rysselberghe. Ka's
refusal of a complete sexual relation at the end of 1911 had
brought matters to a crisis: to be kept on tenterhooks by her was
evidently more nerve-racking than to be kept firmly at arm's
length by Noel. Since chastity had pushed him over the brink, it
made sense to Rupert that physical possession of Ka would
restore him to health. He kept telling her that his vacillations
between her and Noel, lust and love, were now over; he wanted
only her 'deep breasts' and other charms:

> It's funny, I still think, your idea that one doesn't – or that I
> didn't – love you physically, very strongly. When I felt last

year, my whole conduct was wronging you, it wasn't, you
know, that! It was that it'd come over me that I perhaps only
loved you physically and very much as a friend, – that I'd
still to 'only connect' lust and an immense comradeship. But
I didn't imagine I hadn't *those*, you know! It's *possibly* true
that mere prettiness and champagne stir the penis most. But
physical passion includes the penis but is more, it's hands
and thighs and mouth that are shaken by it as well. And
that's stirred by different things: strong beauty and passion
and – undefined things.[28]

If he could set aside Noel, loving and possessing Ka would
restore his sanity and achieve his manhood. But somehow he still
couldn't envision a mature and mutually committed life with her
– only a few months of wandering around the Continent, after
which they would go their separate ways. To a well-brought-up
young lady like Ka, this cannot have looked reassuring. Henry
was married already, while Brooke was proposing a good deal
less than marriage. If she accepted his offer, her future prospects
would be seriously dimmed. Rupert, thanks to the double
standard, had much less to fear from a romantic liaison.
Nonetheless Ka bravely set off for Munich, with Justin Brooke
for company, on 16 January. She had convinced herself that she
owed it to Rupert to be his mistress – and that she owed it to
herself to end her 'extraordinarily randy condition of virginity'.[29]
In the city of three thousand artists, safe from the prying eyes that
surrounded her in England, she would take the plunge into
bohemia.

The Moment of Transfiguration

On the night of Tuesday 30 January 1912, Rupert and Ka both
set off by train. In the morning they would meet at Verona,
halfway between Cannes and Munich. Rupert had set his heart
on meeting in Italy. From Verona, he fantasised, they might slip
away to Venice and be lost to the world for months. But, when
they met, it was more as patient and nurse than as lovers. Ka
realised at once that Rupert was too weak to travel. She took him
back to Munich the next day and installed him in the same rooms

he had had the year before, at 3 Ohmstrasse. There, his landlady took over the task of fattening him up with Ovaltine and bromides. Ka was staying elsewhere with friends of Rupert, the Kanoldts. The two of them cannot have had much chance to be alone, especially when Hugh Popham turned up and accompanied them on their daily outings.

After a week Ka and Rupert went to stay overnight at Salzburg, but they still held off from the final act.[30] At last, on Saturday 17 February, they left for a weekend at the Starnberger-see. On the way, Ka confessed to Rupert that just before she left for Germany she had spent the weekend at a country house where Henry was a fellow guest. The news sent Rupert into a frenzy of jealousy and humiliation, since his whole relationship with Ka rested on the assumption that she had renounced her interest in Henry. But he was at least moved to claim her fully for himself.

As lovers, they must have been painfully awkward and uncertain. Ka had gritted her teeth and 'equipped herself' for the deed, presumably with the 'irrigator' that James Strachey had earlier recommended to Rupert.[31] Coping with this implement, and with the ghostly presence of Henry, cannot have made for a carefree night of love. Still, they had together crossed over a threshold. Recalling the event a month later, Brooke's most vivid impression was of initiation:

> I'm pitiful seeing the useless wasted spoilt old maids who
> creep down this road: and the young maids with their dirty
> suppressed decomposing virginity: and then I'm proud at
> them 'Ka is not like you, and won't be. She knows.' . . . I
> remember the softness of your body: and your breasts and
> your thighs and your cunt. I remember you all naked lying to
> receive me; wonderful in beauty. I remember the agony and
> joy of it all: that pleasure's like a sea that drowns you wave
> by wave. I've the strength of an army, now. And I love you,
> in all the ways of love.[32]

However exciting their new sensations, they did not have the strength of purpose to cast off their previous commitments in Britain. Today, their counterparts might just stay on the Continent and live together while the spirit moves them. In 1912, the predominant concern for Rupert and Ka must have been: what would their families and friends think? what would their land-lady think? what would *everybody* think? And the sexual act itself was so hedged about with taboos that it created as much tension when enjoyed as it did when denied. Even its basic nature remained, to Rupert, something of a mystery:

> The important thing, I want to be quite clear about, is, about women 'coming off'. What it means, objectively – What happens. And also, what *you* feel when it happens. Have you (I'd like to hear when there's infinite leisure) analysed, with the help of that second night, the interior feelings you were yet dim about the first night (at Starnberg.)? And can you discover by poking about among your married acquaintances? . . . It's only that I want to get clear – perhaps it's a further physical thing we've to explore.[33]

But everything was done in a hurry, and only four days after the weekend at Starnberg they were on their way back to England. Ka could not manage the strain of being both Rupert's lover and his nurse, while tacitly keeping a place open in her emotions for Henry. She wrote to James Strachey that she was miserable and unsure of what to do with Rupert. He had to be fed and cosseted like a fractious child, but one with an adult capacity to wound and disturb. Rupert was also writing to James, telling him that he was leaning with all his weight on Ka. 'It is infinitely wicked,' he confessed, 'but I'm beyond morals. I really rather believe she's pulled me through. She is stupid enough for me to be lazy and silly enough for me to impose on her.'[34] To help Rupert feel better, Ka had to listen to endless diatribes about her filthy behaviour with Henry. When Dudley Ward came from Berlin to visit them, he had calmed Rupert down and lightened Ka's burden. The most sensible plan, Ka felt, was to share the task of propping up Rupert between herself, Dudley and Mrs Brooke.

They left Munich on 21 February; when they arrived at Victoria the next day Ka returned to her sister's flat, while Rupert went on to Rugby. Now the understanding was that Rupert would spend two months recuperating in England. In May he and Ka would stay together again in Berlin, where Dudley could be counted on for support. Each would be 'in pawn' to their families while in England – especially Rupert, who was too feeble to look after himself at Grantchester and would have to be sequestered at Bilton Road. His mother got on his nerves, but she would protect him from others who would get on his nerves more, and from the dangerously exciting social life he had led for the past year.

Rupert now developed a new obsession: that Ka was as exhausted as he was, and should therefore submit to a similar invalid regime. When she moved to 38 Brunswick Square on 1 March, she should not 'look after Adrian Duncan Maynard Woolf Sidney-Turner or any other inhabitant'.[35] In the event, she stayed with her sister – perhaps because Virginia had suffered another nervous breakdown in February, or else because Rupert had objected so fiercely to her moving into Bloomsbury. For he had now appointed himself the guardian of her every move:

> Ka, you've once given yourself to me: and that means more than you think. It means so very importantly that you're not your own mistress. And that, far more truly and dangerously than if I had you under lock and key – and with my 'physical superiority'. It means that you're not as free to do anything as you were. It means you mayn't hurt yourself, because it hurts me, like Hell. It means you mayn't make mistakes, because I pay. It means you mayn't foolishly and unthinkingly get tired and ill and miserable: because you make me tired and ill and miserable.[36]

Rupert's real concern upset him too much to be stated in plain terms. He was terrified that Ka might drift back into Henry's orbit and, now that she had given herself to one, give herself to another. But in asserting his male prerogative, Rupert fell victim to his own premises. If women were so weak that they required constant male supervision, it followed that *any* man could make them do what he wanted; and most of the time he could not be physically present to make sure of Ka. Having defined her as will-less and faithless, he had to live with the nightmare of what might happen to her in the moral quagmire of London.

Ka, whether out of a desire to be honest or a streak of malice towards Rupert, promptly reported that she had spoken to Henry at a social gathering. 'I wish to God you'ld cut the man's throat,' he fired back. '. . . See very little of the man, for God's sake. And don't be more of a bloody fool than Nature made you.' Her contacts with Lytton Strachey aroused an even deeper, and more complex, fury. 'I'm glad Lytton has been having a bad time,' he fumed. 'Next time you have one of your benignant lunches with him you can make it clear to him I loathe him – if there's any chance of that giving him any pain.'³⁷ Yet his most devoted male companion in these difficult months was James Strachey, now that Jacques was married and Dudley settled in Berlin. Stuck at Bilton Road with the Ranee, Rupert needed James's weekend visits, but knew that anything he said to him was likely to go straight to Brunswick Square and environs. 'I can't "talk" to James,' he told Ka. '*I* suppose he knows little, and misunderstands. . . . And I feel, rather wrongly, suddenly – that he's a Strachey – a brother, anyhow, of Lytton Strachey. He loves you: but it may be it's only his love for you that matters to him, not you. You know how the Stracheys feel? James *is* better than the rest. But one can't tell.'³⁸

Whether or not James was better, he was unshakably loyal. 'God damn you,' Rupert wrote to him before one of his visits, 'God bum roast castrate bugger and tear the bowels out of everyone. . . . You'd better give it up; wash your bloody hands. I'm not sane.'³⁹ James came anyway, as he always would until he was beaten off. Writing Virginia a letter of sympathy about *her* breakdown, Rupert regaled her with a piece of Rugby scandal:

> Church circles are agitated by what happened at Holy Trinity three Sundays ago. In the afternoon there is first a Choral service, then a children's service, then a Service for Men Only. Two fourteen-year-old choir boys arranged a plan during the Choral Service. At the end they skipped round and watched the children enter. They picked out the one whose looks pleased them best, a youth of 10. They waited in seclusion till the end of the Children's service. They pounced on their victim, as he came out, took him, each by a hand, and led him to the vestry. There, while the Service for Men Only proceeded, they removed the lower parts of his clothing and buggered him, turn by turn. His protestations were drowned by the Organ pealing out whatever hymns are most suitable to men only. Subsequently they let him go. He has been in bed ever since with a rupture. They were arrested and flung, presumably, into a Reformatory. He may live.⁴⁰

In telling Virginia this, was Rupert mad, or just bad? Probably he was unaware that she had been sexually abused as a child by her half-brothers, and had a continuing phobia about being molested.[41] Nonetheless, to write in this vein to someone in her condition was insensitive at best, sadistic at worst.

Noel seemed to be the one person towards whom he still had a conscience. Unfortunately, he literally had nothing to say to her:

> I've not written yet. I'll tell you what I say – that is, what I *tell*. Of course! I shan't tell much, now. It's only I *ought* to have written at the beginning of January. I could only put her off then. 'I'm ill. Wait. I'll write later.' And it's so *beastly* of me leaving her in the air. I can't write much more now. But – though she's not a person to care or be even scratched – silence is so damned grim, sinister: *I* know. I shall just, I think, say better: that I'm not going to see her (once, perhaps, if letter writing's a nuisance: but practically not) till after a Period: that the Period means anyway some more weeks here and anyhow, some month or months abroad: that I shall know more clearly, and be able to be clearer, after a bit; and so on. The *Status Quo*: in fact.[42]

Noel's life, however, was not standing still. The previous October she had moved to London to study medicine at University College – a continuation of her childhood passion for zoology. Now nineteen, and living a much less cloistered life, she was bound to form new attachments. She was corresponding with Feri Békássy at King's, was being treated to tea and Wagner by James Strachey, and had other admirers in the offing. All this attention she treated rather offhandedly; her real dedication was to her studies, which she pursued with her typical single-mindedness. From time to time she heard about Rupert's illness, but treated the news with a mixture of wariness and suspicion that it was just another pose. In the Olivier household, he commented sarcastically, it was 'not done, or thought of' to get upset about his kind of misfortune.[43]

Ka was overflowing with sympathy, but having her come to Bilton Road posed dangers of its own. If she and Mrs Brooke disliked each other, Rupert would be torn between them. If they liked each other too well, it would raise the spectre of an official engagement and marriage. He got Ka invited, after much hesitation; then he told his mother she had been at Munich, and another storm broke. Mrs Brooke had suspected Bryn of having a tryst with her son there (in fact, she was rock-climbing in Wales). Was it Ka, then, who had kidnapped Rupert from her care at Cannes? It took all his dramatic skill to convince his mother that Ka was only a casual acquaintance whom he had met in Munich by chance. Meanwhile, he was regaling Ka with boasts of the 'ferocious tempestuous ocean of lust' that he had in store for her.⁴⁴ Somehow, though, it was not tempestuous enough to make him defy his mother and marry Ka. And when she came, the first time they had seen each other in a month, he could only lash out at her for her past misdeeds. Once she had left, he collapsed and cried himself to sleep. 'Everything's gone from me –', he lamented, 'love for Noel, writing, everything – is swept away.'⁴⁵ The only thing he had left was her renewed promise to be with him in Berlin in May. But, back in London, Henry fell off his horse and Ka volunteered to apply fomentations to his wounds every morning. Once again, Rupert began to bombard her with letters that swung back and forth between indignation and despair.

By the end of March, he was finding life at Bilton Road unbearable. 'Mention *nothing* connected with my life,' Rupert told Geoffrey Keynes before he came to visit, 'no names, nothing, for the Lord's sake. Relations between the Ranee and me are peculiar. And one must be very cautious.'⁴⁶ He learned that he had failed to get his fellowship, though it was hinted that if he applied again his chances were good. Dr Craig had forbidden him mental work, but writing seemed to be the only occupation open to him for the time being. His thesis could be resubmitted without much revision, so he had no further need to grind away in libraries. If he stayed at home, his mother would prevent him doing anything, and would keep most of his friends away as well.

It was time for a break-out, clearly; but Rupert was not really fit to be about on his own. Despite his hatred of Lytton, he was still writing him strange letters – including one proposing to 'abduct Bryn for Sunday to the Metropole at Brighton – and go shares'.⁴⁷ To sustain himself 'on the outside', he would need continuous help from his friends – for example, Jacques and Gwen:

I can't sleep. I'm leaving this Hell. I've got to defer the Deluge a month or two yet. I'm going – I don't know where

– with J. Strachey for the weekend. . . . I'm entirely depraved
and extremely unpleasant – but can I sleep in your Studio?
. . . I'm much less bother than last time.[48]

Where he really wanted to go, it was becoming evident, was
back to Noel. After he finally wrote to her, she had agreed to see
him in London. He told Ka that his love for Noel was 'gone . . .
swept away', but Ka must have known him better than he knew
himself. She could see that the woman who had not yielded to
Rupert would always stand higher in his heart than the one who
had:

> I shall see her once – I'm so ashamed (she's, you'll under-
> stand, *good, fine, wonderful*) – before I leave England. And
> then, you see, I may not see her for years, or ever, again. . . .
> I'm sick with a sort of fear, of seeing Noel. She – you don't
> know what she stands for – stood for to me – Do you I
> wonder understand about love, Ka? – it's rather a holy thing
> – I shall say (for a certain amount I *must* tell her) 'I've taken
> away my love from you, Noel. I've given all my love to Ka.
> And she –' Perhaps Noel'll ask 'what's she done with it?' (as
> one asks after a dog one sold last month) – I daren't look at
> her.[49]

Looking for the Exit

Rupert fled from his mother's house on Thursday 28 March. He
had dinner in London with James and Bryn; Noel had said she
would be there, but sent a last-minute excuse instead.[50]
Whenever Rupert showed signs of being 'elevated' (the Olivier
term for excited and emotional), Noel would quietly make
herself unavailable. He went on to spend the night at Jacques'
and Gwen's studio flat in Baron's Court. Rupert had decided that
it was time to take them into his confidence, and get them to share
his obsession about Ka's flirtation with Henry:

> I can't bear that I should go about knowing some things
> alone. Jacques and Gwen and Justin – I feel I *must* tell them
> the horror, the filthy filthy truth. It's unbearable, suffering
> alone. I want to see their pain –. . . And you – you'd see their

faces – or be able to talk to them – people who *love* you – about things. Now, you see, it's so twisted. I'm the only decent person in 1912 you know – everyone else is in 1911.[51]

The next night Ka came to see them, and, after she left, Rupert told Jacques and Gwen the story of Lulworth and its aftermath. He told them, too, that he and Ka were going to Germany in a month as man and wife, and that he wanted to marry Ka but she wouldn't have him. Having got this off his chest, he left the next morning for a long weekend at Rye with James.

What Rupert did not say, however, was that he and Ka had slept together at Munich. Jacques solemnly advised him that they would both see things more clearly when they were no longer virgins. Jacques and Gwen were inclined to see the whole affair as a bad case of premarital jitters, with one partner emotionally faithful and the other wavering. The reality, of course, was far more complex – and put Rupert in a much worse light.

As soon as Rupert was out of the way, Ka came over for a tête-à-tête with Gwen. Jacques claimed to be too ill to see her, but was in fact too angry. They both felt that Ka, after the fiasco of her broken romance with Jacques, had gone against the grain of her nature by plumping for female independence, free love and the company of degenerate intellectuals. Gwen, especially, was now peddling an unashamedly conventional brand of Neo-paganism:

> I think there's been too much nonsense about these Stracheys. Treating them as equals and all that. Its sentimental and encourages them. They *are* parasites you know, all of them. . . . I for one am a clean Christian and they disgust me. . . . You seem to me to have absolutely no fineness of instinct about a certain goodness (there's no other word) which is essential. You have forgotten God. You think in your arrogance that you can manage your own life – But there is a humility more important than any intelligence. You have not the mind to govern your instincts – you are terribly muddled by education and talk. . . .
> PS Why do all these people think that you are only good enough for a mistress and not to be married? You *are* you *are*; and to be loved all your life. . . . Jacques says Rupert has wanted nothing in the world but to *marry* you, for ever so long.[52]

Becoming a married woman had made Gwen much more outspoken – in fact, downright aggressive. Her stock of ideas was relatively small, but she made up for this by the ferocity with which she proclaimed them. She prescribed for Ka what had worked for herself: marriage, and large doses of hard work. Ka, in her state of wilful self-assertion, was a loose cannon, dangerous to all her friends and especially dangerous to Gwen, since who knew when she might again throw herself at Jacques? As a Darwin, Gwen demanded of Ka earnestness and sober commitment; as Jacques' wife, she condoned libertinism in the man but was appalled by it in the woman.

Jacques was less overbearing, but just as emotionally grievous. In the name of their love – which he claimed still continued – he asked Ka to reconsider her whole course of action since they broke up:

> All last year, you were trying very hard to get on to your own feet. You thought, you think now, that you've done it. Well, have you? Perhaps you have; but I think you're standing on your head. You've made yourself strange and distant and secretive, imagining no doubt, that was independence. . . . It seems to me you've crushed and smothered your old simplicity and goodness and openheartedness.

In Jacques' view, Rupert truly loved Ka, despite his current state of muddle and hysteria; but her love for Henry was 'not convincing, not inevitable'. Going to Germany was a dangerous half-measure. To escape disaster, they must take a single, bold stroke:

> If I were Rupert I'd not have you for a month, for a mistress. It's but a sop to your conscience. It should be all or nothing. You give him all except the one thing he wants, which is your love. . . . I think it's cowardly these reservations. Marry him first even if you must leave him afterwards one day. But these back-doors – that's not facing life.[53]

Both Gwen and Jacques were now unshakably convinced that their two friends belonged together. Years later, they were still waiting for Rupert to return and claim Ka's heart; when he died, much of the tragedy for them was that this reconciliation had been forestalled. They kept making excuses for Rupert's erratic passions. In any case, they felt that only Ka could give him the 'ballast' he needed. They viewed Bloomsbury as a rival and in many ways an enemy camp. Ka was too impressionable, anyway, to run in that company. She was not an intellectual, not sophisticated enough to treat sex as a game. Months later, Gwen showed little repentance for the harsh words she and Jacques had flung at their old friend:

> at the time we both felt that a great shock – a sudden cold bath, was the only thing that would bring her to her senses. ... I think what *I* did was a mistake – but I think it was Jacques's letter, however cruel, that did it. Rupert thinks so I believe.
>
> The bottom of it, was not to save her from H.L., but to save her to herself – to save her the remorse of leaving Rupert whom she loved with all her heart for a man whom she never loved at all. It was that conviction that made us write. You didn't see her as I did – half an hour after Rupert had finished sobbing out his story, come to the house all smug and self-satisfied and happy, saying she was 'very sorry' for Rupert – and somehow impenetrable to everything. She was never unhappy till after that.[54]

Everything Gwen did in the matter was founded on the conviction that she knew Ka much better than Ka, at that point, could know herself:

> It was [Ka's] first going to Rupert at Munich that shocked me – not her going if she had admitted it was for love – but her going and saying 'I don't love you – I nearly hate you, I love H.L., I came out of pity'; she did it out of a mixture of real and unadmitted love for R. and a sort of false intellectual vanity and desire for self abasement.
>
> Rupert loved her then – if she had been honest then – if she had married him (then or within a month or 2 afterwards) – he would have loved and respected her always. Its an intellectual vanity – her actions have been instinctive all through – her words were simply rubbish. In this matter all through she has been simply pushed and driven by her sex. It was that pure and simple with H.L. (By the bye, your admiration theory doesn't work there. He never admired her or even loved her – he went about saying she bored him; and he finally refused to have her to live with him ever. He only desired her.) I expect you think we have been cruel to

Ka – but remember Frances you have only seen her now in a
more honest state of mind – you didn't see her 4 or 5 months
ago – when she lied and lied.[55]

The Raverats' judgement of Ka may not have been fair, but
what mattered was that she was coming to agree with it. Her
wide-eyed devotion was bound to irritate anyone so restless and
cynical as Henry. He was starting to complain about her to his
intimates and she must have sensed his dissatisfaction. Ka was
becoming more receptive to Rupert's protestations of love, and
more inclined to believe that marriage would pull them out of
their emotional swamp. Unfortunately, any real move towards
marriage was guaranteed to make Rupert shy away from her,
though neither she nor the Raverats understood this feature of
his emotional make-up.

No sooner had Rupert gone off to Rye with James than he
again started to play the ardent and repentant lover:

There are two newly-married couples. The husbands have
both retired, just now (9.0). How it brings the old days back,
eh. . . .
   Have they got Irrigators? Are they using Oatine? The
dears! . . . I feel mentally better for being beastly to you. . . .
I'm loving you extraordinarily. . . . Oh my God, I *want* you
so tonight. Your nakedness and beauty – your mouth and
breasts and cunt. – Shall I turn in a frenzy and rape James in
the night? I'd burn you like a fire if I could get hold of you.[56]

Next day came more of the same, coupled with the demand that
'You'd better marry me before we leave England.' But Ka was
asked to reply 'chez Noel' at Limpsfield. 'I'd like to get rid of that
woman,' Rupert told her, 'before I came in to you. I'll crawl in for
comfort – the old game! I'm sick about Noel. I, even I, find my
theories true – she gets hold of one – oh, I know what I'm doing,
it's all right! I admire her rather extraordinarily.'[57]

Caught in his eternal balancing act, Rupert decided to see Ka in
London on Monday afternoon before taking the train to Limpsfield that night. Ka, after seeing him, would leave for her cottage
at Woking. In the meantime, however, she had been exposed to
the full blast of Gwen's and Jacques' disapproval. Seeing Rupert
again was more than she could face. She begged off the

rendezvous, saying she was too tired, and then stayed at her sister's flat instead of leaving town. On the train that was taking him to see Noel and Bryn, Rupert erupted again:

> Are you wanting to make me wild before I see Noel, lest I should be too nice to her? or do you want to get rid of me by killing me – can't you do it quicker easier ways? . . .
>
> I'm going to do the hardest and one of the worst things ever done tomorrow. A thing you hardly understand. And all the time I, the filthied blasphemous I, will be agonizing about you. . . .
>
> Wire that all's right, that you're in Woking. . . .
>
> Gwen Jacques and a thousand more yourself me decency love honour good fineness cleanness truth –: you'd sacrifice them on your lust – and such lust – I'm frantic. I shall see you thank God or I'll kill myself – on Wednesday.[58]

Rupert was speaking in code, because he could not bear to speak directly. When he forbade Ka to tire herself, what he meant was that she must stay away from London, and particularly from those parts of it where she might encounter Henry. His own 'blasphemy' lay in renouncing the chaste Noel for the fallen Ka. At Limpsfield, he was struck by how supportive and calm Noel was – given his unexplained neglect of her over the past several months. 'She is amazing,' he informed Ka, 'I didn't know such people existed. I go sick and blind to think she may be a woman.'[59] That is, vulnerable to the passions that had already entered Ka and, in Rupert's eyes, degraded her.

Having stayed an extra day at Limpsfield, Rupert turned up at Woking on Thursday 4 April for a much less happy meeting. The passionate scenes he had imagined at Rye fizzled out as soon as they were face to face. 'I'm going to leave Ka alone,' Rupert reported to Jacques, 'till she's rested and ready for Germany. I found her (I came yesterday) pretty bad. To rest, as far as she will, is the best thing for her: (and for me). She sees – anyhow – what other people think.'[60] What other people thought, evidently, was that Ka and Rupert should marry; and Rupert told Jacques that he had set himself a deadline to do just that by 10 May, the day before Dudley Ward and Annemarie von der Planitz were due to wed.

*   *   *

In the week after he left Bilton Road Rupert saw all of his closest friends, decided that he and Ka should get married – and also started to sprinkle his letters with hints that he was going to kill himself. Behind this flurry of activity lay a new crisis: he was afraid that Ka was pregnant. When James gave Rupert directions for contraception the previous April, in Munich, he had told him (wrongly, of course) that the safest time for intercourse was halfway between periods. Rupert's consummation with Ka was probably delayed accordingly, until 17 February 1912, when they had been in Munich for two weeks. Her period was due at the end of the month, and by the middle of March Rupert was trying to reassure her:

> Do I see you've been fretting over the non appearance of your month, *allerschuhteruste*? I suppose it was my fault, upsetting your damn inside. But I sort of think you've been half-fearing we'd mismanaged the machine, and that your wellknown fecundity had been set off.[61]

From Rye, on 30 March, Rupert noted that she must be 'at, or nearly at', her period.[62] Then, the letters say nothing more. But there is no reason to doubt Cathleen Nesbitt's report: that Ka had a 'still-born' child, and Rupert felt very guilty about it.[63] She might have got pregnant when she was with Rupert near Berlin at the end of May; but February seems more consistent with the surviving evidence.

If he had the threat of becoming a father hanging over him, one can understand better why Rupert's actions, in his remaining two weeks in England, were so totally erratic. He could not go back to Ka, and would not go back to his mother. Luckily the faithful James stepped in and took him down to Mrs Primmer's at Bank. She was 'the best cook in England', Rupert said, which would help his 'stuffing' cure. But his main reason for going must have been to revive memories of his secret rendezvous with Noel and Margery, three years before. That was Easter 1909; now he had come back to spend Easter in the forest again. The contrast between past and present, however, made him flatly suicidal. 'It is thought by those who know me best (viz. myself)', he wrote, 'that I shall die. Nor do I greatly want to live.'[64]

Two months later, Rupert told James that he had decided 'on

April xth' to buy a revolver, but had found that in England it was not easy to get one.[65] In London he would not have had any problem, so perhaps it was in Brockenhurst that he made his vain search, after putting James on the London train on Tuesday the 9th. He was all alone, and had no idea of where he might go next. He had asked Bryn to come and look after him, but she was off climbing in Wales with the Hubbacks and Hugh Popham. What better way to die, after all, than to shoot himself in some glade where he had walked on a spring morning with Noel, in the days of his innocence three years before?

Lacking the necessary weapon, however, he had to go on living for a while. The next morning, a letter came from Bryn and he went off to Brockenhurst again, waiting several hours for her train. On arrival, she found that Rupert had made no explanation to Mrs Primmer about a single young lady coming to join him. But no objections were made, so they had four days in the forest together. On the rebound from killing himself – on the rebound from everything that had happened in the past year – Rupert now fell in love with Bryn. 'For three whole months,' he told her later, 'I'd been infinitely wretched and ill, wretcheder than I'd thought possible. And then for a few days it all dropped completely away, and – oh! how lovely Bank was! – I suppose I should *never* be able to make you see what beauty is to me, – physical beauty – , just even the *seeing* it, in spite of all the hungers that come.'[66]

Bryn threw Rupert into a rapture by showing up in the nick of time, and by giving him kindly affection. It is unlikely that this included anything more than a sisterly kiss or a few melting looks. Rupert wanted to make love to *her*, certainly; but he was too shy to make his feelings or desires clear – and Bryn surely would not have yielded to them anyway. She cared for Rupert, and felt responsible for him when she was with him; but she was thinking more and more about marriage, and Rupert was obviously too shattered to make a proper husband for anyone.

Why had they never made a couple in better days? More glamorous than Ka, more accessible than Noel, Bryn would seem to be a perfect match for Rupert. At the beginning, they were perhaps too alike to make a pair: too sought-after for their looks, too backward in finding their own path in life. And Bryn had no academic pretensions – so that Rupert compulsively sneered, behind her back, at her lack of brains. When he fell in love with Noel, Bryn may have been mildly jealous; but she and Noel were basically a close and loyal pair, and Bryn never wanted to cut her sisters out.[67] Rupert, however, saw Bryn as a last-minute saviour from his troubles, and he was clearly not restrained by the consideration that his honour was already engaged – and over-engaged – to Ka and Noel.

Rupert and Bryn left the forest together on Sunday the 14th for London, where they had tea with Virginia Stephen at Brunswick Square. She reported to Ka that Rupert was 'slightly Byronic' (deadly modifier!) and that Bryn 'has a glass eye – one can imagine her wiping it bright in the morning with a duster.'[68] The eye was not literally glass, of course, but the image catches Bryn's special mixture of glamour and insensitivity. After tea, Rupert and Bryn went down to Limpsfield to spend a few more days together. Since Noel was there too, his penchant for playing a double game around the dinner table must have been satisfied to the full.

On Thursday, his last day there, Rupert got a letter from Ka saying that she no longer wanted to go to Germany with him. His letters had become fewer and more distant, he was spending all his time with the Oliviers, and there was no indication that his moods had settled down. Unfortunately, Ka's refusal made them all the worse:

> I wonder why you want me to kill you now rather than later. Isn't it rather insolent of you, when I've rather resolutely gone away to get well *for* Germany, to make the beginnings of my success an excuse for trying to shirk Germany? . . .
> 'Not the right and only thing' 'not absolutely free' . . . 'it may bring the most awful misery' are your funny little reservations and irrelevancies. . . .
> My dear, you don't seem to recognize where we are. I suppose it's because you have had no pain worth calling pain. You twixt sentimentality and weakness – *I* don't know – played with mud. It raised a storm, that – you were startled – in the end tossed *you* a bit. At that you shrink in 'quietness' and 'peace', hastily, and demand a four month's respite. Things may have blown over by then
> Oh Child, it won't do. You *must* realise that we're *en route*. You can't back out because you're tired or a little bruised.[69]

At Easter 1909 Margery and Noel Olivier, with Dorothy Osmaston and Evelyn Radford, went for a reading party to Bank, in the New Forest. Rupert Brooke and Dudley Ward came to visit them. From left: Rupert, Evelyn, Margery, Dudley, Noel. The photograph of Rupert with Brynhild (left) was probably taken at the same time.

At play on the Cam during May Week, June 1911. Rupert (seated, in striped blazer) *has Dudley Ward on his right; on his left, Margery Olivier, Dolly Rose, Brynhild Olivier, Edw Pye.*

At work at the Fabian Summer School, Llanbedr, 1908. From left: James Strachey; Margery Olivier looking across the room; below her Ben Keeling (killed at the Somme); Rupert; Arthur Colegate; Rivers Blanco White, reading book; Amber Reeves, his future wife; at right, Clifford Sharp, first editor of the New Statesman, *who married Rosamund Bland in 1909.*

autumn 1909 Rupert was emotionally involved with two people at once – not an unusual
uation for him. One was Noel Olivier, the elusive object of his ideal love; in a poem, he
agined her chastely asleep, 'One white hand on the white/Unrumpled sheet.' The other was
ormer schoolmate, Denham Russell-Smith (here aged about sixteen). Rupert found him
istful, immoral, affectionate, and delightful.'

hel Pye, a friend of the Oliviers from Limpsfield, painted the Neo-pagan camp at Beaulieu
ver in 1910. A.E. Popham described the work (or a near copy of it) to Brynhild Olivier, his
ture wife: 'On the extreme left the boat comes to her muddy moorings and I am seen
shipping the rudder, then Harold [Hobson] is seen grumbling on his way to fetch wood,
en the big tent and Ka and you cooking then Dudley [Ward] and the Financial Times and
upert and all.'

Brynhild Olivier was usually the manager of the Neo-pagan camps. She and Justin Brooke share kitchen duty at Clifford Bridge, Dartmoor, in 1911.

Camp at Clifford Bridge. From left: Noel Olivier; Maitland Radford, doctor and friend of D.H. Lawrence; Virginia Woolf, in Neo-pagan-style headscarf; Rupert.

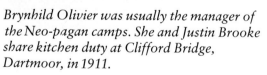

Noel Olivier with gypsy scarf in front of a borrowed Bedales tent, Beaulieu River, 191

Rupert contemplates the ground, Clifford Bridge. Lytton Strachey, who preferred his comfortable lodgings at Manaton to sleepi by the river, pointed out to Rupert that the ground was 'rather an awkward shape for sitting on.'

Bathers, *a woodcut by Gwen Raverat, 1920.*

Noel in pigtails (left), *probably at a millpond near Rothiemurchus, September 1913. The photographer may have been Lytton Strachey, who found Noel 'incredibly firm of flesh, agreeably bouncing and cheerful'.*

Frances Cornford (below) *in Neo-pagan robe and attitude, Cley-next-the-Sea, Norfolk, a few days after the declaration of war, 1914.*

Jacques Raverat, Ka Cox, Gwen Raverat, Frances Cornford in a Norfolk barn, probably October 1912.

Jacques in the country, around 1913.

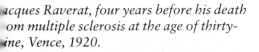

Henry Lamb around 1908, in his Augustus John period. An artist, and rival to Rupert for Ka Cox's affections in 1912, he had 'evil cat's eyes' – and a goatish disposition.

Ka Cox and Will Arnold-Forster, whom she married in 1917.

Jacques Raverat, four years before his death from multiple sclerosis at the age of thirty-nine, Vence, 1920.

Brynhild Olivier in the early years of her marriage.

The photographer Sherrill Schell made Rupert's image into one of the first modern icons of beauty, endlessly reproduced for popular worship. This photograph, taken when he was twenty-five, suggests the man Rupert might have become if he had survived his ordeal of youth – the Rupert expected by Virginia Woolf to become Prime Minister.

Noel Olivier as a young doctor, perhaps in the grey suit she wore for her wedding, December 1920. After Rupert Brooke's death she told James Strachey that there w now no chance that she would marry for love. Virginia Woolf was fascinated by Noel's eyes: 'strange eyes in which a drop seems to have been spilt – a pale blue drop with a large deep centre – romantic eyes, that seem to behold still Rupert bathing in the river at Christow: eyes pure and wide, and profound it seems. Or is there nothing behind them?'

The most Rupert would concede was that they might have a
week or two of celibacy when they first met in Berlin. Before they
could thrash it out, a Hardyesque chain of errors intervened: one
of Rupert's letters arrived at Woking after Ka had left for
London, another was confiscated by her sister Hester. When
Rupert came to London on Thursday evening, ready to confront
her, he found no message at his club, while Ka thought he was
cutting her because of her misgivings about Germany. On Friday
she spotted him on a passing bus and they met later in Trafalgar
Square, where Ka 'collapsed and had to lean behind a lion,
against Lord Nelson's pediment, till the crying was over. I think
she thought I'd suddenly decided not to bother about her at all:
and it brought her round with a jerk.'[70] She had been bullied,
against her better judgement, into going on a trip that she feared
would end disastrously for her – which it did.

While Rupert was pressing Ka to go to Germany, the Oliviers
and James were pressing *him* to stay at home. Ignorant of the real
reason, they could not understand why he was setting off for an
indefinite stay in the Prussian capital. Noel told James that she
and her sisters felt a racial distrust of Germany; they feared to
meet a fat and loud-voiced Rupert when he came back.[71] They
succeeded in getting him to miss the train on Friday and go to
Harry Lauder instead. Bryn, who had left the party, weighed in
with a 'lovely hurried note in pencil, saying I must stop in
England, on principle, because it was my Duty as an English
Poet'. After such an appeal, what could Rupert do but propose to
her?

> I, at 1.30 in the morning, and very drunk, wrote a *very* long
> letter, which said 'My dearest, your letter would – if aught
> could – have saved me from making a hole in the water. *Not*,
> heart, because of the *general* grounds for living you
> advance, but (ah God), because your lips (I'm trembling) are
> like a rosebud, and they curve distractingly. I love you so . . .'
> Oh, I was young and mad.[72]

This was how Rupert described the letter to James; but in fact the
letter he wrote was nothing like a proposal. 'Your letter was
incredibly nice to get,' he actually replied to Bryn. 'If anything
could have turned me North instead of South East, it would. But
I'm going. It's the will of God.' He was drunk enough to get the

bearings of Limpsfield and Berlin reversed, and to end with
endearments – though not so fulsome as the ones he invented for
James:

> Your letter (by the way, you *must* not address me as 'R.': it's
> disgusting) was full of Brynnisms – I suppose you wouldn't
> notice it. I wept over it a little, quietly, in one of these black,
> shiny armchairs, this afternoon. I kiss you for it.
>
> Rupert
>
> I'm glad you're so beautiful.[73]

It is small wonder that Rupert's goodbye to Ka the next day,
Saturday 20 April, was 'shy and hurried'.[74] Ka's dealings with
him over the past fortnight had brought her to the end of her
tether, and she went straight to Asheham afterwards for a rest
in the country with Virginia. There she found another guest,
Leonard Woolf. He had proposed to Virginia early in January,
and had been told that she would have to know him better before
giving him an answer. Now they were coming to the point, and it
says much for Ka's nature that Virginia welcomed her company
while making the most important decision of her life. On
Thursday the 25th, Leonard sent in his resignation from the
Colonial Service. Six days later, Virginia sent Leonard a cautious
but encouraging statement of her feelings, and by the end of May
they were engaged.[75] Ka had thus seen two of her friends
working out their future together with steadiness and mutual
respect, despite a problematic sexual relation and Virginia's
nervous instability. It would be hard for Ka not to take this as a
cue. Could she not, like Leonard, bring Rupert to grasp his
destiny, through her powers of understanding and devotion?
Both love and conscience now proposed to her that this would be
her task in Berlin.

IX

The Funeral of Youth

Syphilis of the Soul

For two weeks Rupert waited for Ka at a *pension* in Berlin. Each
day he went out to explore the countryside, looking for a
pleasant village where he and Ka could lodge as man and wife.
Around 8 May she arrived, livelier and happier than Rupert
expected, and no longer infatuated with Henry Lamb. What she
had wanted was to live with Henry as his mistress; what *he*
wanted was to take her to bed occasionally, and borrow the odd
pound as needed. Rupert was still convinced, though, that Henry
would get his hands on Ka again if she tried to live on her own in
London. Nor was he as pleased as he should have been to hear
that she had really been in love with *him* the whole time. He had
insisted on this second stay in Germany because he hoped to cure
his jealousy of Ka by getting complete sexual possession of her.
But once he had removed her from her dangerous acquaintances,
she lay heavy on his hands, for he was too conscious of the other
hands she had passed through. He didn't really like or trust Ka
any more, he told Dudley. 'Noel is the finest thing I've ever seen in
the world; and Ka – isn't.'[1]

Rupert and Ka set off for Neu Strelitz on 20 May, already
aware of how badly their affair had gone wrong. At the *pension*
in Berlin they had not been able to stay together, but in the
country they would present themselves as 'Herr und Frau
Brooke'. From Neu Strelitz they moved to Feldberg, on a lake
where they could rent a boat, then briefly to Müritz, a seaside
resort near Rostock. The trip lasted about two weeks and was cut

short when Ka learned that her sister Margaret's engagement had been broken. Ka hurried back to England to console her, while Rupert returned to Berlin.

In July, when he had returned to Grantchester for a few weeks, Rupert summed up the Berlin trip in a bitter little poem called 'Travel':

'Twas when I was in Neu Strelitz
I broke my heart in little bits.
So while I sat in the Müritz train
I glued the bits together again.
But when I got to Amerhold,
I felt the glue would never hold.
And now that I'm home to Barton Hill,
I know once broken is broken still.[2]

The 'second honeymoon' of Neu Strelitz had turned into another fiasco. Rupert had fantasised hotly for three months about the sexual raptures they were going to enjoy, but when it came to the point he was either impotent or indifferent. Both he and Ka were ill, and the weather was gloomy. But the basic trouble was that he felt emotionally dead. Now that Ka had renounced Henry, and cared only for Rupert, he simply could not respond to her. When he was jealous of her, he seethed with lust, anger and self-contempt; once she was secure, the 'duty' of loving her made *all* his passions suddenly drain away.

To put the icing on the cake, Rupert finally got a reply to his parting letter to Bryn, after forty days. It wasn't 'a' letter, he told James, it was 'the' letter, an absolute smack in the face:

> Refused – oh, Lord. There are some people (including all women) one should never propose to by letter. . . .
> 'Dear Rupert,' it begins. So *that's* something. 'R' is dropped. The words are well-formed. The letters go stiffly up and down. Not much give and take about *her*, a graphologist would murmur. . . . The whole page gives the impression of a thoroughly superior housemaid.
> I'd, of course, in the lonely evenings – oh, you know how one *does* it – been wistfully murmuring 'Banque' to myself. A hundred times *Highland Waters* sounded vaguely from beyond the balcony. A hundred times great beeches

shadowily obscured the gaunt yellow stove. A hundred times I felt – oh, but that, I remember, is a secret.

But she – oh, it had all passed from her, like water from a duck's back, or facts from a philosopher. Bank was past, was nothing. . . . 'I must say that Berlin, just now, seems like a fussy, exhausting irrelevance.' – But earlier than that she's – oh, so painstakingly, so deliberately, – drawn, with precision, the lines, all lines. Did I ever tell you women were vague, sloppy? Not at all, James: not at all. Clear as Euclid. She sizes up and dismisses my letter to her. The emotional one. 'All things considered, disingenuous was, I thought, the word for it.' So that's at an end. . . .

Oh, there are pieces of playfulness in it, which I've not quoted. Oh James: I think that Life's *just* too beastly to bear. Too utterly foul.

But it's the irresistible, false, fondness of the whole that pins me shrieking down.[3]

Ever since their first flirtation at Andermatt in 1907 Bryn had dealt with Rupert as neatly and firmly as she had the rest of her impetuous suitors. Her watchword in all these affairs was simple: to preserve her self-control. At Bank, she had told Rupert how she had fallen helplessly in love when she was nineteen. Whenever she saw the man the room swam and she almost fainted with passion. Her response was to hide herself away until she had 'cauterised' her love; for nothing was worth the humiliation of being at someone else's mercy.[4] Now that she was twenty-five, years of living by rule had given her a glossy and almost impenetrable shell. Rupert's histrionics had small chance of cracking it; and no chance at all when in fact he hadn't proposed to Bryn, only let slip a few drunken hints about his feelings for her.

On 30 May 1912, the day after getting Bryn's letter, Rupert left for Müritz with Ka and tried once again to build a new life on the foundation of her love and steadfastness. It cannot have worked for more than a few days. When Ka had to go back and comfort her sister, she and Rupert agreed to think things over separately and decide their future in a couple of months. But the relationship was doomed, for his sexual interest in her was over.

If Ka conceived while at Munich she would have been three months pregnant by now. When she went back to England from Berlin the immediate crisis was apparently over, which suggests that she miscarried either while Rupert was in Berlin by himself, or soon after she arrived in Germany. Perhaps it happened at Neu Strelitz, where she was ill with some unexplained ailment. That she had an abortion in April or May is possible; but there is no evidence, and a woman of her background would not have found it easy to arrange one.[5] Whatever happened, it seems clear that Rupert was 'off the hook' by the beginning of June.

Once Ka had gone, Rupert was left alone in Berlin to contemplate the wreckage of his life. He had wooed three women and won none; he had failed to get his fellowship; he had nowhere to go and nothing to do. Sex had literally driven him mad; he could neither deal with his own desires, nor tolerate other people's. He told Hugh Popham, who had got a job in the British Museum, that his ambition was to sneak in and spend the night embracing a female mummy; he had heard that most had died of syphilis, but hoped to find a clean one.[6] A schoolboy joke, perhaps; but his reaction to Virginia's engagement to Leonard Woolf cannot have amused anyone but himself:

> I *thought* the little man'ld get her. Directly he began saying he was the only man who'd had a woman she knew, and telling tales about prostitutes – oh, you should have seen the lovelight dance and dawn in her eyes! *That* gets 'em. To him that hath shall be given: from him that hath not shall be taken away even that which he hath. Even that which he *hath*, James: one by one. Two, two for the lily-white balls: clothed all in hair, oh![7]

Rupert had always had a tendency to sexual hysteria, but loving Noel, so clear and firm by nature, had helped to keep it in check. When Ka came over to Berlin, she told Rupert that over the past few months James Strachey had fallen in love with Noel. For Rupert, this was the last straw. He did not fear that James would have much success: he was too neurasthenic, Rupert felt, and too obviously homosexual. But Noel was no longer a cloistered schoolgirl. She was following Ka into Bloomsbury, and wasn't nature bound to take its course?

> it's on the whole better to be in love with her than with most women; because she is much harder and rather honester

than they. She's a very ordinary person underneath the pink—brown mist, you know. And she's just a female: so she may let you down any moment. As she's unusually unemotional and stony, and as she's backed up by her adamantine family with that loony-man at the head, she *may* be fairly safe. ... But I expect, really, she won't fall in love with anybody for at least two years. After that there'll come a day when she'll suddenly feel a sort of collapse and sliding in her womb, and incomprehensible longings. It's when the ova suddenly begin popping out like peas. Then she'll just be ripe for anybody. But not for you, dear boy. Some rather small and very shiny man, probably syphilitic, and certainly a Jew. She'll crawl up to him, will Noel, – to Albert Rothenstein, or Mr Foss (if she has *very* good taste), or Mr Picciotto, or (if he's joined us) Mr Applegate – and ask him to have her. And no doubt he will. I need hardly ask you to visualise it.[8]

Looking across to London from Berlin, Rupert saw a society in which every fence was down. Lytton Strachey, the confirmed homosexual, had ingratiated himself with Henry Lamb by playing the pandar between him and Ka. Rupert's younger brother, Alfred, had welcomed the overtures from the homosexual milieu that Rupert himself had rejected. Virginia, with whom Rupert had bathed naked at Grantchester, was now giving herself to a Jew. And James, along with other homosexual friends of Rupert's, was finding that he could love women as well as men. Rupert could enjoy the company of 'half-men' – he was, after all, half one himself – but he wanted them to stay in their place, which was among their own kind.[9] He was nothing so simple as a sexually repressed puritan. Rather, his desires were so various and contradictory that they had to be rigidly segregated. He hated and feared Bloomsbury because it took a positive relish in bringing together impulses that Rupert believed should never be allowed to meet. All of this lay behind his outburst to Jacques Raverat when Noel went to Virginia's for a weekend: 'I suppose she's got too much sense – and she's got you and other wise people – to get spoilt in any way by the subtle degradation of the collective atmosphere of the people in those regions – people I find pleasant and remarkable as individuals.'[10]

Much of Rupert's turmoil also came from guilt over his compulsive viciousness towards Noel. He had given her, he

admitted, 'evil and wrong in return for fineness . . . I had been so
wicked towards Noel; and that filled me with self-hatred and
excess of feeling seeking some outlet.'[11] But, if he felt such
remorse, why did he go on libelling her? Because she was a
woman and therefore, he believed, bound to be corrupted sooner
or later; whereas a man like James could be relied on, at least for
understanding and loyalty. They had even shared a kind of love,
free from the corruption of sex (or so Rupert saw it), and wasn't a
'brother' worth more than a mere 'penisholder'? James's infatuation with Rupert had ripened into nearly six years of faithful
service and admiration. Some women, like Ka and Bryn, had let
Rupert down; the rest of them would eventually, simply by virtue
of being female.[12] So Rupert still wanted to count James as an
ally. He *did* advise him to give up pursuing 'holes' and go back to
balls (so long as they weren't Rupert's), though he knew James
was probably too hopelessly romantic to do so.[13] For all that, a
break would not be long in coming.

What was Rupert to do now? He thought of becoming a
journalist, like Dudley Ward, or just wandering on to Denmark
or Sweden. But England still held unfinished business. Ka had to
be given an answer in August; perhaps Noel or Bryn might yet
have an answer for him. He wrote to tell Bryn that he felt as if he
had just woken up with a headache after being asleep for six
months, and hinted even more strongly that it was time for them
to have a real affair. Though he tried to make her feel ashamed of
her motto, which was 'hold on tight to nurse', he was playing a
cautious hand himself. He told her nothing about what he was up
to with Ka, or what commitments he had made to Noel. Bryn's
calling him 'disingenuous' had stuck in his throat, but all it meant
was that she knew how many secrets, and how much calculation,
lay behind his façade of boyish impulsiveness. To get through to
her he would have had to drop his mask, and that was the one
thing he feared to do. He had opened his heart more to Ka than
anyone, and she was already paying the price for knowing too
much about him.

   The next step was finally settled by a fit of homesickness for the
land, if not the people, of England. He went down to Cologne to
meet James at a giant exhibition of modern painting and while

there he read *The Four Men*, a rhapsody in the Merrie Englande
vein about Hilaire Belloc's beloved Sussex:

He does not die that can bequeath
Some influence to the land he knows,
Or dares, persistent, interwreath
Love permanent with the wild hedgerows. . . .

It was all very Neo-pagan, complete with Belloc's animus against
the late-coming Jews. The theme stuck in Rupert's mind, and two
years later was reshaped into his most famous sonnet. But Sussex
was never his county. When he went wandering outside Berlin,
looking for a place where he could stay with Ka, it had only made
him nostalgic for the country round Grantchester, which he had
not seen for almost five months. In town he often whiled away
the time at the Cafe des Westens, writing letters or scribbling in
his notebook. The Cafe was full of long-haired intellectuals,
artists and their models, socialists and Natur-menschen (the
German equivalent of Simple-Lifers) in sandals. A dumpy young
woman in a black satin sack once walked through the Cafe,
smelling a scarlet tulip; 'They do the right things,' commented
Dudley Ward, 'but somehow it's the wrong people who do
them.'[14] In this festival of Bohemia, Rupert scribbled a poem that
rejected everything he saw around him. He first called it 'Home',
then 'The Sentimental Exile', and finally 'The Old Vicarage,
Grantchester'.

Mindful of what Bryn called his Duty as an English Poet,
Rupert scorned the orderly German landscape in favour of
England's 'unofficial rose' – and its virtuous rustics. He only
wished that his own morals had been as pure:

In Grantchester their skins are white;
They bathe by day, they bathe by night;
The women there do all they ought;
The men observe the Rules of Thought.
They love the Good; they worship Truth;
They laugh uproariously in youth;
(And when they get to feeling old,
They up and shoot themselves, I'm told).

It was not from feeling old that Rupert had wanted to shoot himself, but because *his* women had *not* been doing what they ought. Although the last lines of the poem may be read today as mere 'Camp', for him they were a strangled plea that the river and meadows might swallow his – and Ka's – sexual guilt:

And laughs the immortal river still
Under the mill, under the mill?
Say, is there Beauty yet to find?
And Certainty? and Quiet kind?
Deep meadows yet, for to forget
The lies, and truths, and pain? . . . Oh! yet
Stands the Church clock at ten to three?
And is there honey still for tea?

Modernist Berlin was the contrary that generated this classic example of fetishising the English past; this elegy, also, for Neo-paganism. For it was never plausible that Rupert, or any other disillusioned young Englishman, might recover his innocence by returning to the great good place where the clock had stopped. In fact, he had become too restless to be able to live at Grantchester for any length of time again. It was lost to him, honey and all, long before the Great War put it out of everyone's reach, embalmed in the last Edwardian summers.

Nonetheless, it was to Grantchester that Rupert now decided to go: the place where he had been just before everything went wrong. 'I haven't bathed since November,' he joked. 'There's a lot to wash off.' Perhaps he could find a herb at the bottom of Byron's Pool that could heal his 'syphilis of the soul'.[15] He wanted desperately to recover his innocence – and to punish those who had taken it from him. On Tuesday 25 June he boarded the ferry, with James, from the Hook of Holland.

Rupert arrived back in England just in time for the Society's annual dinner in London, on 26 June. He got drunk and maudlin with affection for his 'brothers' – except for Lytton, who sat across from him at table – and alarmed E. M. Forster by weeping when he spoke to Bryn on the telephone. The Society, for its part, informally decided to take Rupert under its wing for the summer. He stayed with Eddie Marsh in London, then went to a weekend house-party at Gerald Shove's; later there would be a visit to Roger Fry and a holiday with Maynard Keynes. Ka, meanwhile, was staying quietly with her sister Margaret near Newhaven, awaiting Rupert's decision.

At Gerald's house, on the Thames near Goring, the group of Apostles was carefully chosen to avoid upsetting Rupert. Harry Norton, Goldie Dickinson, Eddie Marsh and J. T. Sheppard were all friends of Lytton, but other than that they had no connection with the storms of the last six months. The atmosphere was not androgynous, as in Bloomsbury, but exclusively homosexual – which Rupert clearly felt more comfortable with. He was in better spirits by the time he met Bryn in London for lunch at Gustave's, then went down for a few days to Limpsfield. Noel was there with Sir Sydney, who had been much impressed by Bryn's reading of 'The Old Vicarage, Grantchester' over the Sunday breakfast table. But Noel and Bryn gave Rupert sympathy only in carefully measured doses. Noel told James that Rupert was at a loose end because he couldn't go on pretending to be ill.[16] He could 'crawl in' for what he craved, but after a few days he knew he would have to crawl out again.

He wandered on to the Old Vicarage, the place of healing that he had dreamed about at the Cafe des Westens. But when he got there it was not term-time, and Rupert still had a nervous horror of being left alone. Few of his friends were on call: the Raverats had gone to France, Ka was spending her days weeping in the country, Bunny Garnett was off to Munich to study botany and meet a young protégé of his father's, D. H. Lawrence.[17] That left only Frances Cornford to rely on, and Rupert always found it depressing to be with married friends after a few days.

Frances was overburdened with Neo-pagan casualties. As she comforted Rupert in person, she also had to cope with pathetic letters from Ka. Justin Brooke was on hand too, suffering from nervous exhaustion and colitis. Though he was still nominally in articles he could not actually bring himself to do anything. Rupert, who was two years younger, felt that Justin had simply failed to grow up. Nonetheless he spilled out to him the story of his affair with Ka – and was given a lecture on how badly he had behaved. After that he tried to avoid seeing Justin at the Cornfords. 'But I saw the "Rupert is so frighteningly sensitive" look coming into F's eyes,' he told Ka, 'and she started pawing me. So I gave in, lest worse should happen. I don't mind, if he doesn't. Also I don't much mind him at Maynard's. It'll at least brighten up that rather dreary party. – unless the females get nervy about him again.'[18]

On the evening of 10 July, a few days after arriving at Grantchester, Rupert went to visit E. A. Benians at St John's College and learnt that Denham Russell-Smith had died at the age of twenty-three. He wrote at once his long, confessional letter to James, about his affair with Denham three years before.[19] There was a hidden motive, one suspects, in his regaling James with such a vivid account of how he had seduced Denham. He wanted to remind James of how firmly homosexual his life had been, and of how much he had been in love with Rupert. For James, he knew, was now shuttling between London and Limpsfield to pay court to Noel. He was thinking of going to Canada (with Justin), Rupert told James; and then what would happen to Noel?

> Noel stays in London, among all you people: a virgin of $19\frac{1}{2}$ with all the bright little ideas about the identity of the sexes that we've all had and that you have. . . . You know, with friends like you and your Bloomsbury acquaintances, she'll go through the same process as Ka. With Virginia buttering her up in order to get her for Adrian, with you, with all the rest, she'll soon be as independent as any man – like Ka. Then any dirty little man could get hold of her – not you, my little friend, for she knows you too well, – but anybody she doesn't know. . . .
>
> This is an instance, chosen because though you don't love Noel, it may be true that you want to bugger her: so it may appeal to you.[20]

The next day he heard that Henry Lamb had quarrelled with Ottoline, and had met Ka. Rupert claimed to be past caring that she was 'crawling in among those people again', but he treated Ka to a tirade about Ottoline and Lamb wallowing in slime together. Another outburst was triggered by the news that Leonard Woolf now knew about the Lulworth débâcle. 'They're a nice set, your friends,' Rupert fumed, '(and mine – or once mine.) How did it come? Did the noble Lytton find it too good a story to resist? Or is it James? I suppose the Jew'll have to tell his wife. And she could never resist a good joke. So it's no good trying to do anything –'[21]

If Bloomsbury was so corrupt, why was Rupert still hanging around them for news and company? Jacques, for one, thought it was high time that both Rupert and Ka made a clean break. They should live in the country, he told them, away from homosexuals and real and pseudo-Jews (by which he meant the Stracheys). He hated Jews, Jacques went on, because they crucified Christ daily.[22] Given that the only Jew in the Bloomsbury group was Leonard Woolf, whom Jacques had never met, his outbursts had only the most slender connection with reality – which did not prevent Rupert from taking them seriously. It was a streak of rottenness within Neo-paganism, even if Jacques, Gwen and Rupert were the only ones in the group who professed the anti-semitic creed.[23]

The Crown at Everleigh

In the spring of 1912, Maynard Keynes had taken a fancy to ambling around the Cambridge countryside on the back of a horse. He liked it so well that he decided to organise a riding party in the summer. As a bachelor fellow of King's he was now prosperous enough to take over a small country hotel for several weeks, and invite his friends to stay for a week or two at a time. It would be more luxurious than the previous year's camp at Clifford Bridge, and this time Keynes would be host rather than guest. With Rupert in eclipse, Keynes could take over as the patron and master of ceremonies for young Cambridge. He would again mix Neo-pagans and Apostles at his party, but this time on his own terms rather than Rupert's.

On 18 July Bryn and Noel met Justin at Waterloo (Daphne was to follow in a few days) and went down to Pewsey in Wiltshire. They were met at the station by Maynard, resplendent in a new riding outfit and boutonnière, and driven five miles across Salisbury Plain to the Crown Hotel at Everleigh. It was a big white foursquare house with a walled garden and croquet lawn, looking directly out to the Plain. Bryn and Noel were given a whole suite of panelled rooms with several large four-poster beds. During the day there were four horses to ride; in the evenings they all read *Emma* aloud.

When the Oliviers and Justin arrived, the other guests were two Apostles – Gerald Shove and Gordon Luce – and Frankie Birrell. It was a cosy little male coterie, with the lively and 'campy' Birrell setting the pace. After Rupert turned up on Wednesday the 24th, Maynard complained to Duncan Grant that he enjoyed his old friends better than his new ones:

> I don't much care for the atmosphere these women breed and haven't liked this party nearly so much as my last week's. Noel is very nice and Daphne very innocent. But Bryn is too stupid – and I begin to take an active dislike to her. Out of the window I see Rupert making love to her – throwing a tiny [illegible] in her face, taking her hand, sitting at her feet, gazing at her eyes. Oh these womanisers. How on earth and what for can he do it.[24]

Rupert was not just flirting with Bryn: he was quarrelling with her too. Earlier in the month, he had invited her to go boating for a week in August. He still had tender memories of their cruise on the Broads three years before, with Dr Rogers as chaperone. Why not do it again on the Ouse, Rupert proposed – with Goldie Dickinson, who was keen to go, or perhaps just the two of them? The day she left for Everleigh, Bryn agreed to go, for the week of 4 August. But she preferred Beaulieu River, where they had camped in 1910, to East Anglia. Rupert should bring Dickinson, and Bryn would meet them there, with a companion who knew how to sail a boat.

Since Rupert had spent many days sailing on the lake at Feldberg, he must have been miffed by Bryn's news that she was bringing an expert with her. At Everleigh he learned that the other sailor would be Hugh Popham. Hugh had turned up at Grantchester the week before, woebegone over a frustrating love affair with Gerald Shove's mother, of all people.[25] Having quietly scuttled Dickinson's participation, Rupert was now less than delighted to find that his romantic cruise with Bryn was going to be 'chaperoned' by Hugh. With some other part of his mind, he was upset by Bryn's plan to leave Everleigh on Monday and walk across country to Poole Harbour – a jaunt of some sixty miles, which she expected to cover in five days. He thought it quite unseemly for a young woman to wander around unaccompanied like that.

Bryn spent the whole day arguing with Rupert about these arrangements. Exhausted, she finally told him that she and Hugh were going to be married:

> I found it almost necessary to give him some explanation of *you* and bless me if I didn't make a comprehensive statement about my feelings and intentions such as would have amazed you to hear! So there's another peg to this queer web one has drawn over oneself. Don't mind my putting it like that – it seems a little true sometimes – tho' its of course only one aspect and an unimportant one. ... I'm sorry about Rupert, but he knows his own bloody character best, I suppose.[26]

Bryn had turned down Hugh's proposal in October 1910, and then pointedly avoided him for a year or more. But somewhere around her twenty-fifth birthday – 20 May 1912 – she took stock of her life and decided that marriage was the sensible thing for her to do. Despite her beauty, or even because of it, she had never formed any deep romantic attachment. She could easily have married into society or into the 'intellectual aristocracy', but she was not comfortable in either realm. Within the Neo-pagan circle, only Rupert and Justin Brooke were possible matches for her; though she was fond of both of them, in 1912 neither of them was fit to make a husband. Rupert was tapering off from a nervous breakdown, he had only £150 a year to rely on, and no fixed home. Justin was potentially rich, but he was at least as nervous as Rupert, and even more uncertain about his career.

Hugh, on the other hand, had just established himself in London with a flat and a job in the Prints Department of the British Museum. He had not shone intellectually at King's, but he was nice-looking, outdoorsy and sensitive – a good second-string Neo-pagan. Most people liked him, though he was already known for being painfully tongue-tied. When he first fell in love with Bryn he was still an undergraduate, two years younger than her and far less mature. By the time he renewed his suit he was more sure of himself, while Bryn had become more vulnerable and uncertain. Looking after Rupert made for a nerve-racking spring. Sir Sydney was going back to Jamaica, and Bryn had more or less abandoned her training as a jeweller. Perhaps she was simply tired of all the excitable young men of the past five years, and thought that Hugh's devotion would ballast her life. Whatever her reasons, she told him, early in July, that she was in love with him. Hugh needed no further invitation:

> I think it is almost impossibly much to ask you to marry me. It means so much more to you, to lose and somehow you seem a being God never intended to marry. But if you love me as you do, you must. There is no intermediate stage, which is satisfactory or convenient, do you think? So do. I don't know at all what you feel about having children and sexual matters generally: one must come to some conclusion on the subject. Do tell me. I don't think you are a person of very strong passions: but it is rather futile to try and separate one's body from one's heart in this way. I don't think I am either. ... Does it sicken you of marriage looking at it coldbloodedly in this way?[27]

This had none of the throbbing sentiment that adorned Rupert's letters to Bryn. On the other hand, it was a straight question that required, and got, a straight answer. Mary Newbery believed that Hugh sensed Bryn's unhappiness, and 'made' her marry him. But no one so strong-minded could be forced into accepting a proposal, even if she did not do so joyfully or wholeheartedly. Hugh did not trail any clouds of promised glory. A modest flat, a modest job and a conventional marriage set the bounds of his ambition. Still, Bryn was dissatisfied with her single life; she was halfway through her twenties, and she wanted children. Hugh must have impressed her as more serious and potentially a better father than any of her other suitors. And so Helen was won.

Rupert was deeply upset by Bryn's news. He flatly refused to come boating at all; in fact, he feared he was again going mad. When Bryn left on Sunday he refused to say goodbye, and the boating trip fell through because she and Hugh couldn't find anyone to chaperone *them*. Instead, they went climbing in North Wales with Oscar Eckhardt. On Monday Rupert had recovered enough to write and ask Bryn if they could go away together one more time, before everything 'closed down' for her.[28] They would have to act quickly, since the marriage date had been set only two months ahead. Adding to Rupert's panic, Noel went straight from Everleigh to climb in Switzerland for several weeks with Daphne and Ka's cousin Ursula Cox. Given the way Rupert had been acting, Noel probably thought that the best way to deal with him was from the other side of the Channel. He was left to fill up the days disconsolately by playing poker with Maynard and Geoffrey Keynes. Elisabeth van Rysselberghe was going to be in England again in a couple of months, and Rupert told her he wanted to see her. 'If I can't give you the love you want,' he wrote, 'I can give you what love and sympathy and pity and everything else I have. And I have a lot. . . . I've had a lot of pain, infinite pain – I know what it's all like. . . . I'm not worth your loving, in any way.'[29]

Ka had also been invited to Everleigh, though not until after Rupert had left. While he and Bryn were having it out, Ka was staying with two aunts at the Swan Hotel, Bibury, in the Cotswolds. She had not seen Rupert for two unhappy months and she simply couldn't stop crying, she wrote pathetically to Frances. All Ka asked was for Rupert to make up his mind about their relationship, and then meet to tell her. What *she* wanted had already been settled, a fortnight after she returned to England in June:

> I love Rupert – I'm quite clear – and I'm waiting quietly now and getting as strong as I possibly can. To see if he has strength and love enough to heal himself and love me again.
> I have broken and hurt and maimed him – I see. O my dear – apart from me – it was wicked, it was awful to hurt so lovely a thing and so lovely a person. If I've destroyed love and strength in him (not for me particularly – but for everyone) there is no atonement and no help – I feel.
> I'm being very quiet – and I don't want to bother him now at all. He knows what it is and what there is to decide.[30]

The day after Bryn left Everleigh, Rupert wrote to tell Ka that he was ready to see her. On the morning of Friday 2 August he wrote asking Bryn not to drop him yet, since there were secrets that he wanted to tell her. Then Justin came by in his Opel and drove Rupert to meet Ka in the woods near Bibury. They talked for three hours while Justin waited in the car. When they returned, Ka was taken back to her aunts, while Rupert and Justin drove on to spend the night at a hotel in Witney. This time, it really was the end of the affair. 'I can't love her, you see,' Rupert told Frances. 'So now it's all at an end. And she's passed out of my power to help or comfort. I'm so sad for her, and a little terrified, and so damnably powerless.'[31] He went on to Rugby, and wrote Ka a letter that renounced his love, but not his grievance against her:

> It's no good. I *can't* marry you. You must see. If I married you, I should kill myself in three months. I may, I daresay I shall, anyway. But if I marry you, I'm certain to. . . . You keep comparing your coming to Germany then [i.e. in February], with my marrying you now; and my emotions then, with yours now. There is no comparison. You had two ways before you, a dirty one and a clean one; coming to Germany was not even deciding; it was only giving the clean one a chance. You refused to marry me. You refused to forswear filth. . . .
>
> I felt ashamed because you were better and honester than I (ashamed – and yet superior, because you are a woman.). Yet it's not my lack of strength that makes me want not to marry you. It is my strength. . . . When I found that I wasn't too dead for a sort of love, – but that it wasn't for you, that you *had* killed my love for you too dead, – it seemed to me useless to prolong waiting any longer.[32]

To break with Ka cleanly would not have been in character for Rupert. He remained obsessed with the sexual wound that she had inflicted on him, and went on trying to punish her for it. But the hope of marriage was gone, the child was gone and, except for one accidental collision, he would not see her again for two years.

Cleaning House

'I was once in love with 3 people,' Rupert said later, about the events of 1912, 'and that wasn't all jam.'[33] It wasn't all jam for others, either. Rupert's vacillations between Ka, Noel and Bryn broke the easy companionship that the Neo-pagans had once shared. No one had the heart to make a summer camp in 1912, nor would they ever assemble again with Rupert at their head. After five years, most of them wanted to reduce their stakes in the group. Several now believed in marriage more than in friendship; all had seen too much grief within their circle to have faith in their old dream of lives without age or care. They disagreed about politics, religion, the suffrage and many other things. Some had simply realised that they didn't like each other much. Jacques, for one, had seen it coming. 'Youth is a very deceitful thing,' he had told Frances a year before. 'It makes one think so many people so much nicer than really they are, just because of that insolent flush of hot young blood. Middle age finds them all out in all their nakedness of soul – and body.'[34]

Frances felt that the immediate need was to get all the emotional invalids on their feet – which also meant keeping them apart from one another. When Rupert came to her from his painful farewell to Ka, she told him bluntly that he should leave England for at least a year, and go far beyond reach of Ka or Noel. Picking oranges in California, or similar unthinking manual work, was the best thing for him. He was, she felt, 'all jangled and neurotic and terrified of everything. . . . If he doesn't go off and work hard (till he's so tired at night he can only just crawl to bed and sleep) I feel he'll become contemptible and drifting or lose his self-respect irrevocably.'[35] In principle Rupert agreed, though it would be nearly a year before he actually set sail. He was not going to marry Ka or Noel, but neither was he going to leave them alone; and he also had his vendetta with Bloomsbury to pursue. He was supposed to go on a restful holiday in Scotland with James, but as the time approached Rupert bombarded him with abusive letters:

> To be a Strachey is to be blind – without a sense – towards good and bad, and clean and dirty; irrelevantly clever about a few things, dangerously infantile about many; to have undescended spiritual testicles; to be a mere bugger; useless as a baby as means, and a little smirched as an end. . . . It becomes possible to see what was meant by the person who said that seeing you and any member of the Olivier family

together made them cold and sick. But then I suppose you can't understand anyone turning cold and sick to see any body with anybody else – except through jealousy, and that makes hot –; can you? It doesn't happen in buggery.[36]

Soon James was invited to Bilton Road for the *coup de grâce*. 'The explosion', he reported to Lytton, 'has had every motive assigned to it except the obvious one. Oh lord there *have* been scenes. And the dreadful thing is that he's clearly slightly cracked and has now cut himself off from everyone. It's all a regular day-out for a cynic – but unluckily I'm not one.'[37]

The 'obvious motive' was James's dogged and unrequited courtship of Noel. Although Bryn was now the main object of Rupert's sexual ambitions, his casting off of Ka filled him with remorse that he had ever faltered in his ideal love for Noel:

> I fell in love again with Noel with the frenzy of weakness and the desperate feeling that, after the impossible filth and pain, things might yet go well with me – a mad vision – if that came off. So it was bad with me when it appeared how utterly she'd fallen out of love with me. I felt I *couldn't* live. All August and half September I'd tossed about among things; but generally coming back to that plan of suicide.[38]

By this time, all Rupert's chickens were coming home to roost. 'He thought I wouldn't mind if he went off with Ka,' Noel confided to Mary Newbery, 'but I did.'[39] At Everleigh, Rupert's blatant flirting with Bryn must have opened Noel's eyes to what was up in that quarter, if she had not known already. Perhaps he *wanted* her to see, and be jealous. We can be sure, in that case, that his strategy backfired. Her immediate departure for Switzerland left Rupert standing.

Later in the summer, Noel stayed with Gwen and Jacques at Prunoy. While she was there, Rupert spilled before Jacques the accumulated sour grapes of his involvement with the Oliviers:

> [Noel] got tired of me about a year ago, and also she's extremely romantic, in the young woman's way, of conceiving love as only possible towards a person you don't know. She's rather frightened, now, I think, of going on flirting; so she wants to be rid of me, very much. She's one of these virgin–harlots of modern days; a dangerous brood. . . .

Yes, Margery is the only decent one of the family (though Bryn's been extraordinarily nice to me.)[40]

At this point, however, Bryn decided she had been nice for long enough. Rupert had told her that he was going to go to America, or shoot himself; in either case, they should meet for a last walk before she got married and never saw him again. Bryn replied that he wrote a lot of nonsense; but since they were both to be in Scotland, she agreed to meet him at Carlisle to go walking for a day or two at the end of August. 'If they object to us in inns,' Rupert joked, 'I shall say you're my aunt.'[41] At the last moment, though, Bryn stood him up. She got a mild case of flu and found she couldn't face any more emotional sessions with Rupert:

> I'm better now and think it was rather disgraceful of me – but no good could have come of my seeing him. He's evidently got to get through this – what ever *this* is, by himself. I cant help being slightly muddled by his rhetoric even after all these years and dont say the things I meant to when I'm with him, so what's the good? One comes away feeling baffled and exhausted.[42]

When Noel came back from Prunoy, in mid-September, Rupert got another dusty answer. 'She refused for hours', he told Ka, 'to consider seriously even the possibility she might love me again. It was only the sight of my agony (she's rather soft, besides stupid) that made her offer to wait a year before finally deciding against me. I've gone off on that.'[43] During her stay with the Raverats Noel probably learned more about how deeply and compromisingly Rupert had been involved with Ka. Her offer to reconsider in a year was little more than an excuse to slip quietly away. Soon Rupert dropped the pretence that he and Noel were on a trial separation. In October he told Ka he hated Noel, and by January 1913 she was marked down for the snub direct. At the Shaw/Belloc debate, he informed Ka, he 'unluckily ran into that swine Noel. However we put up our noses and cut each other, which was good fun.'[44]

On 3 October 1912 Bryn became Mrs Hugh Popham, after an engagement of two and a half months. She had got married briskly enough, but already her friends were hearing about her misgivings. The wedding itself was a little pinched: Sir Sydney and

Lady Olivier were in Jamaica, and Rupert's antics discouraged Bryn's friends from making any great celebration. Though she had wanted a church wedding she settled (at Hugh's insistence) for the registry office, with a going-away supper afterwards at the Richelieu restaurant on Oxford Street. Bunny Garnett, James Strachey, Arthur Waley and Ka were among the guests, but Rupert stayed in his tent at Rugby. Garnett recalled Bryn, in a rust-coloured tweed dress, 'glowing with beauty' as she went off with Hugh from Paddington. Later, however, she confessed that she had sat in the train and 'looked at her husband with a sinking feeling'.[45]

Rupert must have contributed to her depression by sending her an unconventional wedding present: a long letter bewailing their five years of lost opportunities. In this secretive, shy and ignorant world, he told her, he was queerer and shyer than most – and with 'more to be dishonest about'. So, in all, they had barely come within hearing distance of each other:

> Oh but come, don't even you, my dear 'sensible' unmorbid straightforward Bryn, think that everyone *is* infinitely incomprehensible and far and secret from everyone, and that approach is infinitely difficult and infinitely rare? One tells, some times, some people, a *few* things, – in a misleading sort of way. But any *Truth*! . . – – Oh, Bryn!
> One of the great difficulties, and perils, you see, in ever telling anyone any truth, is the same as in ever loving anyone, but more so. It gives them such a devilish handle over you. I mean, they can *hurt*. If I love a person and say nothing, I'm fairly safe. But if I tell them, I deliver myself bound into their hands.[46]

Rupert would not claim that he had loved only her all this time, but his joy in seeing her beauty and knowing her had been one of the good things in his life. After Bank, especially, he had wanted passionately to explore the joys of the body with her, and he knew she had the courage to carry off an affair finely. But he was sick, and too shy to ask her directly. His hopes of going away with her in August had collapsed when she told him, at Everleigh, that she was engaged. Rupert had lectured her on the importance of marriage in a way that she found 'dreadfully conventional'. At the same time, he now admitted, he had wanted to inveigle her into an affair before the wedding came and made it too late! Bryn's caution had prevented that, and here was Rupert sitting in his mother's house at Rugby, consumed with jealousy of Hugh – for possessing Bryn's fineness and beauty – and lonely envy of their shared life. But Bryn, during Rupert's lifetime at least, had made her bed and settled into it.

The same could not, unfortunately, be said of Ka. Ottoline Morrell saw her in July, and thought her 'evidently devoted to Rupert – and missing him very much after having lived with him as his wife. ... She says she feels so tied to him – and that is I believe the effect on women *much* more than on men. – I don't know if once or twice would have that effect but I think any length of time would.'[47] Ka's closest friends, the Raverats, still cared deeply for her, but they no longer respected her. They agreed with Rupert that she was, for the time being, incapable of making her own decisions. Gwen did not even want to see her at Prunoy – because of the danger that Ka might fall in love again with Jacques!

> she has such a respect, admiration, and trust and love for Jacques; she is so pushed by loneliness and misery and sex. ... I think that sort of panic of loneliness and self hatred may drive her to do anything – to give herself to anyone who says a kind word or has a cold in the head; or (above all) says in an authoritarian tone 'Come here.'
>
> Thats been really the worst pain to me in this affair: my growing feeling of Ka's untrustworthiness. I shall get to believe in her again some day – and I think Rupert's feelings are absurd and exaggerated; but she has so lied to herself (and to us and to Rupert) that I cannot trust her any longer quite as I used to.[48]

Frances felt the Raverats should have been more sympathetic to Ka, and not pressed her so hard to marry Rupert. But she agreed that Ka should be kept away. 'She's got a frightening amount of sex,' observed Frances, 'and it isn't under control. She ought never to have lived this strange modern life.'[49]

Frances's and Gwen's view of the whole affair was really close enough to Rupert's, except for the hysteria. It is unclear whether Gwen knew about Ka's losing the baby; however, she told Ka how much she longed to have babies herself, and assured her she *would* have them someday. For now, she urged Ka to consider training as a nurse or midwife:

> that sort of work might fill a little corner of the hole that is waiting for the babies. And then you know, you're a born nurse – and one who is bound always to have sick people all round you – and it's such really good and important and interesting sort of work. And it would be something at which you would be really really good, and a knowledge which could never under any possible circumstances fail to be useful. Because Ka you're the woman we shall all go to when we are sick and tired – why not make a real profession of it?[50]

There is some irony in Ka being pushed towards nursing, when her rival Noel was already studying to be a doctor. In any case, she was too shattered by her affair with Rupert to do any regular work for years to come. Though friends and family gave her some help, mainly she had to get through the aftermath of Rupert's rejection on her own resources – 'honestly and truly suffering', Frances felt, 'and bearing it with real courage and simplicity'.[51]

By the autumn of 1912 most of the Neo-pagans were embarked on separate lives. Ka was living mainly in London, and trying not to cross Rupert's path. After a honeymoon in Holland and Belgium Bryn set up house with Hugh in Regent Square – around the corner from the London School of Medicine for Women, where Noel was studying. Gwen and Jacques took their own advice and went to live in the country, at Croydon near Cambridge. Before they came back to England from Prunoy, Gwen admitted that she had no desire to take in lame ducks, as Frances always seemed willing to do:

> I don't a bit want to see anyone ever again. I feel as if I'd only just left them a minute ago, all grovelling and wallowing about like tadpoles in a pool. When you look at each one of them separately, they're very very nice, but as a whole they're incredibly wearisome. . . . I don't want to see poor turbid Rupert or sad Ka.[52]

Rupert could not face a winter at Grantchester: it was too

lonely and haunted by memories of better days. London was the only real choice for a fresh start, but he was short of cash and needed to steer clear of Bloomsbury. The easiest solution was to take up Eddie Marsh's offer of the spare room in his flat at Gray's Inn. Eddie was a fellow Apostle, he adored Rupert, and he knew lots of people who didn't know the Stracheys. His affectionate but entirely sublimated homosexuality was somehow reassuring to Rupert, as in his schoolboy friendship with St John Lucas. For the rest of Rupert's life, the Old Vicarage was his sentimental but not his actual home. His two real homes belonged to other people – his mother and Eddie – who sheltered him in exchange for first claim on his company. Both kept the Neo-pagans at a distance: the Ranee was too stern, Eddie not stern enough, with his epicene manner and snobbish devotions (Jacques was cruel but deadly in calling Eddie 'a valet to his heroes'!).

A few days after his parting interview with Noel, Rupert was installed at Gray's Inn and active in Eddie Marsh's literary schemes. On 19 September they had a business lunch at the flat with Wilfred Gibson, John Drinkwater, Harold Monro and Arundel del Re. It was the launching pad for *Georgian Poetry*, the wildly successful house organ of what Orwell skewered as the 'beer and cricket' school of English poetry. Rupert was a better poet than most of the Georgians, and less simple-minded about his enthusiasms, but they were the birds with whom he chose to flock. The literary expression of Neo-paganism now became only one strand in a larger, and coarser, pattern.

All that remained was for Rupert to find a new romantic interest, who clearly had to be a virgin and unsmirched by 'this strange modern life'. Two days after the *Georgian Poetry* lunch he went to the first night of *The Winter's Tale* and was smitten by the actress who played Perdita, Cathleen Nesbitt. Perhaps it was equally Cathleen's part that charmed him – a young girl whose purity rises above a hell of jealousy and betrayal. It would be three months before Rupert actually met Miss Nesbitt, but she marked his path out of the sexual wasteland of the past year.

Or should one say that he needed a replacement for Noel in order to stay in that wasteland, while cherishing the dream of getting out? In September and October Rupert renewed his ties with Elisabeth van Rysselberghe, who was now studying at the

Royal Horticultural College in Swanley, Kent. He decided to go back to Berlin to stay with Dudley in November. Having prepared his escape-route, he persuaded Elisabeth to go away with him the weekend before he left. Such a trip required careful planning, he told her: 'England's a queer place, and I mustn't be seen by my relations spending the weekend with a young woman. ... Dress Englishly. ... have you a ring that looks like a plain gold one? If it has a gold band you can wear that outside and the rest inside – turned round. It's only England!' To avoid another kind of mishap, he would send her a book on contraception.[53]

Elisabeth came up from Kent on Friday afternoon, 1 November. Her instructions were to get a taxi at Victoria – telling the driver to go to Hampstead if anyone she knew was in earshot – and meet Rupert in the tea room at Waterloo. From there they would leave to spend the weekend in Dorset.[54] Everything went according to plan, except for the bodily joys that Rupert had been looking forward to so eagerly. As had happened with Ka at Neu Strelitz, the sex was incomplete and disappointing. Rupert was angry, or indifferent, or simply beastly; he went off to Germany on the Tuesday, leaving Elisabeth broken-hearted, though still in love with him. Unhappily for her, it was precisely her love and desire for Rupert that stirred up his old resentments.

Early in October, Rupert had accidentally run into Ka at the Second Post-Impressionist show; as luck would have it, she was talking to Henry Lamb. 'Sickened and enraged,' Rupert snubbed her.[55] From now on, he vowed to denounce the 'miasmic atmosphere' of intellectual London. Asked to speak to the Apostles the next Saturday night, he gave a talk that amounted to a declaration of war. His theme was his new-found passion for active goodness, rather than ethical contemplation as he had learned it from Moore:

> I think, now, that this passion for goodness and loathing of evil is the most valuable and important thing in us. And therefore it must not be in any way stifled, nor compelled to wait upon exact judgement. If, after ordering your life and thoughts as wisely as possible, you find yourself hating, as evil, some person or thing, one should count five, perhaps, but then certainly hit out. . . . I see the world as two armies in mortal combat, and inextricably confused. The word 'He

that is not with me is against me' has gone out. One cannot completely distinguish friend from foe. The only thing is to thwack suspicious heads in the neighbourhood. It may contribute to winning the battle. It is the only battle that counts.[56]

This was really a picture of Rupert's own emotional state, out of which he created a similarly disordered world. But he could not go on as he had done over the past year. He had to deny his own darker impulses, or else go down into his underworld and perhaps never come out. If he could no longer be a happy pilgrim, he must turn into a crusader. He could still have allies and, when war came, comrades; but the ideal of a life based on friendship, which he had tried to live for the past five years, had gone out of him. With its departure, the Neo-pagans had broken camp.

X

Epilogue

The highlights of the Neo-pagan year had been their ceremonial assemblies for a play or a summer camp. But in 1912 Rupert's breakdown created so much tension in the group that neither play nor camp was possible. The gathering at Everleigh was Maynard Keynes's show, and Rupert and Ka could not be there at the same time. When Rupert left for America in May 1913, the Neo-pagans might have closed ranks around a new leader; as it turned out, they only split into smaller groups and drifted further apart.

The Oliviers still hung together, despite any jealousy over Rupert's parallel attentions to Noel and Bryn. Early in the summer of 1913 Bryn, Daphne and Noel went canoeing on the Severn, upstream from Bridgnorth, with Hugh Popham, Bunny Garnett, Harold Hobson and Paulie Montague.[1] Together these friends made up a junior division of the Neo-pagans, but they had fewer links with Cambridge, and little concern for ideology beyond enjoying themselves in the open air. If they were looking for a philosophy of life, they turned towards Bloomsbury rather than to Rupert. Bunny had become friendly with Adrian Stephen, and through him was getting a toehold in Bloomsbury society. Meanwhile Adrian, like James Strachey, had fallen in love with Noel. Bloomsbury was absorbing the Neo-pagans it liked, and who were willing to like it in return.

This takeover by Bloomsbury was confirmed by Vanessa Bell's and Maynard Keynes's plan for a reprise of the 1911 camp at Clifford Bridge. They called in Noel as technical adviser and arranged to meet at Brandon, in Norfolk, for the first half of

August 1913. The campers included Molly MacCarthy (who soon got ill and fled to London), Roger Fry, Adrian Stephen, Gerald Shove and Duncan Grant – who came equipped with a camp stool, an easel and a bottle of champagne. The leading spirit clearly was Vanessa, even though she slept in a farmhouse rather than under canvas. Since her miscarriage in Turkey two years before her nerves had been bad and she had become a patient of the ubiquitous Dr Maurice Craig. But she thrived at Brandon, finding it an 'amazing fresh air cure'.[2] To Virginia, who missed the camp because she was in a nursing home with another breakdown, Vanessa passed on her impressions of Noel, Margery and Daphne:

> all ... were evidently in rude health and spirits. They are very young and crude but also very nice. There is no doubt, I think, but that Noel is much the most interesting of them – in fact I think she *is* rather a remarkable character, but I don't know if she'll ever fall in love with Adrian. They were all very friendly and easy and I found it possible to adopt a pleasant grandmotherly attitude towards them. ... I lectured them on life and morals and I only hope it did them good but the young are very crude and cruel aren't they? It will take years before they really reach to our point of mature wisdom and of course they haven't had any of the experiences we had had at their age.[3]

Ka also turned up at the camp and was soon called on by Leonard to help him with Virginia, who had had a relapse while staying at Holford in Somerset. Given Rupert's truculent posturings, Bloomsbury was bound to sympathise with Ka over the break-up of their affair. Even after Rupert went to America, Jacques and Gwen took it on themselves to continue the feud. In March, Virginia had complained to Gwen about 'the spirit of neo-paganism' that breathed so fiercely in her letters.[4] Probably she meant Gwen's insistence on the value of living a passionately monogamous life in the country, keeping clear of intellectual London. Underlying this prescription, however, were other attitudes that Virginia knew the Raverats held: scorn for feminism, an aggressive patriotism and a large dash of new-found religiosity (when Ka was suffering through her loss of Rupert, Jacques recommended that she try saying the Lord's Prayer).

The most intimate and hurtful issue must have been the Raverats' dislike of Virginia's marrying a Jew. When Noel went to Brandon Jacques called it a 'Jewish camp'; he warned her against 'pollution' and against leading a promiscuous life in London. Since Leonard didn't go, there were actually no Jews at the camp – only the odd Strachey, whom Jacques imaginatively insisted on counting as Jewish.[5] Still fighting Rupert's battles, the Raverats kept old wounds open and ensured that the carefree Neo-paganism of 1910 and before could not be revived. The Grantchester clock might be stuck at ten to three in Rupert's poem, but the Neo-pagans were now all adults, and for them the clock had surely moved on. Those who were turning to Bloomsbury could see that its values gave staying power to friendship, whereas the Neo-pagans were being driven apart by failed loves, outside enterprises like *Georgian Poetry*, and the friction of irreconcilable differences.

Rupert Brooke

In the early months of 1913, Rupert seemed to have reached a happier state. His literary career was on the rise, propelled by the runaway success of *Georgian Poetry*. He was in love with Cathleen Nesbitt and his Neo-pagan connections were mainly with the Raverats, who shared his prejudices and did not threaten his emotional stability with painful memories. The affair with Cathleen was ardent but strictly Platonic, by mutual consent. Having been once bitten, Rupert was twice shy of mixing the whisky of lust into the spring water of ideal passion. His decision to leave England for a year, despite his fair prospects at home, was an attempt to purge himself completely of his unhappy affair with Ka. When he came back he would be free to make Cathleen his wife. But the time of settling down never came, and the two years of life remaining to him were shaped by two great expeditions: one to a sensual paradise in the west, one to the wars in the east. Each was a search for oblivion, to release Rupert from conflicts that arose in his motherland but could not be resolved there.

All through the months of wooing Cathleen, Rupert was

secretly meeting Elisabeth van Rysselberghe, who came up regularly from Swanley to London. As the débâcle of their November 1912 weekend receded, his letters became more ardent. In May, shortly before he was due to sail for New York, Rupert was pressing her to join him in a final consummation of their love. She had more physical passion, he told her, than anyone he had ever known. Earlier, he had divided his love between the sensual Ka and the unattainable Noel. Now it was similarly divided between Elisabeth and Cathleen, and with a similar result: that his love for neither woman was complete.

Elisabeth chose to deny Rupert the going-away present he sought. Once he was on the boat, he wrote her with a frankness he had never risked before:

> I'm in love, in different ways, with two or three people. I always am. You probably know this. I'm not married to anybody, nor likely to be. A year and a bit ago I was violently in love with somebody who treated me badly. The story is a bloody one: and doesn't matter. Only, it left me for a time rather incapable of loving anybody.
>
> As for you, child: I have two feelings about you now, which alternate and mix and make confusion. I like to be with you. . . . But quite apart (in origin) from all that, you – – move me to passion. . . . The fire in you lights the fire in me – and I'm not wholly responsible. Only, my dear, that's all there is: those two things. I don't want to marry you. I'm not in love with you in that way.[6]

He *would* like to live with her sometime for half a year, Rupert continued, so long as it was on his own terms. Meanwhile, he advised her to get over her love for him and become independent.

'I have been so great a lover,' he would begin a poem, later; but the poem is about beloved things and sensations, rather than people. Rupert's shipboard letter to Elisabeth was belated, but at least it let *her* know where she stood. When he defined his feelings for Cathleen Nesbitt, he did not do so to her, but to Eddie Marsh:

> My general position, you know, is queer. I've had enough and too much of love. I've come to the conclusion that marriage is the best cure for love. If I married, perhaps I could settle down, be at peace, and WORK. It's the only

chance. Therefore, marry soon. Anybody. Cathleen's character is very good, and I'm very fond of her. Why not her? – On the other hand, she's an actress.

Oh, hell, she does mix with a rotten crowd. I hope to God she won't get spoilt. She's very simple – I hope I don't shock you, writing so coldly. I'm fierier, near her, I assure you. . . .

(This is the sort of letter that doesn't look well in a Biography.)[7]

When Rupert arrived in San Francisco on his journalistic tour of North America, he was undecided whether to sail on westwards or to resume his English life, after only four months away. He tossed a coin, and spent the next seven months in the Pacific. For three of those months he was in Tahiti, which gave him the best of his poems, and probably the most unbroken happiness of his life. He lived mostly at Mataia in a ramshackle hotel next to a lagoon, where he could spend half the day naked in the water or on the beach. What made him linger there, long after he was supposed to leave for Europe, was the company of a young Tahitian called Taatamata. She was vaguely attached to the hotel; it would be unfair to call her a prostitute, but the English idea of female virtue had no relevance to her life of easy sensuality. Through her, Rupert came to agree with Gauguin's saying: 'In Europe you fall in love with a woman and eventually end up by having sexual relations with her; in Tahiti you first have physical relations, after which you proceed to fall, quite often just as deeply, in love.'[8]

Taatamata's charm comes across touchingly in a letter that reached Rupert nearly a year after he left Tahiti: 'je me rappeler toujour votre petite etroite figure et la petite bouche qui me baise bien tu m'a percee mon coeur et je aime toujours ne m'oublie pas mon cher. . . . I send my kiss to you darling.'[9] Rupert was disappointed not to have a son by her, though she might possibly have had one without his knowing of it.[10] The poem she inspired, 'Tiare Tahiti', is probably the best thing he wrote. It begins with Rupert's old Platonic fantasy of rising above all the 'foolish broken things we know'. In the changeless world to which death is the doorway, there will be no more lovers, only Love itself. But then he suddenly embraces what his poetry had always evaded, the sexual here and now:

Taü here, Mamua,
Crown the hair, and come away!
Hear the calling of the moon,
And the whispering scents that stray
About the idle warm lagoon.
Hasten, hand in human hand,
Down the dark, the flowered way,
Along the whiteness of the sand,
And in the water's soft caress,
Wash the mind of foolishness,
Mamua, until the day.[11]

At the end of his affair with Ka, Rupert had longed to cleanse himself in Byron's Pool. Water washed away sex; it was the element of purity, even when he bathed naked with Noel or Bryn. But in the lagoon at Mataia bodies plunged to be united. There, Rupert's lifelong guilty conscience about sex was dissolved – for the time being. Inevitably, he achieved his only real sensual happiness with a woman who was as far removed from his mother as it was possible to get.

Tahiti was a cultural as well as a physical revelation for Rupert. Neo-paganism in Edwardian England was necessarily a pose more than a programme; it pointed to what *should* be rather than what could actually be lived out. Geoffrey Keynes had sentimentalised over Rupert as one of the 'wise and childlike children of the sun', but this was a fantasy of escape, generated by reaction against the 'unhappy consciousness' of modern man.[12] In Tahiti Rupert found the true Children of the Sun, and he lived for three months the nearest thing to real paganism still existing in the world: 'the ideal life, little work, dancing singing and eating, naked people of incredible loveliness'.[13] He threw himself headlong into this pagan joy, yet when it was over there remained only wistful memories and a few charming poems. He came back to England with all his old feuds and obsessions intact. Once again, his need to wall off one experience from another had prevented the healing that Taatamata might have given his divided heart. 'The South Seas are heaven,' he wrote to England, 'but I no angel.'[14] When he arrived home in June 1914, he was as itchy and aggressive as when he had left.

                    *   *   *

In London again, Rupert was more than ever a protégé of Eddie
Marsh. His intellectual friends were the Georgian poets Wilfred
Gibson, Lascelles Abercrombie, Walter de la Mare. Socially,
Marsh brought Rupert into high Liberal circles; he became
intimate with Winston Churchill and with the sons and
daughters of Asquith, the Prime Minister.[15] Sentimentally he
returned to Cathleen, whom he had also met through Marsh. She
was a glorious woman, Rupert told her, for him to adore. But by
September, inevitably, he had another sort of woman to go to bed
with. This was Lady Eileen Wellesley, daughter of the Duke of
Wellington. Rupert met her when Marsh took him to dinner at
the Duchess of Leeds'. He was conquering London society as he
had conquered Cambridge six or seven years before.

    Naturally, the Neo-pagans felt mistrust of Rupert's grand new
friends. For his part, he acknowledged his old companions
without trying to revive the old life they had shared. He saw the
Raverats and Cornfords when he found time for them; Ka he met
soon after coming back, and made with her an uneasy truce. She
was still carrying a torch for him, while he wanted no more than
an intermittent friendship – one that would make the old wounds
a bit less tender. At the beginning of August, Rupert thought of
going with Jacques to a camp organised by Noel at Helston,
Cornwall. Bryn would be there with her husband and baby son,
along with Margery, Geoffrey Keynes, Bunny Garnett and
Frankie Birrell. But Rupert had promised to stay a week in
Norfolk with the Cornfords first, and by the end of it he was not
interested in camping out, for war had been declared.

    Rupert went to war as he had gone into London society at the
end of 1912: under the patronage of Eddie Marsh. The connection determined both his fate and his fame. In August 1914 the
professional army in Flanders was too busy to be encumbered
with volunteers. But Eddie was Private Secretary to the First Lord
of the Admiralty, Winston Churchill, and he arranged for Rupert
to be commissioned in Churchill's own little amphibious army,
the Royal Naval Division. Rupert arrived in Camp at the end of
September 1914 and a week later was sent into battle, on a futile
five-day expedition that tried to save Antwerp from the German
advance.

Rupert's brigade did no fighting, and was pulled back after two days in the front line. But on the retreat he found his calling as a warrior, when his troops marched alongside the refugees who had abandoned their homes under German bombardment. 'I'll never forget that white-faced, endless procession in the night,' he wrote, '. . . crawling forward at some hundred yards an hour, quite hopeless . . . the old men mostly weeping, the women with hard drawn faces, the children playing or crying or sleeping.'[16] Those five days were Rupert's first and last experience of actual war. He knew it only as a quixotic sortie in aid of the old and the weak, and his belief in the absolute purity of his mission could hardly have survived a month in the trenches.

The retreat from Antwerp created the certainty and exultation of Rupert's sonnet-sequence '1914'. War had released his generation from shame, he wrote; yet the shames he described were peculiar to himself:

To turn, as swimmers into cleanness leaping,
Glad from a world grown old and cold and weary,
    Leave the sick hearts that honour could not move,
And half-men, and their dirty songs and dreary,
    And all the little emptiness of love!

The war let him feel that the whole nation had joined him in spurning homosexual and pacifist Bloomsbury. What the common reader could not know, however, was that Rupert hated Bloomsbury for its complicity with his own sexual guilt, and that *this* was what it would take a war to wash off. When preparing to sail for the Dardanelles in February 1915, he asked Jacques whether he should 'marry without being particularly in love, before going to the front'. He decided *not* to marry Cathleen Nesbitt because, as he confessed, he feared being stuck with her after the war.[17] War was an antidote to love, and it was war he preferred.

D. H. Lawrence found in Rupert's '1914' sonnets 'the great inhalation of desire' for death.[18] One can see well enough why he looked to death as the only way to cut the Gordian knot of his tangled emotions. Yet how did his despairing and private way of escape become, in the eyes of his country, the essence of a whole generation's self-sacrifice? How did someone who never fired his gun in anger and died of an infected mosquito bite become the most famous British hero of the war, the only one still alive in the popular imagination?[19] (So alive that nine people out of ten now will tell you that Brooke was killed, rather than that he died in bed.)

Rupert's fame began three weeks before his death, when Dean Inge recited 'The Soldier' in his sermon at St Paul's.[20] Such fame was already ironic, since Rupert had long professed a Neo-pagan scorn for orthodox Christianity. Yet Inge had rightly seen that the war sonnets were steeped in Christian mythology: the sleeper who awakes to a spiritual call, the unstained young man who is both victim and redeemer. One could also find in the sonnets the enticing myth that death purged away the sins of the flesh, so that war itself could be seen as a long-awaited cleansing of national guilt.

In the mythologising of Rupert, it is impossible to disentangle ideal motives from expedient ones. The British Expeditionary Force, made up of the 'Old Contemptibles' that the country had never loved, had suffered casualties of more than fifty per cent in the battles of 1914. Conscription was not yet politically acceptable, so an army of volunteers had to be raised. Two and a half million young men rallied to the colours, filling the gap between the Regular Army of 1914 and the conscript army of 1917–18. Rupert stood for the ideal volunteer, beautiful and courageous, the flower of his country's youth. In fact, the image only fitted a narrow elite of public schoolboys, but these were indeed the spearhead of the struggle. A typical British infantry battalion had no more than thirty officers to lead eight hundred other ranks. If the subalterns gained the lion's share of glory, they earned it, by their actual dreadful fate. They were two or three times as likely to be killed as the men serving under them, and forty thousand had died by November 1918.[21] Six hundred and eighty-two Old Rugbeians were killed, a number equal to the school's total enrolment in 1914.

Rupert's glory did more than draw young men into the war after him; it also provided a rosy image of what war was like, and why it was being fought. The war was begun by cavalrymen, but when the trench and the machine-gun took over Kitchener said, 'I don't know what is to be done; this isn't war.'[22] Early in March 1915, a British offensive had failed at Neuve Chapelle; on 22 April, the day before Rupert's death, the Germans used poison gas on the Western Front. The leaders of the British war effort were starting to realise the horror of the enterprise to which they had committed themselves. By attacking Gallipoli, Churchill hoped to outflank the bloody stalemate in Flanders. The reality there was the machine-gun, gas and high explosive, the sordidness and mutilation of the trenches. Everything about the Rupert Brooke myth was designed to deny that reality and to suggest that the Gallipoli expedition would restore cleanness and nobility to war. When Rupert was being buried in an olive grove on Skyros, one of the funeral party felt that he was reliving 'the origin of some classic myth'.[23] Churchill felt the death deeply, no doubt, but he also saw how the myth of it could serve his political advantage, for his tribute in *The Times* coincided with the first landings at Gallipoli.[24]

The myth struck deep into the imagination because it focused a cluster of powerful archetypes on to the body of a single handsome young man. By the time of Rupert's death Britain knew that he was not just a knight of Christian purity, but a Crusader too: a local interpreter wrote on Rupert's cross, in Greek, that he was a 'servant of God ... Who died for the deliverance of Constantinople from the Turks'. Byron had sacrificed himself for the same cause. Now another Cambridge poet, who had loved to swim in Byron's Pool, had shared Byron's fate. And Byron brought in, also, the whole force of classical myth. He had sung of 'The Isles of Greece'; Rupert had died among them. Yet it all served to exalt Gallipoli over the Western Front – where in fact the war would have to be decided, and not in any classical style.

'Bright Phoebus smote him down,' wrote D. H. Lawrence. 'It is all in the saga.'[25] Rupert's death was first reported as caused by sunstroke, and had not Phoebus Apollo, the golden-haired god of poetry, struck down Marsyas for boasting that he could sing as well as the god? Then there was the old saw that those whom the gods loved died young, quoted by Lascelles Abercrombie in his *Morning Post* obituary. In death as in life, Rupert was the supreme *ephebos* of his tribe – the naked young man of godlike beauty and grace. Adored by a ruling class steeped in the classics and in idealised homoeroticism, Rupert stood for what was at stake in the war – and for the price it exacted. 'Joyous, fearless, versatile, deeply instructed,' said Churchill's tribute, 'with classic symmetry of mind and body, he was all that one would wish England's noblest sons to be in days when no sacrifice but the most precious is acceptable, and the most precious is that which is most freely proffered.'

The way of Rupert's death served the myth better than if he had actually died in battle. Unblemished by wounds, the hero's body had been carried by his comrades to a grave lined with flowers and crowned with a wreath of olive. One of those comrades, Denis Browne, was killed in the trenches of Gallipoli six weeks later. In a letter anticipating his death, he had seen how the story would come down to posterity. 'I'm luckier than Rupert,' he wrote, 'because I've fought. But there's no one to bury me as I buried him, so perhaps he's best off in the long run.'[26] In April 1915 Britain needed a death like Rupert's, to blot out the terrible knowledge of what death in war had become. And his death needed a life to match: the young Apollo, carefree with his friends under the apple blossom at Grantchester. The real story is far from golden, but more worth the telling.

Ferenc Békássy

Two months after Rupert's death another young poet and Apostle died in battle, a few hundred miles north of Rupert's tomb on Skyros. When war broke out, Feri Békássy was in England. He had been at Bedales and King's since he was twelve, but he was determined to return home and fight for the Austro-Hungarian Empire. There was a week's gap between Britain declaring war on Germany and the declaration of war on Austria–Hungary. This gave Feri his chance to avoid internment and make his way to Budapest. However, the banks were closed and he lacked money for his fare. He applied to Maynard Keynes for a loan. Keynes tried to argue him out of going but, when he failed, provided the money. Keynes had been Feri's friend and sponsor at Cambridge, and probably his lover also. To send him off to his death appealed to both of them, one suspects, as a quintessentially Apostolic thing to do.

Still only twenty-one, Feri was carried along in the exuberance of the early months of the war. 'There's a difference', he wrote to Noel Olivier from Budapest, 'between poets ... and other people, that poets take hold of the feelings they have and won't let go.' He was still in love with Noel, still very much the sensitive and idealistic young Bedalian, but the war seemed to him the natural outlet for his aspirations. 'I'm going gladly,' he told Noel, five days before he set out for the front. 'I know it's very worth taking the risk and I am sure to get something good out of the war unless I die in it. It's part of the "good life" just now, that *I* should go: and the sooner one gives up the idea that the *world* can be made better than it is, the better.'[27] As a landed aristocrat, Feri naturally went with the cavalry; on his horse's head he put three red roses, because they appeared on his family coat of arms. Four days after he arrived at the front he was killed fighting the Russians at Dobrovouc.

Jacques and Gwen Raverat

Late in 1912, the Raverats came back from Prunoy to settle in England. They wanted to be near Gwen's father, who was mortally ill, and they had decided that the English countryside was the best place for them to work at their art. Ten miles outside Cambridge, at Croydon, they found a farmhouse to rent. Rupert and Justin were regular visitors, but the Raverats saw little of the Oliviers from now on, and Gwen was still wary of Ka. Although they tried their hand at large oils, sculpture and fresco, their best work proved to be Gwen's woodcuts, small-scale but charming scenes of domestic life or nature. Just before he left for America, Rupert sent two of these woodcuts to Bryn and Hugh Popham, as a belated wedding-present and a recognition that Bryn was now firmly someone else's wife.[28]

The war made Jacques and Rupert firmer allies than ever. Jacques passionately supported the French cause and loathed such 'pro-Germans' as the Stracheys, Gerald Shove or Bertrand

Russell. But he found that he was not healthy enough to be a soldier. For the past couple of years he had suffered from spells of overwhelming fatigue.[29] When he failed his medical in August 1914 he tried unsuccessfully to enlist as an interpreter, then went to France to seek a place there. After three months of frustration he returned to England and at last received a firm diagnosis of his mysterious symptoms. He was told that his breakdown on the way to Switzerland in December 1907 had been the onset of a gradual 'disseminated sclerosis of the spinal marrow'.[30] The syndrome of disseminated sclerosis (now called multiple sclerosis) had been described by Charcot in the nineteenth century, and by 1914 clinical studies had noted the highly variable course of the disease. When Jacques' doctors assured him that his case was mild and would not progress they were probably trying to keep his spirits up, since they had no reliable way of helping him or predicting how long he would live. The prescribed treatment was injections of lymph, combined with a course of psychoanalysis from Dr Hayden Brown to settle his nerves. He would not kill his Prussian, but his hands were good enough for him to go ahead with his painting. He and Gwen found a new house at Weston, near Stevenage, and went back to work.

A few months after his diagnosis, Jacques could barely walk. By the middle of 1916 his legs had given out altogether and he could only move around outside in a little cart. He must have realised by now that his illness could not be treated, and would progress steadily until it killed him. Meanwhile, his father lost most of his money in a dubious speculation and the Château of Prunoy was sold in October 1917. Jacques and Gwen no longer had the prospect of becoming rich, though they still had enough between them to live in reasonable comfort. Despite the collapse of Jacques' health they were still able to have two children, Elisabeth in 1916 and Sophie in 1919.

As he lost his health, Jacques also had to cope with lack of success as an artist. He exhibited rarely, sold hardly at all, and gained no real foothold in the British art world, whereas Gwen's woodcuts were in steady demand. Jacques could hardly expect to be in the swim, given that he rejected every new movement in art since Cézanne. 'What *I* like,' he told Ka, 'in common with all decent Europeans (this includes French, English, Italian, Russian and the Balkan peoples; no others) is nice pictures of pretty things with a decent human feeling about them. And I like a coal scuttle to *be* a coal scuttle and not a monstrous abstract black form. The rest is rot.'[31] Opinions of this sort, said with tongue only partly in cheek, were not the way to make a career in 1914.

Jacques' major intellectual contact during the last ten years of his life was with André Gide. He and Gwen met Gide for a holiday in Florence in March 1914, after which they became regular correspondents.[32] In September of the same year the Raverats spent several days at Gide's country house at Cuverville, Normandy. Gide was very taken with Jacques, calling him 'une nature exquise, d'une bonté sublime et fondante'; but he also found him a serious intellectual influence.[33] Jacques pressed on Gide the lesson of Rupert's affair with Ka:

> j'en avais vu sortir deux êtres que j'aimais, si misérables, si douloureux, l'*esprit* sali, empoisonné, révolté, pleins d'amertume. ... Et l'anti-puritanisme, l'immoralisme par théorie me semble vraiment au moins aussi néfaste que le contraire. (il y a un peu le même rapport que du sentimentalisme au cynisme)[34]

It is a tribute to Jacques' charm — or perhaps to Gide's flexibility — that this frontal attack on Gide's position was taken in good part. Jacques even convinced Gide that the Devil — an active, personal principle of Evil — really existed. This was an important shift in Gide's moral universe, which up to then had been based on his rebellion against ascetic Christianity. Like Nietzsche, Gide had been trying to establish a new paganism. Jacques helped to move him back towards his Christian origins.[35]

When Rupert died Gide wanted to publish a memorial volume in France, including his own translation of some of Rupert's poems. The project came to nothing in the end, perhaps because of opposition from Rupert's mother (Gide was, after all, a notorious figure in both countries). In the summer of 1918 Gide came to England for a long-awaited visit and stayed several times with the Raverats at Weston. But during the three months that Gide was in England his friendship with Jacques became strained. Jacques did not hit it off with Gide's companion, his

seventeen-year-old nephew Marc Allégret. Nor did he approve
when Gide became friends with several of the Bloomsbury circle.
Jacques apparently did not realise that Gide was in love with
Allégret, and he told Gide that it was unfair to jeer at Lytton
Strachey too much because 'He's like so many others, don't you
know, who don't like women.'[36]

In 1920 Jacques and Gwen returned to France and settled at
Vence, in the Midi, where the climate made Jacques' daily
routine a bit easier. In June of that year Jacques had a reunion
with Gide in Paris, and was told of Elisabeth van Rysselberghe's
affair with Marc Allégret.[37] Perhaps this led to some coolness
between the two friends; Gide was often in the south but excused
himself, in his inimitable way, from visiting Jacques:

> je sentais presque cruellement, en songeant à vous, l'insuf-
> fisance de mon paganisme. . . . Bref j'étais comme quelqu'un
> qui décline une invitation à diner, parcequ'il n'a pas d'even-
> ing dress. . . . Malgré mon silence et mon éloignement, je
> pense bien souvent à vous, et à ce qui faisait la qualité si rare
> de mon amitié pour vous; elle venait je crois de ceci que, près
> de vous, je me sentais meilleur. –
> Donc, au revoir peut-être.[38]

Still, when Gide finally set aside his quibbles and went to Vence
Jacques found that he could not hold a grudge against him. 'He *is*
an old charlatan,' Jacques observed, 'though still extraordinarily
seductive.'[39]

A more important reconciliation for Jacques, in his last years,
was with Virginia Woolf. They had been out of touch for nearly
ten years when, in the summer of 1922, Jacques sent her a letter
praising her collection of stories *Monday or Tuesday*.[40] Knowing
that Jacques did not have long to live, Virginia wrote to him
regularly and affectionately until the end. Both of them now saw
the pre-war days as distant enough to be transmuted by memory
into art. Jacques was writing a memoir of Bedales and Cambridge; Virginia was at work on *Mrs Dalloway* (a dialogue
between middle age and youth); while Gwen had already completed her own *roman-à-clef* of Cambridge and after. Virginia
had named Neo-paganism; in a way she had even invented it.
With Jacques' help, she now wanted to fix its place in her whole
vision of the past.

Jacques told Virginia that he had abandoned the religiosity that had disturbed her in 1913. He now loathed 'mystic religion' and wanted only to savour the last fragments of his life; while Gwen had reverted to being a proper Darwin – that is, a 'militant atheist'. 'What matters', he continued, 'is [people's] reactions, sensations, actions, passions and pleasures. Thats the sort of things that seem real to me if you ask. And then immediate, particular and concrete things, like boots and trees, and mackerel. I'm sure that neither practical life nor general ideas have any reality at all.' The 'grand attack on Bloomsbury' that Virginia asked about was more Rupert's hobby-horse than Jacques' or Gwen's:

> It was rather a flight from it all – because I suddenly felt as if I couldn't breathe in that air a moment longer. . . . Did I really have convictions 10 years ago? If I did I must have caught them in the English air and from my English friends; for I'm sure they were not natural to me; and I assure you there's very little left of them now, in spite of having married a Darwin – (or perhaps because). (But seriously I suppose Rupert had more to do with it than anyone, in those days.)[41]

And what had Neo-paganism really amounted to? The problem, Jacques explained, was that it was all too nebulous to describe in a linear medium like writing:

> One could perhaps, in the middle of a large sheet of paper write the word Neo-Paganism and then radially bits of sentences like this:
> Shame at the absurdities of my youth.
> Apologies if they really annoyed you.
> But almost impossible to believe that you can have taken them seriously.
> My own annoyance in those days, because I fell so short of that ideal.
> A desire to defend it.
> A desire to counterattack.
> Etc etc
> And all this, you see, simultaneously; though even so its only what happens on the surface.
> Now in painting its all quite different. . . .
> Well, I can easily believe that I must have been, shall we say, a very difficult young man. Very proud and obstinate

and umbrageous. But what you call condescension and flippancy was very often only a mask to hide extreme diffidence and fear of seeming ridiculous to you. You never realized, my dear Virginia, how much I admired you.

Jacques also wanted to make some amends for inflicting his anti-semitism on Virginia. 'It's true', he told her, 'that I've very often found that things and people that I disliked were Jewish; but I did make friends rather intimately with one Jew in Paris years ago; and I always wanted to know your husband better, (I do like *some* Jews), though I dare say we should have disagreed in most of our opinions.' It was not so much a retraction as an admission that he could not afford to let his prejudices come between him and someone who had been so kind to him, and whose letters helped to revive memories of happier days. For now, in plain fact, he felt he would be better off dead. 'I have not the advantages', he confessed, 'of either death or life; not of life, because I have lost almost every pleasure in the world. Not of death because I am still damnably capable of feeling pain. Please do not repeat this.'[42] The worst moment, for one who had loved the mountains, came when he gave away his boots, two years before the end. He died on 7 March 1925; the paralysis had taken ten years to use up his strength.

To Gwen it seemed that the two friends, Rupert and Jacques, were summed up in the different ways they had died:

> [Rupert] didn't really care about life. He was ambitious but he didn't love things for themselves. All that about bathing and food and bodies was a pose. He didn't care – not like Jacques. And when a fly bit him, he just died out of carelessness. And so I wouldn't call him substantial, as you do, unless you mean the schoolmaster side of him – the responsible practical fatherly man. He *was* a schoolmaster. For instance, he tried so hard to prevent all the friends whom he considered young and innocent from being enticed into your bawdy houses at Bloomsbury. Of course Bloomsbury disliked him; how could they help it, when he thought them so infinitely corrupt and sinister that no one (except himself) could be trusted to enter their purlieus and come out unsmirched. I don't quite know why he thought Bloomsbury so devilishly poisonous, but he did – (and was it

perhaps true that they weren't very good for the-not-very-
strong-in-the-head such as Margery Olivier? or the vain and
credulous and cotton wool-stuffed such as Ka? . . .)

But Jacques wouldn't have gone and died like Rupert . . .
though he had lost nearly all possible physical pleasures,
yet he could somehow taste the memory of them in his
impotence with more force than Rupert ever could their
reality in all his youth.

And yet, somehow life has seemed duller ever since
Rupert died.[43]

In Jacques' last years Gwen had fallen in love with a neighbour
at Vence, the painter Jean Marchand. He was married, however,
and would not make the break to live with Gwen. She returned to
England in 1925, living in London and later Cambridge with her
daughters. Though she suffered periods of depression, she had a
life rich in friendship and artistic production. Her novel about
the Neo-pagans never appeared but in 1952 she published *Period
Piece*, a lively memoir of her family life in the first generation of
married dons at Cambridge. She died in 1957, aged seventy-two.

Elisabeth van Rysselberghe

Elisabeth was still at the Royal Horticultural College when
Rupert returned to England from the South Seas. They met for
lunch at Simpson's, but Rupert had his hands full elsewhere and
made no effort to resume their affair. Elisabeth was kept dang-
ling, much as before, until he wrote to her from his troopship in
the Mediterranean. It was 8 March 1915, the day when he wrote
to a number of friends to settle his affairs. He had arranged
for her letters to be destroyed if he died, he told her, but she
should not care for him afterwards. She did care, however, all her
long life. A photograph of Rupert was always by her and she
guarded his letters and memories, without revealing them to
anyone else.

Elisabeth's mother, Maria, painted the affair with Rupert in
romantic colours:

they loved each other without any concern for the future, or
for a permanent attachment. I think this attitude to love is

deeply engrained in Elisabeth's nature, but that it was reinforced by Brooke's influence.[44]

In fact, they shared no future because Rupert was by temperament unable to commit himself fully to any woman. Elisabeth's one-sided devotion to Rupert was doomed to find no substantial return.

Maria van Rysselberghe confided the whole sad story to André Gide, adding that Elisabeth was 'inconsolable' at not having borne Rupert a child. Eight years later she had her child: by a greater writer, but one whose character had something in common with Rupert's mixture of puritanism, sensuality and evasiveness. In November 1916, while returning to Paris from the funeral of Elisabeth's godfather Emile Verhaeren, Gide passed to Elisabeth a note written on a ticket: 'Je n'aimerai jamais d'amour qu'une seule femme et je ne puis avoir de vrais désirs que pour les jeunes garçons. Mais je me résigne mal à te voir sans enfant et à n'en pas avoir moi-même.'[45] In the spring of 1920 Gide's young companion Marc Allégret fell in love with Elisabeth; Gide was delighted by the connection and hoped that they would have a beautiful child, the precursor of 'a new humanity'.[46] After his hopes were disappointed, he and Elisabeth decided to have a child together, though his paternity would have to be kept secret from his deeply religious wife, Madeleine. Elisabeth gave birth to a daughter in April 1923 and married Pierre Herbart in 1931. She led a retired life in the Midi, seeing only a few faithful friends and working in her garden from dawn to dusk; a person of 'great integrity and loyalty', her daughter recalls. Like Noel Olivier, Elisabeth made no public acknowledgement of her old love for Rupert. She died at the age of ninety in 1980.

Frances Cornford

After 1911, Frances became guardian of the Neo-pagan tradition at Cambridge. With her large house and sympathetic nature she provided a comforting refuge for Rupert, Ka, Justin and the Raverats (her ties with the Oliviers were not so close). She wrote poetry when she could, but bearing five children between 1913 and 1924 left little time for a continuous literary career. Since the years of breakdown in her teens she had remained emotionally fragile. At the end of the war she collapsed again, following the birth of her son Christopher, and had to spend two years at cures or in nursing homes, unable to see her husband or children. Religion consoled her, and in 1924 she was confirmed in the Anglican Church.

When Rupert sailed for the Dardanelles he had asked both Jacques and Dudley for a son to be named after him. Neither was able to oblige, but eight months after Rupert's death Frances had a boy whom she named Rupert John Cornford. The 'John' was after John Swan, a Durham miner whom the Cornfords had met through the Workers Educational Association, and as the boy grew up his usual name became John rather than Rupert. Francis Cornford, brilliant as scholar and teacher, was painfully shy with his family. Frances was at the other pole, with overflowing maternal feelings that often flared up into conflict and that focused on her first son. Her dramatic instinct had marked out Rupert for the mythic fate of a 'Young Apollo' in 1907; now that he was dead, did she hope to bring up John as a worthy successor?

Whether by design or chance, so it turned out. Twenty-five years after Rupert turned heads on the King's Parade, John Cornford became the most glamorous figure of *his* Cambridge generation.[47] But 1933 demanded a harder image than 1908. At seventeen Rupert had affected the style of a decadent poet, tossing off witticisms over curiously scented cigarettes. John Cornford's choice of rebellion, at the same age, was to join the Young Communist League – much to his parents' dismay. They persuaded him to consult Godwin Baynes, now a leading Jungian analyst. 'Although there are obvious signs of nervous stress,' Baynes reported to Frances, 'I was very much impressed with the central steadiness of his mind. The discipline of every function to the ruling idea is apparently complete and I must say it is a very extraordinary discipline.'[48] The 'ruling idea' was an absolute identification with communism, and it made John a magnetic figure to his fellow undergraduates. He founded the early student radical style: a black shirt with a tie in solid colour, scruffy tweed jacket, decrepit flannels held up by a large leather belt. John was strikingly handsome – but darkly so, the reverse of Rupert's ingenuous blondness. Rupert had been loose and casual, John was driven. In a frenetic undergraduate career he wrote poetry, worked up to twelve hours a day at politics, had two serious love affairs (one of which produced a child), and took a starred First in history.

The Spanish Civil War began on 18 July 1936, a few months after John Cornford's graduation. Brushing aside his parents' misgivings, he set off for Spain. He arrived as a journalist but soon joined the POUM, the first Englishman to serve in the Loyalist forces. After he had returned home to gather more recruits, John's father sent him off with his First World War revolver – a quixotic gesture reminiscent of Maynard Keynes's loan to Feri Békássy. John was killed on the road to Cordoba, probably on his twenty-first birthday, 27 December 1936. There was no funeral service and no tomb, for his body was never recovered. No sermons were preached in Britain to glorify him and his cause. But he, like Rupert, had written a poem for his generation, one that imagined his death and made a plea on the strength of it. Though there was no mystical patriotism in the poem, it told what youth had learned of love and sacrifice since 1914:

'To Margot Heinemann'

Heart of the heartless world,
Dear heart, the thought of you
Is the pain at my side,
The shadow that chills my view.

The wind rises in the evening,
Reminds that autumn is near.
I am afraid to lose you,
I am afraid of my fear.

On the last mile to Huesca,
The last fence for our pride,
Think so kindly, dear, that I
Sense you at my side.

And if bad luck should lay my strength
Into the shallow grave,
Remember all the good you can;
Don't forget my love.

Frances lived out her life at Cambridge, writing poetry and cherishing her memories. She died in 1960.

Justin Brooke

In the last pre-war years Justin still turned up regularly at Neo-pagan gatherings; he travelled to the Alps with the Cornfords and Ka, to Hungary to visit Feri Békássy. Yet he always seems present but not accounted for, someone who was liked rather than loved. His character was an odd blend of diffidence and imperiousness: he proposed to Ruth Montague, the young sister of his schoolfriend Paulie Montague, but when she asked for time to think about it he abruptly withdrew his offer. He suffered from colitis and had periodic nervous collapses. The scheme of becoming a lawyer petered out and in 1913, when he was twenty-eight, he finally bowed to the yoke and entered the West Country office of Brooke Bond. When he invited Noel to visit, in 1916, she confided to James Strachey that she found it harder to get on with Justin than with any of the old group, for he was *nothing* but a link to the past.[49]

As he passed thirty, however, Justin started to find his way. At the beginning of 1916 Sybil Pye reported that he had been completely cured by the fashionable psychiatrist Hayden Brown.[50] This may have been an exaggeration, but in June 1917 Justin was fit enough to join the Inns of Court Officers' Training Corps. Later that year he married Doris Mead, a young schoolteacher he had met on holiday in Wales. He was commissioned in the Dorsetshire Regiment on 1 May 1918, and saw active service in France. After the war he went back to Brooke Bond, living in a Georgian house full of antiques near Bath with his wife and four children. His father had retired by now and Brooke Bond was being run by Justin's older brothers. It was a settled and prosperous life, but he was not at ease in it. In 1927 he went for treatment to another psychiatrist, H. Crichton Miller, who told Justin's story to Frances Cornford:

> He uses his wife as a mother substitute to facilitate his role of invalidism. All goes well. Then I replace the invalid role by a phantasy of efficiency: at the same time a young governess is brought to live in the house. J.B. falls in love with her and covets her as the one to facilitate his *new* role of virility and achievement. He then proceeds to rationalise and exagger-ate until he accepts his retreat from parental responsibility as a kind of Knight-Errant's Quest! Alas! alas![51]

Justin's life came down around his ears. Doris divorced him and his brothers decided that a divorced man was not morally fit to be an executive of Brooke Bond. (Later, when one of the brothers also got divorced, Justin had the satisfaction of forcing him to resign in turn.) He moved to Suffolk, married the governess, and invested his capital in growing fruit.

As a farmer, Justin had found his niche at last. There is an admiring portrait of his work in Adrian Bell's novel *By-Road*, where Justin is thinly disguised under the name of 'Rayner':

> Rayner was to me the idea of what that pre-war, younger generation's optimism might have become, had not the war come. That optimism, like a June day with wind, of which Rupert Brooke stands (not fairly) as a sort of symbol. Rayner was of that generation, and those of his friends who had survived. He somehow had preserved, or resurrected, that June morning.[52]

Justin had a deep affection for traditional country life, but he realised that people could not stay on the land without employ-ment. He was an expert botanist who pioneered fruit-growing in a part of England previously thought unsuitable. The orchards produced massive harvests, which were delivered by a fleet of vans to nearby cities. In the depths of the slump Justin provided jobs for a hundred and fifty people, most of whom would otherwise have had to move away. He kept a link with his youthful passion by staging plays in the village, recruiting the locals to act in them. Justin's projects translated the Neo-pagan dream into a blueprint for social action. He did not merely live in the country, but tried to strengthen the rural community by providing capital and adapting it to the modern world. In his work on the land he managed to be both a Neo-pagan and his father's son.

Justin lived into his late seventies: a cheerful hedonist, a striking figure at Old Bedalian gatherings and, according to Adrian Bell, a 'devout atheist'. In 1955 Geoffrey Keynes roused the surviving Neo-pagans when he quarrelled with Dudley Ward. Keynes had made an edition of Rupert's letters; they had actually been set in type when Ward, who was also one of Rupert's literary trustees, vetoed their publication. Frances Cornford took Dudley's side, and Justin went to try and change her mind. 'I have argued with Frances without avail,' he reported to Geoffrey. 'I tell her she is trying to build up a Rupert Myth – as a sort of young Galahad. These Darwins are, at heart, dreadful Victorian "Moralists" and of course poor Dudley – "my God, man" is a non-conformist by birth and tradition. Frances' only defence was that the public would not understand and would regard Rupert as a libertine. So he was!'[53] But the victory went to those – led by Keynes himself – who did not want it to be said out loud.

Ka Cox

When Rupert cast her off in August 1912 Ka drifted miserably for five months, staying with relatives in the country or with her sister Margaret in London. She was liable to collapse in tears at the least upset, and Rupert's stream of reproachful letters did nothing to heal her wounds. However, she was not so sad that she lost her appeal to young men. One Arthur Dakyns fell in love with her, and in October Geoffrey Keynes also proposed. Both suitors were gently repulsed and early in January 1913 Ka set off for Berlin, keeping her bargain with Rupert that each should leave England.[54]

Ka spent several months with the Wards in Berlin, helping Annemarie after the birth of her son Peter. In the spring she set out by herself for Poland and Russia. Before leaving she told Frances, pathetically, that she could go on from Russia to California if Rupert fell ill and needed her. But when he arrived in

New York Rupert sent her a letter saying he would not write again. She needed to get completely clear of him, he told her, so that she could fall in love and marry someone else. 'I know I've done you great wrong,' he confessed, '. . . It's the one thing in the world I'm sorry for: though I've done a lot of evil things.' His parting gift to her was a bronze statuette of a madonna and child by Eric Gill. 'You'll be the greatest mother in the world,' he told her. 'And I'll not be anything but sad, till I've heard you're happy and with a child of your own.'[55] It was a poor recompense, he realised, for their own lost child.

Ka returned to England late in July 1913. After the Bloomsbury camp in Norfolk she spent much of the autumn nursing Virginia Woolf at Asheham. Later she worked briefly in publishing, but she had no pressing need to find a profession, nor any strong desire to realise herself in that way. When Rupert returned in June 1914 they resumed an uneasy friendship. He had his hands full with Cathleen Nesbitt and Eileen Wellesley. He told Ka that he didn't want to see her too often, and looked forward to her getting married – to someone else, naturally. Yet when he was making plans in the event of his death, on the way to the Dardanelles, it was Ka that he called 'the best I can do in the way of a widow'.[56] Perhaps he *might* have married her in the end, he mused.

The Raverats certainly believed that Rupert, if he had lived, would have gone back to her. Ka probably had the same conviction, though she kept aloof from any link with Rupert's posthumous fame. When he died, Jacques and Gwen were staying at Conduit Head to paint a fresco while the Cornfords were away. They asked Ka to come up from London to mourn with them. 'We must all draw nearer together,' Jacques pleaded, '– I mean, we who knew him really.'[57] But Ka did not come, nor did she meet Noel to share her grief. Jacques, for his part, was angry with Noel for consorting with the Bloomsbury pacifists. Even Rupert's death wasn't cause enough for a Neo-pagan reunion, and when the Oliviers camped at Porthcothan in August 1915 Justin was the only one from the old group who turned up.

At the beginning of 1916 Ka went out to Corsica for six months, to work at a camp for Serbian refugees. Her sympathy and practicality must have made a strong impression since she was later offered an OBE, which she refused. During the rest of the war she worked as a civil servant on Allied shipping. In the spring of 1918 she fell in love with Will Arnold-Forster, a shore-bound naval officer and would-be painter. They married on 9 September. Unfortunately, Ka's Bloomsbury friends did not judge Will a worthy successor to Rupert. 'What one instinctively says about [him] is "What a Whippersnapper!"' said Virginia Woolf. 'Its the effect of his little mongrel cur's body; his face which appears powdered and painted like a very refined old suburban harlots; and his ridiculous little voice.' Ka kept on about how 'mad and wild' her husband was, but Virginia could see that he was 'as mild as a Guinea pig – a neurotic Guinea pig'.[58]

When Will went into hospital for a minor operation, Clive Bell and Mary Hutchinson speculated that he was having his parts enlarged. He managed, despite the jeers, to father a son – though when he went to visit Ka the nurses thought he was the baby's brother. Not surprisingly, Will disliked Ka's Cambridge and Bloomsbury friends. In 1920 the Arnold-Forsters turned their backs on London and settled near Zennor in Cornwall. Their house, Eagles Nest, had a spectacular view of the moors and the sea. Will painted, worked for the League of Nations and stood unsuccessfully as a Labour candidate for St Ives. Ka gardened, raised her son Mark and played hostess to a stream of guests. Virginia was often nettled by Ka's increasing snobbishness, and by her naive insistence that Will was as romantic a young man as the one she had lost in 1915. Bertrand Russell once described Ka as 'agreeable but not interesting'; that became Virginia's judgement too, except that she was still fascinated by Ka's Neo-pagan years.[59]

Gradually Ka lost touch with many of her pre-war friends. Gwen was still close, but Justin and the Oliviers had gone their own way after Rupert's death. Ka and Noel felt a silent rivalry, one suspects, over what each had shared with Rupert – though he had left both of them, in different ways, unfulfilled. Each kept more than a hundred of his letters, though neither left any memoir of their affairs with him.

Ka died suddenly of a heart-attack at the age of fifty-one, on 22 May 1938. In her diary, Virginia wrote a long, meditative epitaph for her friend – as if making a sketch for a character in a novel:

> Her own identical life ended when Rupert died. So I think. After that she was acting a part very carefully and deliberately chosen. Maternity, Will, public life. Hence some squint; she was never natural, never with me at least. And I was self-conscious; remembering how she had seen me mad. She used to come to Asheham, to Holford: condescending, patronising, giving up her own pleasures to tend me and help L. I don't think I was ever at my ease with her.... But at the same time that was her role: to help; to lift lame dogs; to entertain; to arrange; manage; receive confidences. And what was wrong with all that? only that after Rupert's death she was playing a part. Yet this is superficial. For there was a trustiness in her; a stable goodness; a tenderness.[60]

Margery and Daphne Olivier

David Garnett described the adult life of the Olivier sisters in two cryptic sentences: 'Many of the chief motive forces in human society inspired disgust or contempt in them. Later, when these forces took hold of them, they found life hard to endure or to accept.' Having suffered in youth from the Oliviers' pride, Bunny was primed to view their later lives as a fall.[61] The young sisters had enjoyed an extraordinary sexual power and self-sufficiency – assets that were bound, in the nature of things, to decline. Only for Margery, however, did this decline become a long-drawn-out tragedy. She was the most intellectual of the four sisters, and might have become one of the brilliant 'new women' of the suffragette era. But her studies were interrupted by her stays in Jamaica; she did not take her economics tripos until June 1911, when she was twenty-five, and achieved only a Third. Nor was she able to settle on a career afterwards. Perhaps she was too close to her father in temperament, and felt overshadowed by his commanding position in the political world. On the other side – the women's sphere – she was constantly balked by the dazzling good looks of Bryn, who was only a year younger. The gap in Margery's front teeth, a minor but conspicuous disfigurement, made her even more vulnerable to comparison with her sister.

Margery had been left in the cold in 1909 when Rupert used her as a stalking horse to approach Noel, and in 1912 she fell in love with Hugh Popham and lost him to Bryn. When the engagement was set, in July, Margery had a furious quarrel with Bryn. She looked as pale as tallow, Noel reported to Rupert, with suspicious and fearful and desperate eyes.[62] There was no open break between the sisters; they went on going as a party to the Russian Ballet or the Opera, and Margery could still charm acquaintances like Vanessa Bell. But during 1913 her discontents turned into serious eccentricity. She convinced herself that H. T. J. Norton, the mathematician and Apostle, was in love with her, and wrote him letters that took this for granted. After Vanessa's camp in Norfolk, Margery's parents took her away to Germany. They realised that she was anxious and depressed, but were reluctant to hand her over to psychiatrists. Her condition gradually deteriorated, and in 1916 she was treated by Dr Head after she began talking about imaginary marriage proposals.[63] A few years before, she had joked about how tiresome it was to go around with Bryn, since every young man who saw her fell in love with her. Now Margery, in a pathetic identification with her rival, was suffering from the delusion that she possessed the same power to break all hearts.

After Norton, Margery fell in love with James Strachey, who was already deeply in love with Noel. In 1917 Dr Caesar Sherrard proposed that Margery should live quietly by herself in the country, and she was installed in a cottage at Tatsfield, Kent. Sherrard had a dashing young nephew named Raymond whom he asked to keep an eye on his patient. Margery promptly fell in love with Raymond, whereupon Bryn turned up and once again cut her older sister out. Margery was sent to board at a farm; this worked until 1920 when she had a fit of rage and went around smashing all the windows. Her parents then tried to take care of her themselves at their new home at Ramsden, near Oxford, helped by Daphne, Bryn and Hugh. Margery's mania now focused on her father: she cut up his clothes and violently attacked him, giving him a black eye. The next year was a nightmare of nursing homes and futile searches for a cure. There were plans to take Margery to Zurich to see Jung; and James Strachey, now studying with Freud in Vienna, asked the master for his advice. Nothing worked, and at the beginning of 1922 Margery was committed to Camberwell House, a mental hospital in London. Noel, by now an MD, signed the order. The diagnosis, in the jargon of the day, was 'Dementia Praecox Paranoides'. Margery lived on for more than fifty years in various institutions, a hopelessly disoriented schizophrenic. The first-born of the sisters, she was the last to die.

Daphne Olivier had always been an attendant nymph rather than a central player in the Neo-pagan festivities. Pretty enough, she could not quite capture the attention and love that Noel drew. She studied literature at Newnham but her real passion was for singing, though her voice was not strong enough for a professional career. At the beginning of the war she had a brief affair with Bunny Garnett – the only one of the sisters he was able to ensnare. Perhaps coincidentally, she had a nervous breakdown in the summer of 1915 and was sent off to be 'stuffed' by the ubiquitous Dr Head. She did not marry until she was in her mid-thirties, to an Oxonian named Cecil Harwood who was some seven years younger than herself. They had become disciples of Rudolph Steiner in Germany, and in the year of their marriage they established the first Rudolph Steiner school in England.[64] Daphne taught at the school for a while, then occupied herself with domestic life and the care of her five children. She died of cancer in 1950.

Brynhild Olivier

For the first years of her marriage Bryn's life ran true to form. She lived with Hugh Popham in Regent Square, Bloomsbury, within walking distance of his work at the British Museum. There were parties with boisterous charades for her sisters, Bunny, Frankie Birrell and the rest – including Rupert, once he got over his pique at her marriage. In the winter everyone went to the Russian Ballet; in summer there was usually a camp. Bryn's first child,

Hugh Anthony, was born in March 1914, followed by a daughter, Olivier, and another son, Tristram. By 1917 Hugh Popham had enlisted in the Army and gone out to Port Said. At this time Bryn first met Raymond Sherrard. As soon as the war was over she wanted to live in the country with the children. They moved to Draycott, in the Cotswolds. Hugh stayed on at the Museum and came home on weekends. It cannot have been a coincidence that Raymond Sherrard lived in Draycott too.

Sherrard was eight years younger than Bryn. He was sturdy and handsome, a 'romantic soul' who roared around the countryside on a motorbike and had a big scar on his head — thought to be a war wound, but actually caused by falling off the bike. By now Bryn seems to have accepted the outside consensus that Hugh was a bit of a dry stick, and she felt stifled by the 'dumb and beseeching quality' of her husband's love.[65] The outcome, so Virginia Woolf maliciously reported to Jacques Raverat, was that 'Poor Hugh ... spent his Sundays making wooden beds, for Sherrard to step into on Monday when he'd gone.'[66] The Pophams moved from Draycott to Ramsden, where Bryn's parents were now living and trying to cope with Margery, but soon a divorce became inevitable.

Hugh stayed on at the British Museum and married Rosalind Thornycroft (a cousin of Bryn's) after she was divorced from Godwin Baynes in 1921. Bryn commented that it was 'bloody unenterprising' for Hugh to marry again so close to home. Her own life was more eventful. When Sherrard was cited as co-respondent he was promptly dismissed from his job at the Agricultural Economics Research Institute in Oxford. He and Bryn married and settled on a small farm at Rushden, near Letchworth. Bryn had three more children with Sherrard, and a hard struggle to keep the wolf from the door. She had fifty pounds a year from her father; Sherrard lacked capital and was not notably competent at farming, despite having studied it at Cambridge. At Rushden they went bankrupt, and again later. Bryn dealt out rough justice to her flock of children, cooking over a paraffin stove. For a while she ran a milk round, making the deliveries and washing the bottles herself. Rupert's poem 'Menelaus and Helen' had dwelt meanly on the theme of beauty's obliteration by domesticity; but there is no sign that Bryn was deeply disappointed with her haphazard country life, or that she pined for the days when she had played Helen at Cambridge. She was certainly not cowed by her troubles: once when trying on a hat in a village shop she told her son to run down and tell the train to wait until she got there – 'the way they did things in Jamaica'.

In the thirties, Bryn's life became tragic. Tragedies breed further discord; there are conflicting accounts of what happened, and no way to determine the 'right' after so many years. By all accounts Sherrard was a charmer, but to the Olivier way of looking at things he was also a crook. Sir Sydney was made Lord Olivier and Secretary of State for India in the first Labour government of 1924. His unbending righteousness would not see a place for someone like Sherrard in the Olivier dynasty. Noel had a story that when Sherrard was on the verge of bankruptcy he applied for a government subsidy for his cattle, then showed the inspector his neighbour's herd and claimed it as his own. Probably he thought it a good yarn, since the story got about. When bailiffs came to seize his goods he built a pyramid of his best china in front of the door, and told them that if they forced their way in they would smash it all. Some people might think desperate remedies fair enough when you have three young children to feed; others, like Noel, might find his tricks contemptible. Like many charmers, Sherrard inspired strong loyalty or strong hate – and sometimes one after the other. That seems to have been Bryn's experience of him. In her forties she found herself married to a man in his thirties who, to the cold Olivier eye, looked like a weakling and a philanderer. She tried to subdue him and tear him down. Their children, adoring the child in him, favoured their father's side.

When Sherrard went bankrupt again in the early thirties Bryn asked George Bernard Shaw for help. He was an old friend of Lord Olivier's and had known Bryn all her life. Shaw and H. G. Wells clubbed together to give her a thousand pounds, with which she bought Nunnington Farmhouse at West Wittering, Sussex.[67] Towards the end of 1933 she fell ill with aplastic anaemia, rapidly progressive and incurable. It was misdiagnosed as Lymphadenoma and treated, uselessly, with X-rays; the glands in her neck swelled up and disfigured her. 'B's case is very dreadful,' Lord Olivier wrote to H. G. Wells, 'for she loves life and, for her friends, alleviates it.'[68]

Sometimes Bryn had only enough money to take the bus one way into Chichester for treatment, and walked back seven or eight miles in agony. Perhaps Sherrard did fail her and run to other women for comfort. Certainly as an undischarged bankrupt he could hardly provide decent medical care for his wife and keep three children as well. Lord Olivier and Noel took charge of Bryn's case; loathing Sherrard, they pushed him aside. On Wells's advice they sent Bryn, in the summer of 1934, to the Rigiblick clinic in Zurich. But nothing availed and she died on 13 January 1935 in St Bartholomew's, London – very magnificently, Noel said. She was forty-seven. A few days later she was buried in the churchyard at West Wittering, with all the Oliviers around. Noel never spoke to Sherrard again.

Three days before she died, Bryn was persuaded by her parents to make a will leaving her whole estate to Noel. Meanwhile, Sherrard and her three younger children were living at Nunnington Farmhouse. On Lord Olivier's application to the High Court, a policeman was sent down from London with an eviction order. When he arrived, Sherrard refused to leave and barricaded himself in the house with the children. Finally they had to surrender. As they had done so often together on holidays – though now it was mid-winter – they went and camped in a nearby field. Sherrard eventually made his way to Oxford and got a job there. He married again, to a former waitress, and moved to Dorset. There he prospered by buying up old cottages cheaply and restoring them. He died in 1974. Noel took possession of Nunnington Farmhouse and used it for holidays, since her practice was in Middlesex. 'There was a hard streak in the Oliviers,' said one of the evicted children, telling the story fifty years after.

Noel Olivier

In September 1913 Noel gave the Raverats an accounting of her recent suitors. One had simply cooled down, she said – Rupert, perhaps? One had been driven to death, two others to debauch, and there were seven still hanging on. The most tenacious of these was James Strachey, now as hopelessly in love with Noel as he had been before with Rupert. Feri Békássy was still in pursuit, as was Adrian Stephen (though he shortly dropped away and married Karin Costelloe). Noel was twenty-one on Christmas Day of 1913; it was time to think of marriage, but she resisted all the young men who ardently, or meekly, or despairingly sought her love. Her first concern was her studies at the Royal Free Hospital for Women: to become a doctor would confirm the emotional independence that had always been at the base of her character.

When Rupert returned from America Noel was content to be friends with him again, and she was very happy when he came back safe from the expedition to Antwerp in 1914. But each kept the other at arm's length. There was too much wounded pride on Rupert's side, too much mistrust and jealousy on Noel's. After his death, Noel buried their past history deep within herself. The impact of his loss appeared only in her overwhelming nostalgia for the Neo-pagan days – as if, in her early twenties, she knew already that she had seen the best of life. At times she seemed willing to return James's love, but always held back from a final commitment. James, meanwhile, was ardently pursued by Alix Sargant-Florence, who had been a contemporary of Noel's at Bedales. By 1916 Noel was telling James that she was going to take Bryn's advice and marry a successful doctor, since there was no chance now that she would marry for love. Nothing worked for her emotionally, and everything had been spoilt.[69] She qualified as a doctor in the autumn of 1917, exhausted by the war and her years of study. Noel joined the '1917 Club', which was meant to be a rallying ground for the younger generation of intellectuals, but she had no deep interest in politics. In 1918 she found herself in Rugby. She did not go to see the medallion of Rupert in the school chapel, nor did she call on Mrs Brooke. But she saw ghosts there, and had her dream of Rupert, one that came regularly just before she woke up.

During 1919 Noel became involved with Arthur Richards, a 'little ordinary medical Welshman', keen on rugby and other things alien to Bloomsbury. At first she wanted an affair only, but both came to recognise that living in sin would be fatal to their careers. Noel was cheered by the prospect of marriage; in any case, she admitted to James, she could not bear the alternative. On 4 June 1920 James married Alix Sargant-Florence. It was her twenty-eighth birthday, and after the wedding they left for Vienna, where both would train as psychoanalysts under Freud. Noel became engaged in October of the same year and married Richards on 21 December, four days before her twenty-eighth birthday. There was a quiet ceremony at St Martin's, Trafalgar Square; the bride and groom both wore grey suits. At first Noel kept her own name, but she bowed to convention and became Dr Noel Olivier Richards in 1921.

Early in 1923, Virginia Woolf dined with Noel at the 1917 Club. Richards, like Will Arnold-Foster, did not care for Bloomsbury any more than it cared for him. Noel's life now centred on medicine, and Virginia was fascinated by the contrast between her past and her seemingly mundane present:

> She looked at me with those strange eyes in which a drop seems to have been spilt – a pale blue drop, with a large deep centre – romantic eyes, that seem to behold still Rupert bathing in the river at Christow: eyes pure and wide, and profound it seems. Or is there nothing behind them? I as good as asked her. Why didn't you marry any of those romantic young men? Why? Why? She didn't know, said she had moods; all Oliviers are mad, she said. And Rupert had gone with Cathleen Nesbitt and she had been jealous, and he had spoken against women and gone among the Asquiths and changed. But when she read his love letters – beautiful beautiful love letters – real love letters, she said – she cries and cries. How direct and unyielding these young women are. But she is 'over 30' – she would not say how much. And I am 41: which I confess. So we parted.[70]

Noel was in fact a month over thirty when she confided in Virginia. Whoever was to blame, the love between herself and Rupert had slipped away without fulfilment, while its ghost lived on in her secret garden of nostalgia – like all the loves of Noel's youth.

In 1924 Noel had a son, Benedict, followed by four daughters over sixteen years. The three Olivier sisters who married had sixteen children altogether; perhaps the real centre of their lives was what Virginia called 'the bestial and beautiful passion of maternity'. Noel was the only one of the four to find a vocation outside marriage, and to become the 'new woman' that, in 1910, all the Neo-pagan girls had expected to be. As her life filled up with professional duties she became plump and prematurely grey. By 1927, in her mid-thirties, she was telling James Strachey that nature should now have safely and completely disenchanted him of his old love for her. They could settle down to friendship, even if they still cherished memories of their passionate youth.

Then in the spring of 1932, facing her fortieth birthday, Noel belatedly fell head over heels in love with James. She thanked God, she told him, that she had finally woken up and realised that James was the one she should have loved all along.[71] They began an affair that went on through the thirties. Most of their meetings were when Noel went away on holiday with her children and could invite James to come and stay with them. She lived for the times they could be together day and night, but James held back from the deep and continuous connection that Noel craved. He still had a strong partnership with his wife Alix, both personal and professional; unlike Noel, he felt guilty about being unfaithful. They were making, it seemed, a final settlement of their emotional accounts. From 1912 to 1920 James had suffered and beseeched, while Noel would give him only affection instead of the passion he wanted. Exactly twenty years later, they played out the opposite roles. James had gained in sexual power and desirability, while Noel had lost. But what really mattered was Noel's surrender to feelings that she had never had, or at least never yielded to, in her youth. The final irony was that when Noel at last wanted passionate love she met with the same caution and evasiveness that she had dealt out to all who had vainly loved *her*.

After the birth of her fifth child, in 1940, Noel's affair with James petered out. She was fully occupied with motherhood, the war, her work as a paediatrician, and her troop of nieces and nephews. The Neo-pagan days were again closed off in memory. She rarely spoke of Rupert to outsiders, or even to her children. When Christopher Hassall wrote his authorised biography of Rupert she refused to co-operate, nor did she let Sir Geoffrey Keynes see any of Rupert's letters to her for his edition. Noel died in April 1969 at the age of seventy-six, two years after James

Strachey. She made no will, and her Neo-pagan papers have remained inaccessible since her death.

A few months before Jacques died, Gwen Raverat apologised to Virginia Woolf for irritating her with the hearty Neo-paganism of 1912. But why, after all the intervening sorrows, did Virginia still take it all so seriously?

> Anyhow its all over long ago; it died in 1914 I should think, though it was sick before – Neo Pagans, where are they? Here's Jacques and me very old in Vence and Ka so pathetic and lost in Cornwall; and do the Oliviers exist or not? Frances I believe carries on the tradition in the fields of Cambridge – at least as far as neo-paganism can be combined with evangelical christianity, (which I think anyone but Frances would find difficult.) And all the others are dead or have quarrelled or gone mad or are making a lot of money in business. It doesn't seem to have been a really successful religion, though it was very good fun while it lasted.[72]

On 1 May 1933 three or four survivors of the Clevedon pact could have turned up at Basel station; but of course no one had the heart, or the foolishness, to be there. Another romantic idealist of their generation, Adolf Hitler, had just become Chancellor of Germany.[73] Two years earlier, the past shared by the Neo-pagans had been frozen in time, when a group of admirers had raised at Rupert's grave on Skyros a giant bronze figure of 'a nude young man symbolizing Youth'. Whatever that past meant to them, it surely could not offer a way of escape – the 'Chance of Living Again' that they had dreamed of, walking along the Somerset cliffs in 1909. The lives they had made since then, happy or not, were the reality to which they now had to attend.

Notes and References

Abbreviations and References
AEP A. E. Popham
AG André Gide
AOB Anne Olivier Bell
BA Rupert Brooke Archive, King's College, Cambridge
Berg Berg Collection, New York Public Library
BL The British Library, London
BO Brynhild Olivier
BR Bertrand Russell
BRA Bertrand Russell Archives, McMaster University
CUL Cambridge University Library
DG Duncan Grant
DHL D. H. Lawrence
EM Sir Edward Marsh
EvanR Elisabeth van Rysselberghe
FC Frances Cornford (née Darwin)
FCM F. Crichton Miller
GK Sir Geoffrey Keynes
GR Gwen Raverat (née Darwin)
HAP H. A. Popham
HL Henry Lamb
HRC Henry Ransom Humanities Research Center, University of Texas
JB Justin Brooke
JMK J. M. Keynes
JR Jacques Raverat
JS James Strachey
KC Katharine (Ka) Cox
LRB *The Letters of Rupert Brooke*, ed. G. Keynes
LS Lytton Strachey
MHP Monks House Papers, University of Sussex
NO Noel Olivier
OM Lady Ottoline Morrell
RB Rupert Brooke
SG Sophie Gurney
SP Sybil Pye

VAF Val Arnold-Forster
VB Vanessa Bell
VW Virginia Woolf
Hassall: Christopher Hassall, *Rupert Brooke*
Hastings: Michael Hastings, *The Handsomest Young Man in England*
Holroyd: Michael Holroyd, *Lytton Strachey*
Levy: Paul Levy, *G. E. Moore and the Cambridge Apostles*

Letters for which no location is given are in private collections.

Chapter I: Rugby, Bedales and Cambridge

1. The Clarendon Commission that examined the public school system in 1861–4 considered seven boarding schools: Charterhouse, Eton, Harrow, Merchant Taylors', Rugby, Shrewsbury and Winchester, plus two London day schools, St Paul's and Westminster.
2. Connolly, *Enemies of Promise*, 260.
3. Honey, *Tom Brown's Universe: The Development of the Victorian Public School*, 3.
4. Hope Simpson, *Rugby Since Arnold*, 6.
5. Ibid., 5–6.
6. Honey, 17–18.
7. RB/KC, 'Friday evening' [1 March 1912); BA.
8. Lehmann, *Rupert Brooke: His Life and His Legend*.
9. Brooke still had Lascelles's photograph in his room at Cambridge in 1908; see Charles Sayle's diary, 22 February 1908.
10. The poems are roughly those from 'The Wayfarers' to 'Vanitas' in the *Poetical Works*.
11. *LRB*, 49.
12. Carpenter, *My Days and Dreams*, 72.
13. Ibid., 77.
14. Tsuzuki, *Edward Carpenter*, 33.
15. Ibid., 42–3, quoting from Carpenter's case history in Havelock Ellis, *Studies in the Psychology of Sex*, I, Case VII.
16. Carpenter's doctrine is summed up in his essay 'Simplification of Life', in *England's Ideal*.
17. Ward, *Reddie of Abbotsholme*, 56.
18. Stewart, *Progressives and Radicals in English Education*, 388.
19. Ward, 53. For the Fellowship of the New Life see N. and J. Mackenzie, *The First Fabians* (London: Weidenfeld & Nicolson, 1977).
20. Ward, 72.
21. Ibid., 168–9, 165. One drop-out was Lytton Strachey, though he left because his health broke down under the school's spartan regime.
22. Brandreth and Hendry, eds, *John Haden Badley*, 18.
23. E. L. (Peter) Grant Watson, 'Bedales', in *The Old School*, ed. Greene.
24. Charles Dukes, the school physician at Rugby, recommended morning cold baths for the boys; he warned that warm ones in the evening encouraged masturbation. Honey, 173.
25. Stewart, 389.
26. *La Supériorité des Anglo-Saxons: d'où Vient-il?* and *L'École Nouvelle*.

27. Greene, ed., *The Old School*, 224, 227.
28. JR, *Memoir*, 21B; my translation, here and throughout.
29. Ibid., 32–3. Badley himself was no more dapper: 'He always wore a jaeger shirt with a very old red tie, a waistcoat much too big for him, grey flannel trousers that always looked as if they were about to fall down, and old rubberised bathing slippers.'
30. J. C. T. Oates, 'Charles Edward Sayle', *Transactions of the Cambridge Bibliographical Society*, VIII (1982), 236–69. Sayle's voluminous diary is in the Cambridge University Library.
31. 6 March 1908.
32. 22 February 1908.
33. The Bond was added to make the name sound more impressive.
34. JR, *Memoir*, II.
35. Ibid., III.2.
36. GR, *Novel*, 1.1.3.
37. JS/RB, Friday (30 Nov. 1906?); Berg. After Hillbrow School, James had gone to St Paul's and seen little of Rupert for some years.
38. *LRB*, 73.
39. Ibid., 576.
40. The parallel with D. H. Lawrence is worth noting: the death of his older brother William in 1901, after entering business in London; the defeated father; the dominant, puritan mother; the sensitive, sexually ambivalent second son. 'He's a big man,' said Brooke of Lawrence, when reading *Sons and Lovers* (LRB., 576); while Lawrence would write the most memorable epitaph for Brooke.
41. Back at Cambridge, after describing the death of his brother to St John Lucas, Brooke continued: 'Another thing has happened that hurts a great deal, too; but that affects only me so I suppose it doesn't matter' (ibid., 77). The departure of Lascelles is the most likely explanation of this reference. In July 1909 James Strachey was invited to meet Lascelles at a theatre with Rupert (JS/RB, ?7 July 1909; Berg).
42. *LRB*, 258.
43. Ibid., 81.
44. Hastings, 71.

Chapter II: Young Samurai

1. Dalton showed his staying power by becoming Chancellor of the Exchequer in the Attlee government.
2. RB/EvanR, 3–5 Jan. 1912.
3. Speaight, *The Life of Hilaire Belloc*, 110.
4. Until 1906, the constitution of the Fabian Society allowed it to have no more than seven hundred members; this clause was repealed at the urging of Wells.
5. Keeling was killed at the Somme.
6. *LRB*, 116.
7. Ibid., 308.
8. G. Keynes, *The Gates of Memory*, 87.
9. Rupert, who was not particularly well off, went to the Continent four times

in 1907. One should recall, of course, that the standard wage for an agricultural labourer then was 13 shillings (65p) a week.

10. There were other curious rules. 'I mustn't give you tea (or anything to eat),' Daphne Olivier wrote to James Strachey, 'without the presence of a "chaperon" (to see that I don't poison you, I presume).' Daphne Olivier/JS, 26 April [1912]; BL.
11. *LRB*, 116–17.
12. Laurence's father, an Anglican clergyman, was very different in temperament and interests from his brother Sydney.
13. Interview with Mary Newbery Sturrock (a contemporary of Noel Olivier at Bedales), 25 June 1982.
14. *LRB*, 118.
15. Ibid., 117.
16. Those present included Goldsworthy Lowes Dickinson, Ben Keeling, Gerald Shove, Arthur Waley and Hugh Dalton.
17. Wells, *New Worlds For Old*, 242–3, 303.
18. Quoted in N. and J. Mackenzie, *The Time Traveller: A Biography of H. G. Wells*, 228.
19. Wells, *A Modern Utopia*, 303, 316.
20. Its official name was the Cambridge Conversazione Society; the name 'Apostles' came from the rule that it could not have more than twelve active members. For the history of the society to the First World War see Levy.
21. Holroyd, 278.
22. Ibid., 370. Those who voted on new members at this time were Alfred Ainsworth, J. T. Sheppard, Lytton Strachey, Saxon Sydney-Turner, Leonard Greenwood, J. M. Keynes, A. L. Hobhouse, James Strachey and H. T. J. Norton.
23. I.e. Leonard Woolf, Lytton and James Strachey, Maynard Keynes, Desmond MacCarthy, Harry Norton and Roger Fry. 'The single notable omission [was] E. M. Forster; but [Moore's parties] also included men who were only on the fringes of Bloomsbury like Gerald Shove, Rupert Brooke, J. T. Sheppard, Robin Mayor, Bob Trevelyan, C. P. Sanger, the Llewelyn Davies brothers and Ralph Hawtrey. . . . though Bertrand Russell more than once asked to be invited, he was in fact *never* a member of any of Moore's parties.' Levy, 196–7.
24. Holroyd, 281–2.
25. GR, *Novel*, 1.1.7, where James is portrayed under the name of 'Archie Hamilton'.
26. Holroyd, 168. The Taupe – 'mole'.
27. With the possible exception of Arthur Hobhouse; see p. 139 below.
28. The socialist had no chance of winning, and the Tory was William Joynson-Hicks ('Jix'), a notorious enemy of writers and artists.
29. *H. G. Wells in Love*, 68–9; West, *H. G. Wells*, 306–7.
30. Mackenzie, *The Time Traveller*, 234.
31. *H. G. Wells in Love*, 75; *The Diary of Beatrice Webb*, III, 125.
32. Garnett, *The Golden Echo*, 181.
33. Hassall, 159.

Chapter III: Neo-pagans

1. *LRB*, 139.

242 Notes to pages 39–55

2. *Civilisation: Its Cause and Cure* (London: Swan Sonnenschein, 1906), 46–7.
3. *Sydney Olivier*, 9.
4. *The Golden Echo*, 100.
5. Letter to the author.
6. *The Golden Echo*, 17.
7. Hassall, 175.
8. To recall some others: Spenser, Marlowe, Herbert, Herrick, Dryden, Coleridge, Wordsworth, Byron, Tennyson.
9. He borrowed the joke from *Love's Labour's Lost*, where the King of Navarre asks three of his courtiers not to speak to a woman for three years, in order to enjoy the pleasures of study and their own company.
10. FC, *Memoir*, 31.
11. *LRB*, 136.
12. Hassall, 163.
13. Ibid., 165.
14. Webb, *Letters,* II, 316.
15. Waley, a friend of Rupert's from Rugby, was then going by his original name, Schloss, and had not yet begun to translate Chinese poetry. See Garnett, *Great Friends*. Shove was reading economics at King's.
16. Webb, *Letters*, II, 316.
17. Or, naturally, the Webbs themselves. 'One only becomes thoroughly "adaptable" after 50,' Beatrice told one correspondent, 'before that age, one is so terribly handicapped by one's body.' Ibid., 332.
18. *The Diary of Beatrice Webb*, III, 77.
19. Webb, *Letters*, II, 280.
20. Webb, *Diary*, II, 142. Allen became chairman of the No-Conscription Fellowship during the First World War; Foss was a friend of Rupert's from Emmanuel.
21. RB/LS, 11 Sept. 1910; Berg.
22. Webb, *Letters*, II, 372. The Webbs defined themselves as 'B's' – Bourgeois, Bureaucratic and Benevolent (Clark, *The Life of Bertrand Russell*, 37).
23. Hassall, 168.
24. Frances's father also being called Francis, Gwen Darwin was inspired to write a play for the family Christmas called *The Importance of Being Frank*, in which all the characters were called Frances or Frank (Raverat, *Period Piece*, 252).
25. *LRB*, 339.
26. Besides Rupert and Jacques, Frances Darwin, Gwen Darwin, Justin Brooke, Ka Cox and Daphne Olivier suffered breakdowns of greater or lesser severity; and Margery Olivier became a chronic schizophrenic.
27. JR/KC, 2 May 1908; VAF.
28. JR/KC, 4 June 1908; VAF. Bramwell was the author of *Hypnotism* (London: Grant Richards, 1903).
29. The house is illustrated in Thomas, *Letters to Gordon Bottomley*. Lupton also designed and built parts of Bedales School.
30. JR/KC, 20 Nov. 1908; VAF.
31. *LRB*, 142.
32. RB/JS, 7 Jan. 1909; Berg.
33. RB/JS, ?14 June 1912; Berg.
34. Interview with Angela Harris.

35. When Brooke was still at Rugby, Lytton Strachey took to calling him 'Sarawak' after Sir James Brooke, the Victorian 'White Rajah' of Sarawak; Rupert himself hit on the idea of calling his mother 'the Ranee'.
36. *LRB*, 159.
37. JS/LS, 7 April 1909; BL.
38. *LRB*, 164.
39. Ibid.
40. Hassall, 169.

Chapter IV: 'At Grantchester, Where the River Goes'

1. *LRB*, 171.
2. Ibid., 173.
3. RB/JS, 10 July 1912; Berg.
4. There is a picture in Hastings, 87. Lamb, a Newnham student, later taught at Bedales; she was the sister of Henry Lamb. Robertson became a fellow of Trinity.
5. Hassall, 188.
6. Holroyd, *Augustus John*, 362.
7. Ibid., 95.
8. Garnett, *The Golden Echo*, 166. Baynes's athletic prowess later saved his life while he was studying with Jung. He went out rowing with his master on the Lake of Zurich, and dived off the boat for a swim. When he came back to the boat Jung hit at him with an oar, saying that he had black spots around him; Baynes had to make his own way back from the middle of the lake. (Interview with Anna Anrep.)
9. Walter became Lord Layton, editor of the *Economist*.
10. Garnett, *The Golden Echo*, 170.
11. Badley, *A Schoolmaster's Testament*, 45.
12. Pacifism got a better hearing at Bedales than at most public schools, though two hundred and forty Bedalians would serve in the war (several on the side of the Central Powers), and sixty were killed. But when the War Office offered Bedales a captured German gun after the war it was refused. Ibid., 65–7.
13. *Bedales Record*, 1908.
14. Garnett, *The Golden Echo*, 169. Justin, Ka and Jacques also swam naked in Cornwall on their walking tour the year before.
15. Badley, *A Schoolmaster's Testament*, 169. Frances Partridge (née Marshall), who was at Bedales in 1915–17, reports the rumour that Badley would invite favourite girls for private tutoring and squeeze their hands surreptitiously. He certainly volunteered to coach flocks of naked teenage girls for their life-saving tests. Partridge considered him, in retrospect, to be 'an old hypocrite and a far from admirable character'. *Memories*, 48.
16. Garnett, *The Golden Echo*, 169.
17. E. M. Forster, we may recall, was taught to refer to his penis as 'his dirty' (Furbank, I, 36).
18. Garnett, *The Golden Echo*, 179.
19. *LRB*, 135 (misdated; should be early August 1909).
20. Ibid., 175.
21. Quoted in RB/D. Ward, 'Sunday', BA.

22. Hassall, 196.
23. GR/FC, 25 Aug. 1908; BL.
24. Hubback was a Cambridge undergraduate and Young Fabian who was looked over by both the Neo-pagans and the Apostles, but finally not adopted by either group. He married Eva Spielman.
25. *LRB*, 194.
26. Ben Keeling was invited, but refused (ibid., 184).
27. Ibid., 192–4.
28. Ibid., 195.
29. Ibid., 188.
30. JR/KC, 12 Nov. 1909; VAF.
31. JR, *Memoir*, III, 7. Jacques describes this as a first meeting; he had in fact met her after Andermatt, but his breakdown seems to have effaced the memory of it.
32. Ibid., 8.
33. JR/KC, 24 March 1909; VAF.
34. GR, *Novel*, 2.1.4–5. In this quotation, Raverat's pseudonyms have been replaced with their original counterparts. The narrator of the novel is an imaginary observer, not identified with any of the actual Neo-pagans.
35. *LRB*, 180.
36. Ibid., 181.
37. Ibid., 173.
38. 'Whales': sardines, traditionally eaten at the Apostles' meetings on Saturday night (Rupert had just come from one).
39. RB/JS, 10 July 1912; Berg.
40. With one possible exception; see pp. 139–40, below.

Chapter V: Ten to Three

1. JR/KC, 19 Jan. 1910; VAF.
2. *LRB*, 211.
3. A year after Rupert's death Allen served the first of several prison terms as leader of the No-Conscription Fellowship.
4. RB/JS, 31 March 1910; Berg.
5. *LRB*, 232.
6. Ibid., 248.
7. NO/David Garnett, 13 & 22 March 1910; R. Garnett.
8. *LRB*, 212.
9. KC/JS, 2 Feb. 1912; BL. Godwin and Rosalind had both been at Klosters in 1908.
10. JR, *Memoir*, III, 22–3. 'Yseult' was Noel's pseudonym in Raverat's memoir; he had translated Bédier's version of *Tristan* into English in 1909.
11. RB/JS, ?18 July 1912; Berg.
12. *LRB*, 238.
13. Garnett, *The Golden Echo*, 222.
14. Interview with Mary Newbery Sturrock, who once accompanied her.
15. Hassall's statement that Popham and Bryn were already engaged at this camp is incorrect (Hassall, 229). David Pye became a fellow of Trinity.
16. Ibid., 230.

7. JR, *Memoir*, III, 24.
18. Pye memoir; Hastings, 97.
19. JR, *Memoir*, III, 24. 'Charles Rivers' was the pseudonym for Rupert.
20. RB/LS, 11 Sept. 1910; Berg.
21. GR/FC, Ripon [Aug. 1910]; BL.
22. Webb, *Our Partnership*, 417, 419.
23. Hassall, 227.
24. JR/KC, 19 Jan. 1910; VAF.
25. Similar debates have arisen over the social values and status of Bloomsbury – arguments that started within the group, as family quarrels. See, for example, Stansky and Abrahams, *Journey to the Frontier.*
26. *LRB*, 265.
27. Ibid., 258.
28. Holroyd, 399. Apostolic distaste for leftist sentiment had a long history. As far back as 1896, G. E. Moore had uncharacteristically flown off the handle over another enthusiastic Fabian:

    > Graham Wallas is a beastly fool; that's what I have most on my mind. Hasn't he a sneaking air of conceit as if he thought he knew everything? . . . He has no idea of what real science is; everything is to subserve his wretched utility – educating the masses! Educate them into what? He cannot tell you. . . . He has a fixedly low point of view, and laughs at what signifies the heaven which he never even peeped into, as if there were nothing more ridiculous on earth. (Levy, 179)

    Wallas had been Sydney Olivier's closest friend at Oxford. The Apostles held off the threat of politics until the thirties, when brothers like Julian Bell, Guy Burgess and Anthony Blunt so polarised the Society that it could not function for several years.
29. *LRB*, 259.
30. JR/KC, 25 Aug. 1910; VAF.
31. *LRB*, 256. In the event, Noel did not go to Prunoy this time.
32. JR/KC, Thursday ?7 July 1910; VAF. The phrase 'good as ends' came from G. E. Moore, whom Jacques had been re-reading.
33. JR/KC, 29 Sept. 1910; VAF.
34. JR/KC, 19 Jan. 1910; VAF.
35. JR/KC, 29 Sept. 1910; VAF.

Chapter VI: Foreign Affairs

1. They did not marry until September 1913. Rosalind's father was Hamo Thornycroft, sculptor and son of sculptors. Her mother, née Agnes Cox, was Lady Olivier's sister.
2. JR/KC, 25 April 1910; VAF.
3. BO/AEP, 20 Dec. [1910]; HAP.
4. Lady Olivier wanted Noel to come too, at Christmas, but Bryn talked her into letting Noel stay in England. Bryn felt that being in Jamaica was simply a waste of time – in part because 'the negroes are much too modest to sit as [nude] models' (Hastings, 93; should be Jamaica, Nov. 1910).

5. AEP/BO, 13[should be 12?] Oct. 1910; HAP.
6. BO/AEP, 'Wednesday night' [12 Oct.? 1910]; HAP.
7. JR/KC, 20 July 1910; VAF.
8. JR/KC, 29 Sept. 1910; VAF.
9. JR/KC, 25 April 1910; VAF.
10. GR, *Novel*, 2.2.17; Mary Newbery Sturrock interview.
11. Pearsall, 39.
12. BO/RB, 1 Oct. 1910.
13. For example, 'Dust' and 'The Life Beyond'.
14. RB/KC, 28 Nov. 1910; BA.
15. JR/KC, ?16 Dec. 1910; VAF.
16. *LRB*, 265.
17. Ibid., 270.
18. He had previously stayed there in 1907 with Hugh Russell-Smith. In April 1912 G. E. Moore had his reading party there, though Rupert himself was in Vienna.
19. Geoffrey Keynes joined them for a couple of days during their week-long stay.
20. GR, *Novel*, 2.3.24.
21. Ibid., 2.3.28.
22. *LRB*, 269.
23. Ibid., 270.
24. GR, *Novel*, 2.4.32.
25. JR/KC, 'Chelsea – Monday morning' [late 1910]; VAF.
26. GR, *Novel*, 2.5.36.
27. Ibid., 2.5.38.
28. Ibid., 2.7.54.
29. Ibid., 2.10.82.
30. VW, *Letters*, I, 463 (19 April 1911).
31. JR/KC, Gwithian [April 1911?]; VAF.
32. GR/KC, 'Wednesday' [late April?] 1911; VAF. The word 'least' is under-lined three times.
33. JR/KC, 'Monday' [May?] 1911; VAF.
34. DHL, *Letters*, I, 416.
35. Grohmann, 65.
36. *LRB*, 286. Kandinsky himself was at this time living at Murnau, south of Munich; it is not known if he met Brooke.
37. Ibid.
38. Ibid., 288.
39. The poem is dated 1909 in the *Poetical Works*, but in an unpublished letter to Jacques (6 Dec. 1911; BA) Brooke says it refers to 'Elizabeth'.
40. RB/KC, 31 March 1911; BA.
41. JS/RB, 10 April 1911; Berg. James also applied to his older brother Oliver for advice, and was told that it was safest to stick to married women.
42. RB/EvanR, ?16 April 1911.
43. RB/JS, 20 April 1911; Berg.
44. See Martin Green, *The Von Richthofen Sisters*, for an account of this milieu.
45. *LRB*, 301–2. The compass has thirty-two points and yachts at that time could sail within eight points of straight into the wind (modern yachts can sail within four).

46. RB/KC, *c.* 3 March 1911; BA.
47. *LRB*, 300. He was thinking mainly of Schnitzler.

Chapter VII: Combined Operations

1. RB/JS, 21 March 1910; Berg.
2. JR, *Memoir*, III, 17.
3. Russell at this time was living in Cambridge, where he was a lecturer at Trinity, and preparing to sell his Oxford house. Ray had been a fellow student of Ka's at Newnham; she married Oliver Strachey, and her sister Karin married Adrian Stephen.
4. VW, *Letters*, I, 450. Gwen Darwin was a family friend of the Stephens.
5. Ibid, 466.
6. *OED*, citing a use by Justin McCarthy.
7. *LRB*, 296.
8. VW, *Letters*, I, 446.
9. Ibid., 461.
10. BR/OM, 25 May 1911; HRC. The Keynes would be J.M., the Olivier Margery or Daphne, who were now at Newnham together.
11. VW, *Letters*, I, 461.
12. Ibid., 463–4.
13. *LRB*, 238 (misdated; should be *c.* 1 June 1911). The Germans were Annemarie von der Planitz, who married Dudley a year later, and her sister Clotilde 'van Derp', a professional dancer.
14. RB/EvanR, 19 May & 4 July 1911.
15. On either 5 June (*Bedales Record*) or 7 June (JR/KC, 1 Sept. 1911; VAF).
16. *LRB*, 310 (misdated; should be ?30 May).
17. Ibid., 291.
18. GR/FC, [March 1911]; BL. Eily married Bernard Darwin, the writer on golf.
19. GR/FC, 11 Nov. [1910]; BL.
20. *LRB*, 304 (misdated; *c.* 11 July 1911).
21. Ibid., 305.
22. Ibid., 307 (misdated; should be 20 Sept. 1911).
23. Ibid., 333.
24. RB/EvanR, [14 Aug.] 1911.
25. Taylor made no great mark at Cambridge, or in later life (he became a 'much loved' schoolmaster at Clifton). Levy, 270.
26. JR, *Memoir*, III, 16–17.
27. Ibid., 25–6.
28. RB/JS, 22 Aug. 1910; Berg.
29. JS/LS, 18 Aug. 1910; BL.
30. Holroyd, 547.
31. JS/LS. 12 Sept. 1910; BL.
32. Holroyd, 466.
33. JS/RB, ?27 July 1911; Berg.
34. JS/RB, 1 June 1911; Berg. Skidelsky, 259. At some point around this time, Justin shared lodgings with Duncan Grant.
35. VW, *Moments of Being*, 171.

36. Begun in 1907 as *Melymbrosia*, published in 1915 as *The Voyage Out*.
37. Conversation with Michael Hastings, citing Noel Olivier as source.
38. Vanessa Bell's report on Virginia's initiation into married life was that she 'never had understood or sympathised with sexual passion in men. Apparently she still gets no pleasure at all from the act, which I think is curious' (Bell, II, 6).
39. VW, *Letters*, I, 476.
40. RB/JMK, 22 Aug. 1911; BA.
41. Hastings, 84.
42. Hassall, 282.
43. Skidelsky, *John Maynard Keynes*, 259; VW, *Letters*, I, 477.
44. Hastings, 36.
45. JMK/DG, 6 June 1910; BL. Keynes rented a house at Burford, in the Cotswolds, for August and September 1910.
46. RB/KC, ?16 Sept. 1912; *LRB*, 587.
47. RB/KC, ?16 Sept. 1911; BA.
48. Dudley had met her in Germany, where he had gone early in 1910 to study the roots of international tensions.
49. *LRB*, 318.
50. Ibid., 307 (misdated; should be 13 Sept. 1911).
51. RB/KC, [29 Feb. 1912?]; BA.
52. *LRB*, 320, 323.
53. Ibid., 313.
54. RB/JR, 19 Oct. 1911; BA.
55. VW, *Moments of Being*, 174. Virginia puts the exchange at a time, around the end of 1909, when she and Vanessa began to talk grossly about sex with Lytton Strachey and other male friends; as she recalls those heady days, 'the word bugger was never far from our lips'. Quentin Bell argues that this happened no later than the summer of 1908 (Bell, 124).
56. JMK/[JS?], 19 Oct. 1911; BL. Maynard, James, Rupert, H. T. J. Norton, Shove and possibly Hobhouse had been meeting in London to discuss which embryos should be elected to the Society. In a letter to Maynard around the same time, Rupert refers to someone called 'Four Footmen': could this be a joke on Hobhouse's aristocratic connections and conventional views?
57. RB/KC, ?29 Feb. 1912; BA.
58. RB/KC, 'Wednesday evening' [Nov. 1911]; BA.
59. RB/KC, [28 Nov. 1910]; BA.
60. Freshmen were not supposed to be eligible, but in 1905 Lytton had broken precedent by getting his beloved Hobhouse elected. However, Hobhouse had studied for two years at St Andrews before coming to Cambridge; so Békássy must have been one of the youngest Apostles ever (James Strachey was a few months older when elected).
61. RB/JS, 27–9 Jan. [1912]; Berg.
62. JS/RB, 29 Jan. 1912; Berg. James had been Békássy's sponsor, who gave him the news that he had been elected to the Society.
63. JS/RB, 31 Jan. 1912; Berg. James was disconcerted to be asked by Feri why Justin had never been elected to the Society; he put him off by saying that Rupert wouldn't let him in. The joke is obscure. In 1908, when Justin

was in his last year at Emmanuel, people like Maynard and Lytton would have considered him too heterosexual and not sufficiently clever. By 1911 they were much more receptive to Justin's style. Rupert's concern, no doubt, would simply be to keep his friends in the Society and the Neo-pagans apart.

64. JS/LS, 1 Nov. 1912; BL.
65. RB/JMK, 17 Dec. 1911; BA.
66. Hassall, 292.

Chapter VIII: The Descent

1. FC/GR, 'Saturday' [?18 Aug. 1912]; CUL.
2. In 1920 Virginia Woolf found her 'flushed, lascivious, imbecile', and noted Maynard Keynes's comment that 'she'd had more sexual life than the rest of us put together'. VW, *Diary*, II, 54.
3. VW, *Letters*, I, 378.
4. Holroyd, 505.
5. RB/KC, 'Thursday' ?29 Feb. 1912 (misdated 20 March on letter); BA.
6. RB/KC, 'Saturday noon' [?14 Dec. 1912]; BA.
7. Instead, of course, he resigned from the Colonial Service to marry Virginia Stephen. Details of arrangements at Lulworth are taken from JMK/DG; 31 Dec. 1911; BL.
8. JMK/DG, 5 Jan. 1912; BL.
9. RB/KC, ?29 Feb. 1912; BA.
10. RB/JS, 12 Aug. 1912; Berg.
11. 'The Obelisk has done me in, but eventually I'll subdue it.' HL/LS, 'Thursday' [4 Jan. 1912?]; BL.
12. Holroyd, 472.
13. HL/LS, 6 Jan. 1912; BL.
14. LS/HL, 6 Jan. 1912; Holroyd, 473.
15. LS/HL, quoted in Holroyd, 473.
16. RB/E. J. Dent, 11 March 1912; BA.
17. For example, in the midst of his collapse at Lulworth Rupert wrote (3–5 Jan. 1912) a long and perfectly coherent account of Chesterton's social theories to Elisabeth van Rysselberghe.
18. *LRB*, 671.
19. RB/KC, 'Tuesday noon' [27 Feb.? 1912]; BA.
20. Compare D. H. Lawrence's rage, in 1915, at Bunny Garnett's relations with Frankie Birrell. With both Lawrence and Brooke, bisexuality seemed to produce strong anxieties about sexual roles.
21. RB/KC, 'Wednesday' [April? 1912]; BA.
22. RB/E. J. Dent, 11 March 1912; BA. *'aber etwas langweilig'*: but rather long drawn out.
23. S. Trombley, *'All That Summer She Was Mad': Virginia Woolf and Her Doctors*, 186. See also Poole, *The Unknown Virginia Woolf*.
24. *LRB*, 333.
25. Ibid., 335.
26. Ibid., 334; RB/KC, 'Wednesday evening' [24 Jan. 1912].
27. *LRB*, 339.
28. RB/KC, 25 Jan. 1912.

29. Expurgated from *LRB*, 347.
30. Hassall (321) says they became lovers at Salzburg, but this is contradicted by a letter of early March: RB/KC, 'Friday evening'; BA.
31. For the use of this appliance see Frank Harris, *My Life and Loves*, passim.
32. RB/KC, 'Thursday' [14 March? 1912]; BA.
33. RB/KC, 'Friday evening Rugby' [1 March 1912]; BA.
34. RB/JS, 13 Feb. 1912; Berg.
35. RB/KC, 'Monday noon' [26 Feb. 1912]; BA.
36. RB/KC, 'Sunday' [early March]; BA.
37. RB/KC, 'Tuesday noon' [27 Feb.? 1912]; BA.
38. RB/KC, 3 March 1912; BA.
39. RB/JS, 14 March 1912; Berg.
40. Passage expurgated from *LRB*, 365. On 'Tuesday morning' [?2 April 1912] Rupert wrote to Ka, 'I enclose a letter. Don't tell V. Keep it.' This was probably Virginia's reply, now apparently lost.
41. VW, *Letters*, I, 491.
42. RB/KC, '11.30 a.m. Tuesday' [5 March? 1912]; BA.
43. *LRB*, 363.
44. RB/KC, 'Wednesday evening' [13 March? 1912]; BA.
45. RB/KC, 'Tuesday evening' [?19 March 1912]; BA.
46. Hassall, 333.
47. RB/LS, 27 March 1912; Berg.
48. RB/JR, 'Tuesday' [26 March? 1912]; BA.
49. RB/KC, 'Sunday' [24 March? 1912]; 'Thursday night' [28 March? 1912]; BA.
50. NO/JS, 'Tuesday' [26 March 1912]; BL.
51. RB/KC, 'Friday evening' [22 March? 1912]; BA.
52. GR/KC, 'Wednesday' [27 March? 1912], 'Sunday' [31 March 1912]; VAF.
53. JR/KC, early April 1912; VAF.
54. GR/FC, [late August 1912?]; BL.
55. GR/FC, 'Wednesday night' Prunoy [late July? 1912]; BL.
56. RB/KC, 'Saturday night' [30 March 1912]; BA.
57. *LRB*, 367.
58. RB/KC, 'Monday night' [1 April? 1912]; BA.
59. RB/KC, 'Tuesday morning' [2 April? 1912]; BA.
60. *LRB*, 370.
61. RB/KC, 'Saturday' [?16 March 1912]; BA.
62. Expurgated from *LRB*, 366.
63. Interview with the author, May 1981; see also the American edition of her autobiography, *A Little Love* (Owings Mills, Maryland: Stemmer House, 1977).
64. *LRB*, 372 (11 April). During his visit to Limpsfield, 15–18 April, Rupert also wrote to James Elroy Flecker about 'taking the last step' (Hassall, 337).
65. RB/JS, [?14 June 1912]; Berg. By then, Rupert had acquired a small German revolver.
66. RB/BO, 'The end of September 1912'.
67. Noel, it should be noted, knew that Bryn was coming to Bank, and thought her company would be good for Rupert (NO/JR, 10 April [1912]; CUL).

68. VW, *Letters*, I, 495.
69. RB/KC, 'Thursday' [18 April? 1912]; BA.
70. *LRB*, 377.
71. NO/JS, 20 April 1912; BL.
72. RB/JS, 29 May 1912; Berg.
73. RB/BO, 'Friday evening' [19 April 1912]. Bryn's note to Rupert is lost.
74. RB/KC, [24 April? 1912]; BA.
75. Rupert's only comment on the romance, when told of it by Ka, was 'Woolf is, after all, a Jew.' (Expurgated from *LRB*, 376.)

Chapter IX: The Funeral of Youth

1. *LRB*, 378.
2. Barton Hill is near Grantchester; Amerhold I have not been able to locate.
3. RB/JS, 29 May 1912; Berg. 'proposing by letter': in February 1911 James had received an invitation to tea containing a silhouette of the sender's penis, cut from tissue paper.
4. RB/KC, [24 April? 1912]; BA.
5. A strange letter written while Rupert was crossing to Holland in April may be relevant: '*Flushing* – the lewdness! It means when you (elsewhere than at Woking) persuade it to come off. "Always flush the pan" creeps into my mind.' RB/JS, 22 April 1912; Berg. But this may only mean that Ka's cottage at Woking had an earth-closet.
6. RB/AEP, [June? 1912]; BA.
7. RB/JS, 10 June 1912; Berg. (In his autobiography, Leonard Woolf speaks of sometimes going to prostitutes when he was in Ceylon.)
8. RB/JS, 14 June 1912; Berg. 'if he's joined us': i.e. become an Apostle.
9. The term 'half-men' was used contemptuously by Brooke in the first '1914' sonnet. Before that, he had applied it to Adrian Stephen – another homosexual who, in 1912, fell in love with Noel (RB/KC, Raymond Bldgs Tuesday [?Feb. 1913]; BA).
10. *LRB*, 380.
11. Ibid., 386.
12. When he was not tormenting James, Rupert would often go out of his way to affirm their solidarity against women. On the way to Berlin, for example, there were two women in Rupert's carriage: '"If it came to the straight thing between us" they continually think, "you'd put us down, and drive supremely home, and we'd open our legs, submit, accept mastery, whimper and smirk." Oh! oh! I am touched also to tears for them because they never *quite* know what's up. Women aren't quite animals, alas! They have twilight souls, like a cat behind a hedge. What can one do?' (RB/JS, 22 April 1912; Berg).
13. RB/JS, [14 June? 1912]; Berg.
14. RB/BO, 8 May 1912.
15. *LRB*, 389.
16. NO/JS, ?5 June 1912; BL.
17. Lawrence and Frieda Weekley had eloped to Germany on 3 May, a few days before Ka left to join Rupert in Berlin. In a letter to Bryn on Wednesday 12 June, Rupert refers to 'your Lawrence man' – which suggests

that she had already met Lawrence, presumably when he came down to The Cearne to meet Edward Garnett. Cf. Lawrence's comment to David Garnett in 1915: 'The Oliviers and such girls are wrong.... You have always known the wrong people' (DHL, *Letters*, I, 322, 321). In his fictional account of his first meetings with David Garnett, Lawrence categorises the Neo-pagans as 'that ephemeral school of young people who were to be quite, quite natural, impulsive and charming, in touch with the most advanced literature.... the spoiled, well-to-do sons of a Fabian sort of middle-class, whose parents had given them such a happy picknicky childhood and youth that manhood was simply in the way.' (DHL, *Mr Noon*, 255, 257).

18. RB/KC, 'Thursday' [18 July? 1912]; BA.
19. James found the letter a wonderful description of that kind of copulation – what was known in the Society as the 'Lower Sodomy'; he admitted that he had never experienced copulation with anyone he had been in love with, and assumed it was altogether different. If he had the choice, James continued, he would have settled for Denham's fate. JS/RB, 'Thurs night' [11 July 1912]; Berg. Within two days of the event, however, Rupert was shrugging off his own reaction to the death. 'Denham doesn't make me much more gloomy,' he assured James. 'Just takes a shade more light from the landscape; that's all.... Anyway, death's extremely unimportant really: it turns out. I daresay he did it all rather cleverly. I may see his ghost – I thought there was something last night. It's the only one I'm not afraid of.' RB/JS, 'Friday' [12 July 1912]; Berg.
20. RB/JS, 16 July 1912; Berg.
21. RB/KC, 'Thursday' [18 July? 1912]; BA.
22. JR/KC, June? 1912 and 23 July 1912; VAF.
23. In March 1913 Rupert tried unsuccessfully to get Gwen to contribute woodcuts to *Rhythm*, which she was boycotting because Albert Rothenstein, a Jew, was on the editorial board. This had something to do with Gwen's militant Christianity at this time. However, see below, p. 218, for Jacques' later apology to Virginia Woolf for his anti-semitic outbursts.
24. JMK/DG, 26 July 1912; BL.
25. RB/JS, ?18 July 1912; Berg.
26. BO/AEP, 'Saturday' [27 July 1912]; HAP.
27. AEP/BO, Thursday [?11 July 1912]; HAP.
28. RB/BO, Monday evening [29 July 1912].
29. RB/EvanR, 31 July 1912.
30. KC/FC, 21 June 1912; BA.
31. *LRB*, 390.
32. RB/KC, 'Tuesday' [6 August? 1912]; BA.
33. *LRB*, 437.
34. JR/FC, 'Wadebridge' [April? 1911]; BL.
35. FC/GR, [7 Sept.? 1912]; CUL.
36. RB/JS, 6 Aug. 1912; Berg. An exchange between Hugh Popham and Bryn at this time is worth recording. *Hugh*: 'Are you shocked at homosexual love? I imagine you have read your Uncle Edward Carpenter's books on the subject. All those people Maynard, Francis [Birrell], [Gordon] Luce, and Mottram are – more sentimental than actual.' *Bryn*: 'No – it was no shocking revelation to me about those very charming people. I guessed it,

somehow when I first met one or two of them – and when I was told it for a dreadful fact (by Gwen or Jacques via Margery) about 3 months ago, it did not seem at all relevant. I wondered whether there was some nice feeling wanting perhaps, but I've decided NOT. Homosexuality is, after all such a *Fact*, that sentiment has nothing to do with it.' (Letters of 19 and 22 August 1912; HAP.) V. H. Mottram was a former president of the Cambridge Fabians; made up by the Dramatic Society, he was one of the Keir Hardie impersonators in the spring of 1907.

37. JS/LS, 17 Aug. 1912; BL.
38. RB/KC, 'Friday night' [11 Oct.? 1912]; BA.
39. 'She was dead right to mind,' commented Mary Newbery, 'he didn't love Ka deeply, but went off with her because someone else wanted to.' Interview with the author.
40. RB/JR, expurgated from *LRB*, 397 (misdated; should be 7 Sept.).
41. RB/BO, 21 Aug. 1912.
42. BO/JS, 4 Sept. [1912]; BL.
43. RB/KC, 'Friday night' [11 Oct.? 1912]; BA.
44. Expurgated from *LRB*, 422.
45. Conversation with Anne Olivier Bell, 22 June 1979.
46. RB/BO, 'The end of September 1912'.
47. OM/BR, 10 July 1912; BRA.
48. GR/FC, [14 Aug.? 1912]; BL.
49. FC/GR, 'Saturday' [17 Aug.? 1912]; CUL.
50. GR/KC, 20 Aug. 1912; VAF.
51. FC/GR, 'Saturday' [17 Aug.? 1912]; CUL.
52. GR/FC, [24 Sept.? 1912]; BL.
53. RB/EvanR, [30 Oct.] 1912.
54. It is not known where; presumably Rupert was too well known at Lulworth to pass off Elisabeth as his wife there.
55. RB/KC, [9 Oct.? 1912]; BA. Henry was in need of funds at the time; Ka came through 'nobly', he told Lytton, but that seems to have been the end of their close friendship.
56. 'In Xanadu did Kubla Khan'; BA.

Chapter X: Epilogue

1. Hobson was a year older than Garnett; they had gone walking in Austria with D. H. Lawrence and Frieda the previous autumn.
2. VB/VW, Sunday [?17 Aug. 1913]; Berg.
3. VB/VW, ?17 Aug. 1913; Berg. A few months later, Vanessa had changed her ranking: 'I think [Margery] a most attractive and beautiful creature. She has very brown eyes rather wide apart – a Greek nose – and curious teeth with a gap in the middle but you know all about that. I prefer her I think of the other Oliviers. She seems to me to have had more experience of feeling and more imagination' (VB/VW, ?27 March 1914; Berg).
4. VW, *Letters*, II, 20. Gwen's letters of this period have not survived.
5. NO/JR & GR, 24 Sept. [1913]; CUL.
6. RB/EvanR, ?31 May 1913.
7. RB/EM, 6 Sept. 1913; BA. Geoffrey Keynes obligingly omitted this passage from Brooke's *Letters*, and Hassall from his biography.

8. Hastings, 165.
9. 'I always remember your sharp little face and the little mouth that kisses me nicely you have pierced my heart and I always love don't forget me my sweet . . .' (*LRB*, 654).
10. Her letter was written on 2 May 1914, but was lost in a shipwreck and did not reach Rupert until the following January. It contains the ambiguous phrase: 'I get fat all time.'
11. 'Mamua' was Rupert's pet name for Taatamata.
12. JS/RB, 7 Dec. 1909; Berg. Hastings, 163.
13. *LRB*, 525.
14. Ibid., 529.
15. When Rupert fell ill with flu in February 1915, he spent nine days recuperating at 10 Downing Street.
16. E. Marsh, 'Memoir', in *Rupert Brooke: The Collected Poems*, cxxx; Hassall, 466.
17. *LRB*, 656.
18. DHL, *Letters*, III, 38.
19. Rupert had always been vulnerable to infection, and a bad case of coral-poisoning in Tahiti (from which he might easily have died) left him with even lower resistance. Later there was a rumour, indignantly denied by Geoffrey Keynes, that Rupert had actually died of venereal disease. This was probably just a case of one myth – of a young man without blemish – generating its opposite. Still, Rupert lived with Taatamata in a milieu where venereal disease must have been endemic. Dr Noel Olivier Richards observed that if he did have a strain of gonorrhoea the mosquito bite might well have got infected more easily, and been more dangerous. (Conversation with Michael Hastings, reported to the author, 1 July 1983.)
20. However, Inge complained that a Christian would expect more after death than to be merely 'a pulse in the eternal mind'!
21. Of fifteen officers in Brooke's Hood Battalion, eleven were gone after two months of fighting at Gallipoli. The Royal Naval Division was withdrawn in 1916 and sent to France, where it was again badly mauled in the last stages of the Battle of the Somme.
22. Taylor, *English History, 1914–1945*, 47.
23. Hassall, 513.
24. It is likely that the tribute was drafted by Churchill's secretary, Eddie Marsh.
25. DHL, *Letters*, II, 331.
26. *LRB*, 688.
27. Quoted in G. Gomori, 'Ferenc Békássy's Letters to John Maynard Keynes', *New Hungarian Quarterly*, v. 21, 169.
28. RB/BO, 22 May 1913.
29. In July 1913, however, he made the traverse from Arolla to Chamonix with Geoffrey Keynes, no minor expedition.
30. JR/AG, 22 Jan. 1915; SG.
31. JR/KC, 10 July 1914; VAF.
32. Both sides of the correspondence have been preserved, and an edition by Professor D. A. Steel of the University of Lancaster is in preparation. See also Steel's 'Escape and Aftermath: Gide in Cambridge 1918', *The Yearbook of English Studies*, 15 (1985), 125–59.

33. 'an exquisite nature, with a sublime and affable goodness'. Van Rysselberghe, *Les Cahiers de la Petite Dame* ... *1918–1929*, 45. The *Cahiers* is an intimate record of Gide's life from 1918 until his death, compiled by Maria van Rysselberghe and amounting to nearly 3000 pages of typescript in the original.

34. 'I saw two people I loved come out of [this affair] so miserable, so much in pain, their *spirit* befouled, poisoned, revolted, full of bitterness. ... And anti-puritanism, immoralism as a theory, seems to me truly at least as pernicious as its opposite. (they have about the same relation as sentimentality and cynicism)'. JR/AG, 2 Aug. 1918; SG.

35. *The Journals of André Gide*, tr. Justin O'Brien (London: Secker & Warburg, 1948), II, 84, 187–90. However, Jacques was never *croyant* in the sense of being an orthodox or observant Christian; and he also urged Gide, in October 1911, to read Blake's *Marriage of Heaven and Hell*. Gide was deeply impressed by this work, which helped clarify his interpretation of Dostoevsky.

36. JR/AG, 1 Aug. 1918; SG.

37. See below, 220.

38. 'I felt almost cruelly, when I thought of you, the inadequacy of my paganism. ... In short I was like someone who turns down a dinner invitation because he has no dinner jacket. ... In spite of my silence and distance, I very often think of you, and of what made the quality of my friendship for you so rare; I think it came from the fact that, in your company, I felt a better person. –
    So, *au revoir* perhaps.' AG/JR, 3 Dec. 1923; SG.

39. JR/VW, 13 May 1924; MHP.

40. Jacques may have felt the need to renew old friendships because he had recently broken off with Dudley and Annemarie Ward. This bitter and complex quarrel had also involved Ka and Frances Cornford; the main issues were (a) an abortive affair between Ka and Dudley when she was staying with the Wards in Berlin in 1913 and (b) Dudley's belief that Jacques' libertine ideas about sex had encouraged Annemarie to have an affair with David Pye.

41. JR/VW; 14 Sept. & 4 May 1923; MHP.

42. JR/VW, [Sept.? 1924]; MHP.

43. GR/VW, 22 April 1925; MHP. Gwen had always, one might note, been immune to Rupert's charm. 'I've never at all', she told Frances in 1914, 'had any feeling about him stronger than thinking him a pleasant and amusing companion. I've never known him in the least intimately or loved him at all. But I *cannot* love without respecting. ... And if Rupert got 2 dozen Victoria Crosses it wouldn't change my bottom feeling for him.' 'It seems to me', she wrote later, 'that intelligence with rather muddled instincts is the point of Rupert – and of course the sympathy and beauty of him .' GR/FC, 17 Oct. 1914 and [1920]; BL.

44. Van Rysselberghe, *Les Cahiers de la Petite Dame* ... *1918–1929*, 150.

45. 'I will never really love any woman except one and I can only have real desire for young boys. But I find it hard to bear that you have no child, and that I have none myself.' Van Rysselberghe, *Les Cahiers de la Petite Dame* ... *1918–1929*, 150. The 'one woman' was his cousin and wife Madeleine, though the marriage was never consummated.

46. Ibid., 44.
47. For a detailed account of John's career see P. Stansky and W. Abrahams, *Journey to the Frontier.*
48. Godwin Baynes FC, 10 April 1933; BL.
49. NO/JS, 21 Sept. [1916]; BL.
50. SP/KC, 20 Feb. 1916; VAF.
51. FCM/FC; 16 July 1927; BL. Frances Cornford was also a patient of Crichton Miller's at this time. Miller suggested to her that an exact parallel to Justin's case could be found in Strindberg's *The Father*, then playing in London.
52. Bell, *By-Road*, 71.
53. JB/GK, 19 Dec. 1955; BA. Keynes's edition was not published until 1968, after Ward's death.
54. In August 1914 Keynes proposed again, with the same result. In May 1917 he married Margaret Darwin, younger sister to Gwen Raverat.
55. *LRB*, 476.
56. Ibid., 669.
57. JR/KC, ?27 April 1915; VAF.
58. VW, *Letters*, II, 291, 393.
59. BR/OM, 4 Nov. 1912; BRA.
60. VW, *Diary*, V, 143.
61. Garnett, *The Golden Echo*, 100. One of Noel's daughters (Angela Harris) recalled how Bunny would get hot and red-faced with desire for her mother, and be laughed at for his pains. See also Noel's sardonic account of how Bunny tried to seduce Dr Marie Moralt when she was staying at Charleston; Moralt drove him off – the first time a virgin had ever escaped him, Vanessa observed – though her hands were left covered in slobber. NO/JS, 14 Feb. 1919; BL.
62. RB/JS, 16 July 1912; Berg.
63. See Virginia Woolf's report to Ka: 'Margery Olivier had not been in the room a minute before she said "I've just refused a proposal of marriage!" Nobody knew what to say. For some reason we all felt very awkward. . . . Leonard inclines to think that she suffers from a disease of advanced virginity in which one imagines proposals at every tea party.' VW, *Letters*, II, 83.
64. Founded in London in 1925, later moved to East Grinstead. Harwood was a peripheral member of the 'Inklings', going on walking tours with C. S. Lewis and Owen Barfield, a fellow disciple of Steiner.
65. AOB/Author, 14 June 1983.
66. VW, *Letters*, III, 93.
67. Conversation with Angela Harris, 25 June 1979. When Wells was being pilloried over his affair with Amber Reeves, Bryn had gone out of her way to show support for him.
68. *Sydney Olivier*, 171.
69. NO/JS, 11 Sept. 1916; BL.
70. VW, *Diary*, II, 229–30. Cristow is downstream from Clifford Bridge, where the Neo-pagans and Virginia had camped in August 1911.
71. NO/JS, 1 Aug. 1935; BL.
72. GR/VW, Oct. 1924; MHP.
73. The pre-war German 'Youth Movement' had much in common with

Neo-paganism, but differed in two crucial ways: it was a mass movement (with some 25,000 members in 1913), and it claimed the right to supplant its elders and rule Germany in better style. In brief, the *Wandervogel* were forward-looking rather than prematurely nostalgic. See Wohl, 42–7.

Bibliography

J. H. Badley. *A Schoolmaster's Testament*. Oxford: Basil Blackwell, 1937.
The Bedales Record. Petersfield: Bedales School.
Adrian Bell. *By-Road*. London: John Lane, 1943.
Quentin Bell. *Virginia Woolf: a Biography*. London: Hogarth Press, 1972.
Hilaire Belloc. *The Four Men*. London: Thomas Nelson, 1912.
Robert Best. *A Short Life and a Gay One: A Biography of Frank Best, 1893–1917*. Unpublished MS in Birmingham Public Library.
Jeremy Boissevain. *Friends of Friends*. Oxford: Basil Blackwell 1974.
Giles Brandreth and Sally Henry, eds. *John Haden Badley, 1865–1967: Bedales School and its Founder*. Bedales: Bedales Society, 1967.
Rupert Brooke. *Rupert Brooke: The Collected Poems. With a Memoir by Edward Marsh*. London: Sidgwick & Jackson, 1942.
   Democracy and the Arts. London: Rupert Hart-Davis, 1946.
   The Letters of Rupert Brooke. G. Keynes, ed. London: Faber & Faber, 1968.
   Letters From America. With a Preface by Henry James. Toronto: McClelland & Stewart, 1916.
   The Poetical Works of Rupert Brooke. G. Keynes, ed. London: Faber & Faber, 1970.
   The Prose of Rupert Brooke. C. Hassall, ed. London: Sidgwick & Jackson, 1956.
   John Webster and the Elizabethan Drama. New York: Lane, 1916.
Edward Carpenter. *England's Ideal*. London: Swan Sonnenschein, 1901.
   My Days and Dreams: Being Autobiographical Notes. London: George Allen & Unwin, 1916.
Ronald W. Clark. *The Life of Bertrand Russell*. London: Jonathan Cape & Weidenfeld & Nicolson, 1975.
Keith Clements. *Henry Lamb*. London: Redcliffe Press, 1984.
Cyril Connolly. *Enemies of Promise*. New York: Doubleday, 1960.
Frances Cornford. *Collected Poems*. London: Cresset Press, 1954.
   Memoir. Manuscript in the possession of Christopher Cornford.
Paul Delany. *D. H. Lawrence's Nightmare: The Writer and His Circle in the Years of the Great War*. New York: Basic Books, 1978.

E. M. Forster. *Arctic Summer and Other Fiction*. London: Edward Arnold, 1980.

P. N. Furbank. *E. M. Forster: A Life*. London: Secker & Warburg, 1977–9.

Brian Gardner. *The Public Schools: An Historical Survey*. London: Hamish Hamilton, 1973.

David Garnett. *The Familiar Faces*. London: Chatto & Windus, 1962.
   The Flowers of the Forest. London: Chatto & Windus, 1955.
   The Golden Echo. London: Chatto & Windus, 1953.
   Great Friends: Portraits of Seventeen Writers. London: Macmillan, 1979.

Jonathan Gathorne-Hardy. *The Public School Phenomenon*. New York: Viking, 1978.

Martin Green. *Children of the Sun*. New York: Basic Books, 1976.
   The Von Richthofen Sisters. New York: Basic Books, 1974.

Graham Greene, ed. *The Old School: Essays by Divers Hands*. London: Jonathan Cape, 1934.

Will Grohmann. *Wassily Kandinsky: Life and Work*. New York: Abrams, 1958.

Christopher Hassall. *Edward Marsh*. London: Longmans, 1959.
   Rupert Brooke: A Biography. London: Faber & Faber, 1972.

Michael Hastings. *The Handsomest Young Man in England: Rupert Brooke*. London: Michael Joseph, 1967.

James L. Henderson. *Irregularly Bold*. London: Andre Deutsch, 1978.

Michael Holroyd. *Augustus John: a Biography*. Harmondsworth: Penguin, 1976.
   Lytton Strachey: A Biography. Harmondsworth: Penguin, 1971.

J. R. de S. Honey. *Tom Brown's Universe: The Development of the Victorian Public School*. London: Millington, 1977.

Samuel Hynes. *The Edwardian Turn of Mind*. Princeton: Princeton University Press, 1968.

Fred Ilfeld Jr and Roger Lauer. *Social Nudism in America*. New Haven, Conn: College & University Press, 1964.

Geoffrey Keynes. *The Gates of Memory*. Oxford: Clarendon Press, 1981.
   A Bibliography of Rupert Brooke. London: Rupert Hart-Davis, 1954.
   Henry James in Cambridge. London: W. Heffer, 1967.

D. H. Lawrence. *Mr Noon*. Cambridge: Cambridge University Press, 1984.
   The Letters of D. H. Lawrence, Vols. I, II, III. James T. Boulton, general ed., Cambridge: Cambridge University Press, 1979–84.

John Lehmann. *Rupert Brooke: His Life and His Legend*. London: Weidenfeld & Nicolson, 1980.

Paul Levy. *Moore: G. E. Moore and the Cambridge Apostles*. London: Weidenfeld & Nicolson, 1979.

Norman and Jeanne Mackenzie. *The First Fabians*. London: Weidenfeld & Nicolson, 1977.
   The Time Traveller: A Biography of H. G. Wells. London: Weidenfeld & Nicolson, 1973.

Rita McWilliams-Tullberg. *Women at Cambridge*. London: Victor Gollancz, 1975.

Edward Marsh. *A Number of People*. London: Heinemann & Hamish Hamilton, 1939.

C. F. G. Masterman. *The Condition of England*. London: Methuen, 1960 (1st edn 1909).

George Edward Moore. *Principia Ethica*. Cambridge: Cambridge University Press, 1965 (1st edn 1903).

Gilbert Murray. *A Biography of Francis McDonald Cornford, 1874–1943*. Oxford: Oxford University Press, 1944.

Cathleen Nesbitt. *A Little Love*. Owings Mills, Md: Stemmer House, 1977.

Sydney Olivier. *Letters and Selected Writings*. London: George Allen & Unwin, 1948.

Frances Partridge. *Memories*. London: Gollancz, 1981.

Robert B. Pearsall. *Rupert Brooke: The Man and Poet*. Amsterdam: Rodopi, 1974.

Ann Phillips, ed. *A Newnham Anthology*. Cambridge: Cambridge University Press, 1979.

Roger Poole. *The Unknown Virginia Woolf*. Cambridge: Cambridge University Press, 1978.

Sybil Pye. 'Memoir of Rupert Brooke', in *Life & Letters*. May 1929.

Gwen Raverat. *Novel*. Unpublished MS in the possession of Sophie Gurney.
    Period Piece: A Cambridge Childhood. New York: Norton, 1952.
    The Wood Engravings of Gwen Raverat. Selected with an Introduction by Reynolds Stone. London: Faber & Faber, 1959.

Jacques Raverat. *Memoir*. Unpublished MS in the possession of Sophie Gurney.

Timothy Rogers. *Rupert Brooke: A Reappraisal and Selection From His Writings, Some Hitherto Unpublished*. London: Routledge & Kegan Paul, 1971.

Sheldon Rothblatt. *The Revolution of the Dons: Cambridge and Society in Victorian England*. New York: Basic Books, 1968.

Maria van Rysselberghe. *Les Cahiers de la Petite Dame: Notes pour l'histoire authentique d'André Gide. 1918–1929. Cahiers André Gide, IV*. Paris: Gallimard, 1973.

Charles Sayle, *Diary*. Unpublished MS in Cambridge University Library.

John Hope Simpson. *Rugby Since Arnold*. London: Macmillan, 1967.

Andrew Sinclair. *The Red and the Blue: Intelligence, Treason, and the Universities*. London: Weidenfeld & Nicolson, 1986.

Robert Skidelsky. *English Progressive Schools*. Harmondsworth: Penguin, 1969.
    John Maynard Keynes. Volume I: Hopes Betrayed 1883–1920. London: Macmillan, 1983.

George Spater and Ian Parsons. *A Marriage of True Minds: An Intimate Portrait of Leonard and Virginia Woolf*. New York: Harcourt, Brace, Jovanovitch, 1977.

Robert Speaight. *The Life of Hilaire Belloc*. New York: Farrar, Straus & Cudahy, 1957.

Peter Stansky and William Abrahams. *Journey to the Frontier: Two Roads to the Spanish Civil War*. New York: Norton, 1970.

W. A. C. Stewart. *Progressives and Radicals in English Education*. London: Macmillan, 1972.

J. and A. Strachey. *Bloomsbury/Freud: The Letters of James and Alix Strachey, 1924–25*. Perry Meisel and Walter Kendrick, eds. New York: Basic Books, 1985.

Arthur Stringer. *Red Wine of Youth*. New York: Bobbs-Merrill, 1948.

A. J. P. Taylor. *English History, 1914–1945*. Harmondsworth: Penguin, 1970.

Edward Thomas. *Letters From Edward Thomas to Gordon Bottomley*. R. George Thomas, ed. London: Oxford University Press, 1968.

Stephen Trombley. *'All That Summer She Was Mad': Virginia Woolf, Female Victim of Male Medicine*. New York: Continuum Press, 1982.

Chushichi Tsuzuki. *Edward Carpenter, 1844–1929: Prophet of Human Fellowship*. Cambridge: Cambridge University Press, 1980.

B. M. Ward. *Reddie of Abbotsholme*. London: Allen & Unwin, 1934.

Sidney and Beatrice Webb. *The Letters of Sydney and Beatrice Webb. Volume II: Partnership, 1892–1912*. Norman Mackenzie, ed. Cambridge: Cambridge University Press, 1978.

Beatrice Webb. *The Diary of Beatrice Webb*, Vol. III. London: Virago, 1984.
  Our Partnership. New York: Longmans Green, 1948.

Frank Wells. *H. G. Wells: A Pictorial Biography*. London: Jupiter Books, 1977.

H. G. Wells. *H. G. Wells in Love: Postscript to an Experiment in Autobiography*. G. P. Wells, ed. London: Faber & Faber, 1984.
  A Modern Utopia. Lincoln: University of Nebraska Press, 1967 (1st edn 1905).
  New Worlds For Old. London: Constable, 1908.

Anthony West. *H. G. Wells: Aspects of a Life*. London: Hutchinson, 1984.

Robert Wohl. *The Generation of 1914*. Cambridge, Mass: Harvard University Press, 1979.

Virginia Woolf. *The Diary of Virginia Woolf*. Anne Olivier Bell, ed. 5 vols. London: The Hogarth Press, 1977–84.
  The Letters of Virginia Woolf. Nigel Nicolson and Joanne Trautmann, eds. 6 vols. London: The Hogarth Press, 1975–80.
  Moments of Being: Unpublished Autobiographical Writings. Jeanne Schulkind, ed. London: The Hogarth Press, 1978.

Index

Müritz, 177, 179

National Committee for the Prevention of Destitution, 94–5
National Liberal Club, 73
Neeve, Mrs, 125–6
Nesbitt, Cathleen, 172, 199, 204–6, 208, 209, 226
Neu Strelitz, 177, 178, 180, 200
Neue Künstlervereinigung München, 114–15
Neuve Chapelle, 211
New Forest, 56–8, 95, 172
New Theatre, Cambridge, 46
New York, 86, 205, 226
Newbery, Mary, 87–8, 130, 142, 190, 194
Newnham College, Cambridge, 25, 27, 35–6, 43, 44, 74
Nietzsche, Friedrich Wilhelm, 215
Norfolk, 208
Norfolk Broads, 90, 188
Norton, Harry, 81, 98, 128, 152, 185, 229

Olivier, Bryn, 73, 87, 127, 164–5, 185, 213; childhood, 40–1; background, 27; beauty, 27, 55; holiday in Andermatt, 27–8; friendship with Rupert, 28, 34, 36; and Godwin Baynes, 68–9, 103–4; at Clevedon, 70–1; life in London, 75; rock-climbing, 88; at Cambridge, 90; camping holidays, 91, 132–4, 202, 208; in *Faustus*, 92, 130; visits Prunoy, 99–101, 103; makes jewellery, 104; and Hugh Popham, 104–5; Rupert falls in love with, 173–4, 175–6, 178–9, 182, 188–9; holiday at Everleigh, 187–8; engagement, 189–90, 229; marriage, 195–7, 198; later life, 230–3; death, 233
Olivier, Daphne, 27, 36, 74, 82, 89; childhood, 40–1; camping holidays, 66, 68, 133, 202–3; holidays in Switzerland, 107, 191; breakdown, 155; holiday at Everleigh, 187–8; later life, 230
Olivier, Laurence, 27

Olivier, Lady Margaret, 27, 40, 104, 196
Olivier, Margery, 31, 66, 72, 74, 89; childhood, 40–1; holidays in Switzerland, 27, 82, 107; friendship with Rupert, 54, 56; love for Rupert, 57–8; on Bryn, 70; at Clevedon, 71; tries to keep Rupert away from Noel, 75–7, 87, 108; political views, 96; camping holidays, 203, 208; later life, 228–30
Olivier, Noel, 27, 185; childhood, 40–1; appearance, 36–7, 89; Rupert Brooke's love for, 36–8, 54–5, 56–9, 74, 75–7, 81, 86–91; and *Comus*, 43, 45; character, 54–5, 87–8; camping holidays, 66, 68, 91, 133–4, 202–3, 208; life in London, 75; rock-climbing, 88; engagement to Rupert, 91, 107–8; at Grantchester, 93–4; visits Prunoy, 99–100; James Strachey's love for, 129–31, 180–1, 186, 194, 234, 236; and Rupert's *Poems*, 141; withdraws from Lulworth holiday, 143; and Rupert's breakdown, 156–7, 164, 166; studies medicine, 164, 198; Rupert visits in Limpsfield, 170–1; Rupert's viciousness towards, 180–2; holiday at Everleigh, 187–8; later relations with Rupert, 194–5; Békássy loves, 213; on Justin Brooke, 223; and Rupert's death, 234; and Bryn's death, 233; later life, 227, 233–7; death, 237
Olivier, Sir Sydney, 27, 30, 34, 40, 127, 185, 190, 195–6, 229, 230, 232, 232, 233
Orwell, George, 15, 199
Osmaston, Dorothy, 56, 66
Ouse, River, 188
Overcote, 64

Pacific, 206
Paris, 159
Pater, Walter, 100
Pease, Edward, 29
Pease family, 27, 41

Picture Acknowledgements

The photographs are reproduced by courtesy of Mrs V. Arnold-Forster, Mrs Sophie Gurney, Mrs Elizabeth Hollingsworth, King's College Library, Cambridge and The Brooke Trust, The National Portrait Gallery, London, Dr Benedict Richard and Private Collections. The publishers have endeavoured to acknowledge all known persons and collections holding copyright or reproduction rights for the illustrations in this book.